Return to the Postcolony
Specters of Colonialism in Contemporary Art

T. J. Demos

Return to
the Postcolony

Specters of Colonialism
in Contemporary Art

SternbergPress

Contents

Introduction
Enter: The Ghosts

Let those to whom history has not been friendly bear witness to the process by which the living transform the dead into partners in struggle.
—Black Audio Film Collective, *Handsworth Songs* (1986)

This book explores the photography and film of contemporary artists who have voyaged or returned to postcolonial Africa in recent years. With a focus on the work of Sven Augustijnen, Vincent Meessen, Zarina Bhimji, Renzo Martens, and Pieter Hugo, it considers how they have investigated the specters of past colonial injustices. Those injustices are often repressed in European consciousness and visual culture, yet still frequently and stubbornly emerge in its discourse and representation. The often unrecognized and generally inadequately interrogated historical presence, material traces, and psychic scars of colonialism, passed through generations, also creep up in current forms of economic and political inequalities found between the Global North and South, Europe and Africa—inequalities that colonial relations, of course, played an important role in defining. These traces can be found in the contemporary media images of seemingly senseless violence and poverty in the postcolony, and in the disavowed complicity and unprofessed responsibility of European nations that once ruled those distant lands in the name of political, economic, and social advantage. Given the fact that there is no firm separation from, or clear European conscience in relation to, the colonial past, in many ways, that colonial era never actually ended.

Against the amnesia and misrecognition that characterizes so much of European cultural and political representation, the artists addressed herein might be thought of as conjurers of the "spectral"—to invoke the title of Augustijnen's film *Spectres* (2011)—a term I use to address the haunting memories and ghostly presences that refuse to rest in peace and cannot be situated firmly within representation. Indeed, they typically escape the grasp of the art history of iconographical identification as much as the positivist typologies of scientific knowledge. In using this occult language, my aim is not to embrace a post-secular and antimaterialist metaphysics, but rather to think along with theorists such as Isabelle Stengers, Bruno Latour, and Avery Gordon, sharing their skepticism regarding the self-assured and firm separation between modern science and premodern animism, between objective positivism and subjective belief, between the real and the imaginary. The resulting analysis takes an even more materialist line insofar as it is attentive to the historical and current circumstances and socio-material conditions of colonial and

postcolonial narratives that pose challenges to positivist representational forms. Indeed, it was in a provocative moment of dialecti-
cal materialism sensitive to this enchanted netherworld that Karl
Marx and Friedrich Engels described how a certain "spectre" once
haunted Europe. Moreover, such methodological recourse is de-
manded not simply because of recent developments within philosophical circles—for instance, the recent formation of "speculative
realism," which, building on Latour's position, attempts to move,
on the one hand, beyond the stale oppositions of the postmodern
era between a reality-denying constructivism and a naive objectiv-
ist realism,[1] and, on the other hand, toward a different set of documentary possibilities that bring affect, imagination, and truth into
a new experimental configuration. And it's not simply because this
discourse has been taken up recently within artistic circles—for
instance, Anselm Franke's ongoing research/exhibition project
"Animism," and Okwui Enwezor's postcolonial-engaged documenta 11 (2002), among others—with which my own investigation shares a similar set of interests (exhibitions that extend
earlier artistic invocations and critical conjurings of postcolonial
enchantments and possessions in experimental cinema—for
example, Black Audio Film Collective's and Isaac Julien's work
made in the 1980s and 1990s).[2] Taking up
the language of the ghostly is justified mainly
because the photography and film works that
form my central case studies enact a complex
turn toward the spectral, innovatively and
diversely figuring and building upon what
Jacques Derrida has usefully called a "spectropoetics."[3] They focus our attention on the aesthetic aspects of the problem, whereby beings
and presences enter uneasily into, or insistently
disturb, representation and the stability of its
visual, temporal, and spatial logic. It is for these
multiple reasons that I take seriously these
ghostly matters in contemporary art.

    If these artists investigate the poetics
of the spectral, then they do so in quite diverse
and singular ways, invoking the equally diverse
and singular histories and geographies of colonialism. The approaches, for instance, include
Augustijnen's *Spectres*, in which the Belgian artist investigates the still-extant regime of justification of one collaborator for the crimes of
his country's colonial past in the Congo, which
leads to the witnessing of an apologist discourse

1   See Graham Harman, *Towards Speculative Realism: Essays and Lectures* (Winchester: Zero Books, 2010); and the March 2007 issue on speculative realism edited by Robin Mackay in the journal *Collapse*.

2   See Anselm Franke, "Much Trouble in the Transportation of Souls, or: The Sudden Disorganization of Boundaries," in *Animism*, ed. Anselm Franke (Berlin: Sternberg Press, 2010); Anselm Franke, ed., *Animism: Modernity Through the Looking Glass* (Cologne: Verlag der Buchhandlung Walther König, 2011); Okwui Enwezor et al., eds., *Experiments with Truth: Transitional Justice and the Processes of Truth and Reconciliation,* Documenta11_Platform 2 (Ostfildern: Hatje Cantz, 2002); and Okwui Enwezor, et al., eds., *Under Siege: Four African Cities; Freetown, Johannesburg, Kinshasa, Lagos,* Documenta11_Platform 4 (Ostfildern: Hatje Cantz, 2003).

3   Jacques Derrida, *Specters of Marx: The State of the Debt, the Work of Mourning, and the New International,* trans. Peggy Kamuf (London: Routledge, 1994). See also Avery Gordon, *Ghostly Matters: Haunting and the Sociological Imagination* (Minneapolis: University of Minnesota Press, 2004).

that ultimately condemns itself. Conversely, Brussels-based artist Meessen's *Vita Nova* (2009) opens up the ghost world surrounding the early critic of French colonialism, Roland Barthes, in order to reveal simultaneously the impossibility of any definitive and truthful account of history, and the ongoing need for a historical reckoning, in part by shedding light on the aftermath of France's colonial interventions in West Africa. Meanwhile, London-based artist Bhimji's *Yellow Patch* (2011) crafts a cinema of affect in order to explore an emotional sensitivity to the history, cultural geography, and ghostly presences of twentieth-century Indian migrants who once called Uganda their home and were later brutally exiled during the country's early years of independence (in Bhimji's case, ending up in Britain). Employing a still different artistic approach, Dutch artist Martens traveled to the Democratic Republic of the Congo for his video work *Episode III (Enjoy Poverty)* (2009) to create a performative intervention in the image regime of media, photojournalistic, and artistic representations of poverty, ultimately exhibiting the structural conditions of economic inequality under neoliberal globalization. And finally, for his various photographic series over the last decade, South African artist Hugo journeyed across sub-Saharan Africa to visualize the complex aspects of postcolonial social reality, offering a mix of performative artifice, allegories of horror and dysfunction, and testimonies of creative existence.

In this regard, *Return to the Postcolony* takes account of a convergence in contemporary art of the last few years whereby numerous practitioners in Europe (and in the case of Hugo, South Africa) have begun to explore the complex legacy of colonization, doing so at the moment of the fiftieth anniversary of independence for many African countries. (In the 1960s more than thirty countries gained their independence from nations including Britain, France, Belgium, and Spain.) The artists considered here are of a generation born during the 1960s and early 1970s, and are thus considering the colonial history of their parents' and grandparents' generations. There is also a shared impulse in critically investigating the conditions of neocolonialism that in recent years have thwarted economic development and democratization in equatorial Africa, as in many areas of the Global South, and which connects directly with the European political crisis around migration. This impulse has inspired a kind of "reverse migration" for European artists: to return to the postcolony to seek answers to urgent questions regarding the causes and histories behind the desire of multitudes to travel northward, and to account for the transgenerational haunting for the injustices of the past that continues to inform the present.

By invoking the term "postcolony"—identifying societies that have emerged from the experience of colonization—I remain aware of its chaotically pluralistic qualities, which prevents any single or general definition. As theorized by Achille Mbembe, the African postcolony nevertheless possesses an internal coherence, particularly in terms of the distinctive regime of violence of dictatorial and failed states alike. Mbembe describes that regime as expressive of a "necropolitics"—that is, a mode of governance and economy of death that merges a Foucauldian biopolitics with the Agambenian notion of bare life and the state of exception (visions of which appear variously in my case studies).[4] Yet while the postcolony maintains its own mythologies and fetishes of state and militia power, which Mbembe treats at length, one finds no such unmediated representation of such a reality within the works of the artists considered here—rather each offers a particular approach to the postcolony that is itself typically determined to greater or lesser degrees by European narratives, historical accounts, and symptomatic disavowals (in the films of, for instance, Augustijnen, Meessen, and Bhimji), as well as by the often clichéd mass media representations of central Africa (in the work of Martens and Hugo). As a result, the postcolonial condition emerges as one of "temporal entanglement," which encloses "multiple *durées* made up of discontinuities, reversals, inertias, and swings," including European narratives and representations and African experiences and histories that intertwine and (in)determine each other.[5] Still, in terms of my approach, there is no attempt to suggest a unified picture of postcolonial reality; instead, each artistic project offers its own entrance into distinctive and immensely complex histories and places.

That said, there is an additional internal coherence to the *economic* conditions of the postcolony that many of the projects considered here touch on, insofar as those conditions have come to define neoliberal Africa. As political theorist Graham Harrison observes, "It is fair to say that from the early 1980s, Africa was subjected to a pervasive and concerted project of economic liberalisation: a project that was aggressively advocated, funded and monitored by the World Bank and the IMF." As he explains, "structural adjustment"—a macroeconomic program that privatized industry, opened up states to deregulated free trade, and consequently defunded them—has led to the crumbling of social systems, insecurity, and lack of education and health care funding that we're familiar with today, becoming "in effect, the develop-

4   Achille Mbembe, "Provisional Notes on the Postcolony," in *Fault Lines: Contemporary African Art and Shifting Landscapes*, eds. Gilane Tawadros and Sarah Campbell (London: Iniva, 2003); and Achille Mbembe, "Necropolitics," *Public Culture* 15, no. 1 (Winter 2003).

5   Achille Mbembe, *On the Postcolony* (Berkeley: University of California Press, 2001), 14.

ment orthodoxy for the continent."[6] It is here that we get to one fundamental spectro-ontology—or birthplace of ghosts—of the postcolony. My running hypothesis is that the colonial past still haunts us because it is a past that has not really past. When Mbembe points out how "postcolonial state forms have inherited [...] the regime of impunity" of "colonial sovereignty,"[7] and when Harrison observes that "neoliberalism is one more project in a programme of Western imposition that commenced with colonisation,"[8] it becomes clear that the postcolony is not strictly *post*, but is in fact in many ways *neo*. Indeed, one might say that it has been *neo* ever since Ghanaian leader Kwame Nkruma coined the term in 1965 with his book *Neo-Colonialism: The Last Stage of Imperialism*—if for different reasons in the neoliberal present than during the beginnings of so-called independence.[9] Still, the basic idea is the same: *neo* signifies the continuation of colonial rule by other means, by political and economic control rather than military occupation.[10] It is in this context that we now live, even if it is frequently denied and disavowed by those that typically benefit from such arrangements, and who make the claim that we recognize a New World Order of liberal democracy, freedom, and economic inequality—inviting us to forget the war, suffering, and social dysfunction on which global neoliberalism thrives. Against the veil of mystification that represented the initial years of economic globalization in the 1990s, Derrida claimed, "It must be cried out, at a time when some have the audacity to neo-evangelize in the name of the ideal of a liberal democracy that has finally realized itself as the ideal of human history: never have violence, inequality, exclusion, famine, and thus economic oppression affected as many human beings in the history of the earth and of humanity."[11] One motivating factor behind Derrida's imperative is that if we *don't* cry out, then we face a continual haunting by the catastrophe of the colonial present, which is in fact what we've witnessed ever since.[12]

It is precisely the negations, disavowals, and rejections of historical responsibility and present advantage, occurring in political discourse as much as in cultural representations, that allow and even cause the ghosts to

6   Harrison goes on to point out that "the core policies within SAPs [Structural Adjustment Programs] were: the removal of exchange rate controls and consequent likely devaluation, the reduction of money supply and relatedly reduced public expenditures, increased rates of interest, the removal of price controls and public marketing institutions, and some kind of plan to open the economy more fully to FDI [Foreign Direct Investment] and relatedly privatisation." Graham Harrison, *Neoliberal Africa: The Impact of Global Social Engineering* (London: Zed Books, 2010), 39.

7   Mbembe, *On the Postcolony*, 26.

8   Harrison, *Neoliberal Africa*, 22.

9   Kwame Nkruma, *Neo-Colonialism: The Last Stage of Imperialism* (London: Thomas Nelson & Sons, 1965).

10   See Robert J. C. Young, *Postcolonialism: An Historical Introduction* (Oxford: Blackwell, 2001), esp. 47.

11   Derrida, *Specters of Marx*, 85.

12   Of course, the relation between past and present is not a simple matter, and Mbembe indicates elsewhere the necessity of addressing the aftermath of colonialism: "As far as Africa is concerned, colonialism is over. Apartheid is over too. Africans are now the free masters of their own destiny. This is why from an intellectual and political point of view, there is no turning away from the difficult work of freedom." Quoted in Christian Höller, "Africa in Motion: An Interview with the Post-Colonialism Theoretician Achille Mbembe," *Springerin* 3, no. 2 (June 2002), n.p. Also see Derek Gregory, *The Colonial Present* (Oxford: Blackwell, 2004).

fly free. This recognition of negation as a causality of haunting raises a problem in relation to aesthetics given its definition as a mode and medium of appearance. For how can we account for an aesthetics of the negation of appearance, or the appearance of negation, that determines the spectropoetics found in the works of the artists addressed in the following pages? For Derrida, the challenge is one of developing an appropriate "hauntology"— the study of the haunting of being, and of the being of haunting, which he carried out in reference to Shakespearean literary texts and Marx's writings.[13] Owing to the West's failure to address the suffering and misfortune that are the products of the global capitalism and liberal democracy it triumphantly celebrates, the West has remained haunted by the history of communism and its promise of equality and social justice, even as it thought that that history was definitively concluded with the fall of the Soviet Union.[14] Again, the problem is not one of dealing with spirits from another world; rather, it's a matter of being sensitive to modernity's phantoms—that is, the disturbances and lingering presences, or presences of absence in the orders of visual appearance, through which current social formations manifest the symptomatic traces and uncanny signs of modernity's history of violence and exclusions. For Gordon, "the ghost is a crucible for political mediation and historical memory," one that calls for "an alternative diagnostics" linking "the politics of accounting, in all its intricate political-economic, institutional, and affective dimensions, to a potent imagination of what has been done and what is to be done otherwise."[15]

It is such an "alternative diagnostics" that I also want to deploy in reading the innovative aesthetic terms of these artistic practices concerned with ghostly matters of the colonial past and present. In taking up the colonial histories and experiences, narratives and stories, they challenge the kind of "knowing" neoliberalism desires, and by challenging its epistemology of forgetfulness, they propose ways of enacting politics differently, as well as aligning art with the struggle against forgetting. The advantage being that by reckoning with these phantom presences, the artworks allow us to overcome the dangers of paranoia and depression, as well as surmounting traditional forms of critique that, in claiming access to a greater truth, often only ended in another level of mystification. Whereas Gordon's analysis takes up Freudian psychoanalysis—from the uncanny to the death drive—my own approach investigates ghostly matters in relation to the photographic and

13   Derrida, *Specters of Marx*, 10.

14   This revival of Marxism has been present in numerous exhibition projects in recent years. I explore some of them in my essay, "Is Another World Possible? The Politics of Utopia in Recent Exhibition Practice," in *On Horizons: A Critical Reader in Contemporary Art*, eds. Maria Hlavajova, Simon Sheikh, and Jill Winder (Utrecht: BAK, 2011).

15   Gordon, *Ghostly Matters*, 18.

filmic aesthetics that investigate colonial narratives, the materiality of haunted geographical sites, and the possessions of social figures. It takes seriously the filmic intimations and portents, negations and disavowals of historical and contemporary figures. My modus operandi is to provide close analyses of the works at hand and to think with and believe in them, to be sensitive to their aesthetic interventions and metamorphic transformations, as well as point out their critical limitations when appropriate.[16]

Organized over five interconnected chapters, *Return to the Postcolony* presents a series of case studies that contextualizes the select artist's work within a broader set of artistic developments in Europe and Africa, including contemporary art's relation to the aesthetics and politics of a variously reinvented documentary practice, critical and creative historiography, and postcolonial globalization. It is not surprising that the documentary mode emerges here as a crucial form in relation to the will-to-history in the context of enforced amnesia. Nor is it unexpected that documentary practice would find itself significantly challenged by what Derrida terms the "apparition of the inapparent" and the conjuring of "the untimely," which spectropoetics comprises. How such an aesthetics of the ghostly emerges in contemporary art, and exactly what it means for the reinvention of documentary practice, will be addressed in relation to the singularity of individual artworks—while simultaneously exploring the commonalities between these artists' projects in working toward breaking the spell of the colonial haunting and the political ambition that that shared commitment implies. The first chapter focuses on Augustijnen's film *Spectres*, which deals with the haunting of one Jacques Brassinne de la Buissière. A young diplomat at the time of the "Congo Crisis" in 1960–61, when the first elected prime minister of the country, Patrice Lumumba, was arrested, tortured, and assassinated, Brassinne has as of late turned into an obsessive archivist of the past he lived through. The film develops a complex and critical accounting of his discourse, opening up the trauma of Belgium's past, including the violent history of King Leopold II's nineteenth-century conquest of the Congo. It reveals the still-professed official narratives that whitewash the history of the country's involvement and carefully control its colonial archive. My analysis aims to bring out the importance of the film's investigation of the perpetrator's narrative, by which it resists continuing traditional documentary's longstanding and expected concern with the suffering of victims, and asking where such a focus leaves the viewer.

16   On learning to think with animism, see Isabelle Stengers, "Reclaiming Animism," *e-flux journal*, no. 36 (July 2012): 8. "Reclaiming animism does not mean, then, that we have ever been animist"; only becoming sensitive to the "assemblages that generate metamorphic transformation in our capacity to affect and be affected—and also to feel, think, and imagine."

The second chapter examines Meessen's filmic archaeology of the iconic image of a young African boy saluting the French flag that appeared on the cover of a 1955 issue of *Paris Match*. Roland Barthes famously analyzed the photo in his 1957 book *Mythologies*, wherein the French critic decoded the colonialist message of native devotion to the French Empire. Meessen recently visited Burkina Faso in search of the photograph's subject and found an old man whose memory of his country's colonial days was spotted with gaps, including—as shown in the film's opening scene—his recollection of many of the words to the French national anthem, which was once dutifully sung by the colonized. As it turns out, Barthes had himself "forgotten" to mention the history of his own family's relation to colonialism—and particularly that of his grandfather, Captain Louis Gustave Binger, who "gave" Ivory Coast to France—opening onto a critical and moving account of the specters that haunted Barthes, one of France's most enlightened cultural critics. That history has yet to be fully acknowledged today in cultural, historical, and political discourse in a France that has largely refused to engage its colonial legacy. As well, the film movingly explores the aftermath of the colonial project in contemporary central Africa, where new generations of Africans now salute their own national flags (but in whose interest is a question infrequently asked).

My third chapter considers Bhimji's recent film, for which the London-based artist returned to Gujarat, India, the point of origin for many Indians who left for East Africa during the late nineteenth- and early twentieth-century expansion of the British Empire. Her film investigates the historical intersection of colonialism and migration, and builds on her earlier films such as *Out of Blue* (2002), which traces the remnants of violence and present repression, and conversely the sources of tenderness and beauty, in postcolonial Uganda. That country remains the primal scene of trauma for thousands of Ugandan Asians who were violently expelled by the military dictator Idi Amin during the early years of his reign in 1972, when he attempted to "Africanize" his country by expelling all "foreigners," including some who had lived in the country and whose families had called Uganda home for several generations. Bhimji discovers the ruins of that expansive and transnational geography and fraught history in her allegorical imagery of sights and sounds of present-day Uganda, India, and Zanzibar, which elicits the terror of the colonial past and, paradoxically, the irrepressible desire of a homecoming. Distinct from the film essays of Augustijnen and Meessen, Bhimji's film includes almost no verbal language. Her work conjures the spirits of the past in order to create a new cinematic poetics of affect beyond the linguistic dimension.

The fourth chapter examines Martens's controversial film *Episode III (Enjoy Poverty)* (2009), which documents his intervention in the mediatized representations of the dire economic conditions of the Democratic Republic of the Congo. Proposing something of a Swiftian satire realized in the artist's performance, Martens suggests that the country's greatest "natural resource" is its poverty, for which it receives hundreds of millions of dollars in annual aid from international donors such as the World Bank. Investigating the implications of that scandalous proposal, Martens's film represents a critical exploration of the image industry of photojournalists, critical artists, documentarians, and humanitarians alike, which reveals the paradox of documentary practice based in well-intentioned compassion that risks contributing to, and economically benefiting from, the perpetuation of social crises. It also shows how present economic arrangements that drive African poverty are a carry-over from colonial dominance. As such, globalization remains haunted by the undead existence of Europe's imperial past.[17] In this case, exorcizing the ghosts of this past means discovering our own complicit position within the image regimes that mediate and even generate the reproduction of inequality.

The fifth chapter considers Hugo's documentary photography, for which he visited several sites in Africa, including the infamous Agbogbloshie market in Accra, Ghana, the center of a notorious e-waste dump that "recycles" disused European computer technology. The reality behind such environmentalism is the production of a toxic atmosphere ruinous to West Africa's social and natural ecology. Hugo's imagery of young foragers in these techno-wastelands represents the current-day reversal of years of colonial resource exploitation of African lands: now the obsolete products of Europe are returned to complete the cycle of destruction—both of lives and of environments. In this regard, European viewers are confronted with the specters of their own participation in the socio-environmental destruction of Africa, even as those specters of death and destruction are returned to them in the monsters of Nollywood horror, as captured in another of Hugo's photographic series, which transcribes the experiential deformities and economic alienations into a visual economy of white-eyed zombies and blood-sucking vampires. His imagery of "capitalist sorcery," one of possession and exploitation, offers a glimpse of the imaginary of contemporary neoliberalism.[18] Yet here horror also translates into a creative rewriting of the space of everyday life, and defines an imaginative

17   See David Harvey, *The New Imperialism* (Oxford: Oxford University Press, 2003).

18   See Philippe Pignarre and Isabelle Stengers, *Capitalist Sorcery: Breaking the Spell*, trans. Andrew Goffey (New York: Palgrave Macmillan, 2011).

form of survival and a posthuman futurity amid the crises that otherwise plague the postcolony.

If such a hauntological study necessarily proceeds by rejecting—along with Stengers, Latour, and Gordon—the clear separations between modern science and premodern animism, objective positivism and subjective belief, the real and the imaginary, then it corresponds, in my view, to an innovative approach to aesthetics that joins the factual and the fictional. It is in this sense that I remain sensitive to the novel approaches to the documentary mode here, in that the films and photographs of Augustijnen, Meessen, Bhimji, Martens, and Hugo reject the strict definition of the documentary as a matter of presenting facts in an objective fashion—as in current news media footage, legalistic and military surveillance, and forensic modes of representation—wherein we witness the survival of earlier paradigms of documentary authority, whether ethnographic, scientific, or criminological.[19] My analysis is attentive to the apparitions, the ghostly memories, the spectral figures, and the untimely presences that trouble and disturb those very declamations of historical truth and disavowals of the colonial present that make these artists attuned to what Meessen has termed a "colonial hauntology."[20] As such, it is entirely appropriate that this investigation is conducted in the medium of the moving image, the privileged modern site—along with photography—where we witness "the great Frankensteinian dream of the nineteenth century" wherein the dead appear to return to life.[21] As Franke points out in his own engagement with this line of inquiry in relation to contemporary art: "The Frankensteinian dream does not undo the subject–object dichotomy; rather, it qualifies it. It is the symptom of a bourgeois hegemonic perspective that has internalized the logic of the divide"—between animism and objectivism, between a porous relation between subjects and objects and its rigid separation in modern science—"and turns the tension, the antagonism between *rigor mortis* and phantasmagoric animation into an aesthetic economy endlessly reiterated."[22]

Still, that is not to say that these artworks surrender their purchase on capturing the significance of historical experience and even exposing and contesting the fabrications and lies of neocolonialist revisionism. These commitments have led to the original

19   For more on contemporary art's reinvention of documentary practice, see my book *The Migrant Image: The Art and Politics of Documentary During Global Crisis* (Durham, NC: Duke University Press, 2013). For a useful review of the history of ethnographic photography, see Christopher Pinney, *Photography and Anthropology* (London: Reaktion, 2011).

20   Meessen organized a film screening and discussion series under the title "Hantologie des colonies" from October 8 to November 18, 2011, in coordination with Espace Khiasma in Paris.

21   Noël Burch, *Life to Those Shadows* (Berkeley: University of California Press, 1990), 12.

22   Franke, "Much Trouble in the Transportation of Souls," 34. Franke draws on Latour's *We Have Never Been Modern* and discusses cinema, among other matters of contemporary art, as opening a liminal transit zone between objective and subjective, mechanical and phantasmic worlds.

approaches to what might be variously termed documentary fiction, the film fable, the cinema of affect, the film essay, and the performative documentary.[23] Confronting this blurring of fact and fiction, document and storytelling, it is the language of the literary, speculative, and aesthetic that becomes particularly apt in terms of defining a methodology where truth is not abandoned, but is instead found in the contingencies, conflicts, and shadows of historical discourse, media imagery, and social reality.[24] These films and photographs thus investigate, probe, and analyze what has been done, and in doing so, they provide numerous suggestions—if not ideologically programmatic or politically activist—for what is to be done otherwise. To start, what can be done otherwise is to acknowledge the ghosts, to open up the repressed histories, to admit the colonial present, and to commence this politics of memory in partnership with the dead in struggle. As Derrida observed almost twenty years ago, this is a time of the "learning to live," "to learn to live *with* ghosts. [...] To learn to live otherwise [...] more justly."[25] We are still grappling with that lesson. Enter the ghosts…

23   See Jacques Rancière, "Documentary Fiction: Marker and the Fiction of Memory," in *Film Fables*, trans. Emiliano Battista (London: Berg, 2006). For a useful history of the film essay, which also joins documentary and fiction in a self-reflexive, interrogatory, and critical aesthetic, see Nora M. Alter, "Translating the Essay into Film and Installation," *Journal of Visual Culture* 6, no. 1 (2007).

24   In other words, truth survives as a "matter of concern," to invoke Latour once again, as well as constitutes a "politics of truth" in the Foucauldian sense. See Michel Foucault, "Subjectivity and Truth," in *The Politics of Truth*, ed. Sylvère Lotringer, trans. Lysa Hochroth and Catherine Porter (Los Angeles: Semiotext(e), 2007), 152–53.

25   Derrida, exordium to *Specters of Marx*, xviii.

1. Sven Augustijnen's
Spectropoetics

The world in which we live today is at each moment the world of the past. It consists of moments and relics of what man has done for better or worse; in other words, it is entirely right to say that we are haunted by the past.
—Sven Augustijnen, quoting Hannah Arendt[1]

History will one day have its say; it will not be the history taught in the United States, Washington, Paris, or Brussels, however, but the history taught in the countries that have rid themselves of colonialism and its puppets. Africa will write its own history, and both north and south of the Sahara it will be a history full of glory and dignity.
—Patrice Lumumba, letter to Pauline Lumumba[2]

Sven Augustijnen's *Spectres* (2011), a film of roughly one hundred minutes, takes up the traumatic memories of Belgium's past interventions in the Congo and the haunting that those memories inspire. Most immediately, the period in question concerns the intervention in 1960–61 during the momentous process of Congolese independence when Belgium, under King Baudouin, granted nominal sovereignty to its colonial possession but refused to surrender political and economic control of it, leading to disastrous results. That period of semi-independence cloaking foreign intervention and control is continuous with the longer history of Belgium's colonization of the Congo, beginning with King Leopold II forcibly taking possession of the African country eighty times the size of his own, and creating the "Congo Free State" in 1884, before international pressure obliged him to make it Belgian property in 1908. It is this history that provides an important backdrop to the film. Indeed, at one point the film shows the tombs of Leopold II and Baudouin lying side by side in the crypt of the Church of Notre Dame of Laeken, thereby drawing the connection between colonial and neocolonial eras and indicating the expansive history that bears on the present, which is the film's immediate area of concern.

If the present remains filled with ghosts from that sordid past, chief among them is the spirit of Patrice Lumumba. The first elected prime minister of independent Congo, Lumumba attempted to throw off the yoke of colonial control during his brief time in office before being imprisoned and brutally executed on January 17, 1961, with the alleged complicity of Belgium, the United States, and the United Nations (as well as the Belgian min-

1   In Sven Augustijnen, "An Interview with Colette Braeckman," *A Prior*, no. 14 (2007), the artist quotes Hannah Arendt, "Home to Roost: A Bicentennial Address," *The New York Review of Books*, June 26, 1975.

2   Patrice Lumumba, "Letter to Pauline Lumumba," in *Lumumba Speaks: The Speeches and Writings of Patrice Lumumba, 1958–1961*, ed. Jean Van Lierde, trans. Helen R. Lane (Boston: Little, Brown and Company, 1972), 422–23.

ing group Union Minière du Haut Katanga).[3] It is no doubt that the meaning of Lumumba's contentious historical legacy continues to disturb Belgium's fragile sense of nationality—in addition to French–Walloon linguistic and cultural rifts—divided in this regard between its elite political establishment and its postcolonial immigrant community. As a result, many spirits of the past—Lumumba's in particular—continue to fly free. For some, like the Brussels-based collective Mémoires Coloniales, which continues to struggle for the explicit and critical engagement with Belgium's colonial history, Lumumba represents a beacon of hope for an independent Africa: "His memory must remain alive, his fight a source of inspiration for Africa's emancipatory struggles."[4] For others, such as Arnoud d'Aspremont Lynden, son of Harold d'Aspremont Lynden, the Belgian minister of African affairs during the early 1960s, Lumumba figures as "Belgium's political enemy" to this day.[5] Confronted with such fundamental disagreements over the meaning of the past and its notable figures, we await the realization of Lumumba's vision of a glorious and dignified history of Africa. In the meantime, specters reign.

And the ghosts that appear in *Spectres* are numerous, which is not surprising, given the film's copious and wide-ranging historical references and the volatile situation of the present. As one comes to suspect, Augustijnen's film shows how the haunting lives on especially as a result of fanatical attempts of some Belgians to control the historical narrative, particularly those who lived through the events of the early '60s and remain possessed by the experience today. Obsessed with history, they ignore the present and its shifting attitudes toward past colonialism. Indeed, the film was made during the buildup to and celebrations of the fiftieth anniversary of Congolese independence (marking equally the fiftieth anniversary of Lumumba's assassination). Belgium's current monarch King Albert II participated in the festivities by visiting Kinshasa, but not without controversy. The royal presence in the Congo elicited charges of Belgium's endorsement of Joseph Kabila's corrupt regime and inspired protests in Belgium against the general amnesia regarding the past that continues to inform present neocolonial relations. How *can* the ghosts be laid to rest, we are led to ask, when the events that unleashed them are not entirely concluded, only repressed in the present?

3   See Ludo De Witte, *The Assassination of Lumumba*, trans. Ann Wright and Renée Fenby (London: Verso, 2003).

4   Pauline Imbach, of Mémoires Coloniales, "Patrice Lumumba: Belgium Must Recognize Its Historical Responsibilities," in *Sven Augustijnen: Spectres,* eds. Steven Tallon and Emiliano Battista (Brussels: ASA Publishers, 2011), 116. Translation slightly modified by the author; originally published as an open letter in the daily *Le Soir* on January 28, 2009.

5   Arnoud d'Aspremont Lynden, "Patrice Lumumba: Belgium Did Not Plot His Assassination," in ibid., 126. Originally published as an open letter in the daily *Le Soir* on February 11, 2009.

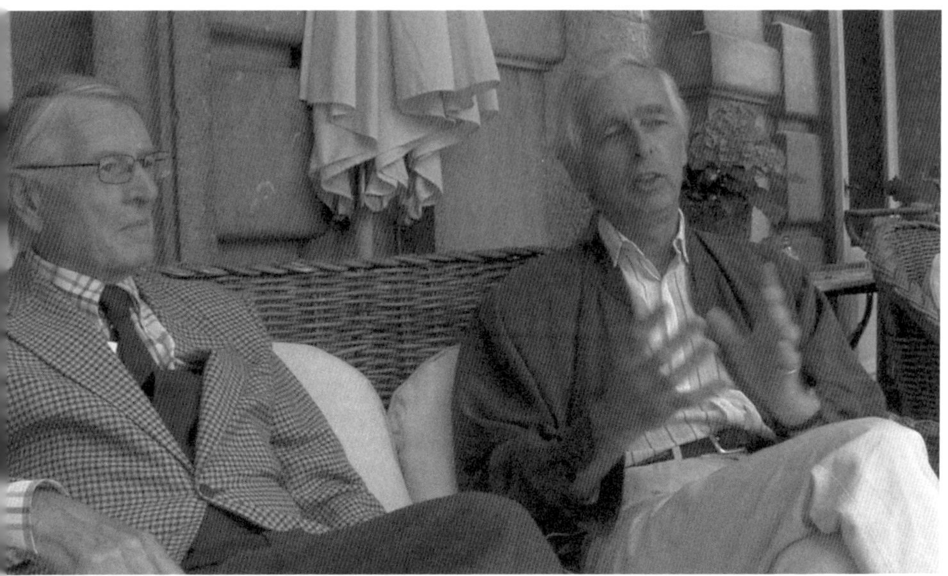

Sven Augustijnen, still from *Spectres*, 2011

Spectres deftly opens up the symptoms of that repressed history, and the history of that repression, by training its camera on one Jacques Brassinne de la Buissière, a young Belgian diplomat based in Elisabethville, Katanga, at the time of the 1960 "Congo Crisis." Brassinne later became a historian of the crisis, submitting his doctorate in 1991 on the circumstances of Lumumba's assassination and coauthoring the book on the subject, *Qui a tué Patrice Lumumba?*.[6] The film takes us to various locations in Belgium and the Democratic Republic of the Congo (DRC), where Brassinne, serving as charismatic guide and central subject of the film, is shown making visits and conversing with other characters about the history that appears to haunt him. Chief among them are Arnoud d'Aspremont Lynden and Jacques Bartelous, chief of cabinet to Moïse Tshombe, leader of the Belgian-supported Katanga secession that brought on the calculated civil war and shook Lumumba from power. Brassinne is also shown meeting Marie Tshombe at the Etterbeek cemetery on the occasion of the fortieth anniversary of the death of her father, and visiting Lumumba's widow Pauline Opango, and her children Patrice, Juliana, and Roland Lumumba, at their family home in Kinshasa.

Spectres focuses on these few individuals, yet the central one is Brassinne, a civil servant who lived in the Congo at the time of the

6   Jacques Brassinne and Jean Kestergat, *Qui a tué Patrice Lumumba?* (Paris: Duculot, 1991).

events in question. In this regard, the film sheds light on the banal and low-level bureaucratic workings of (neo)colonial power and the way functionaries come to identify with their leaders and their respective political agendas long after critical events have past. Nonetheless, more than this narrow focus would suggest, the film's subject continues to implicate those living in the present. At stake is the history of the transitional moment when the era of European colonialism came to a close, transmuting into a more complex form of neocolonialism that continues into the present—a mix of political independence and economic subjection[7]—forming a legacy of injustice, exploitation, and state violence that is the common heritage of contemporary society. To ignore this history would be to misunderstand the development of globalization and its present economic and political inequalities. In this sense, Hannah Arendt's insight remains valid: "It is entirely right to say that we are haunted by the past."

—

In addition to the film, Augustijnen has presented an installation of numerous photographs, documents, and recordings from Brassinne's extensive historical archive on the same subject. These were on display for the first time at WIELS in Brussels in 2011. Further material has been compiled into a book, also titled *Spectres*, which includes an extensive interview with Brassinne, additional historical information and newspaper articles, and supplementary reproductions of Brassinne's many photographs, including images of military operations in the Congo in which he appears[8]—all of which comprises the larger research materials of Augustijnen's extensive project and testifies to the considerable work that went into its development. In the exhibition, a suite of reprinted black-and-white images showing trees and bushes in the Congolese savannah attested to Brassinne's longstanding quest to determine the execution site and burial grounds of Lumumba, which he first identified in 1988 during his doctoral research. Additionally, an audio recording played a 1974 interview with Brassinne for Radio Télévision Belge Francophone concerning his research and conclusions on the subject at the time; and documents, artifacts, and publications (including the four weighty volumes of his doctoral thesis) filled a vitrine. (Augustijnen included the reverse side of one framed photograph of the Congo's independence ceremony on which Brassinne handwrote the misspelled

7   For a precise definition of neocolonialism, see Young, *Postcolonialism.*

8   As Augustijnen has explained to me, these images concern "the reconquering of Stanleyville" by the "Ommegang Brigade" in November 1964; Ommegang was composed of Congolese, Belgian, and former Katangese mercenaries and American troops. See Tallon et al., *Sven Augustijnen: Spectres,* 82–90.

words "L'indépence du Congo"—offering us a telling lapsus.) The material speaks to Brassinne's thoroughgoing, even compulsive attempts at reconstructing and defending his own narrative of the past, one that basically absolves Belgium of all guilt or responsibility for Lumumba's death.

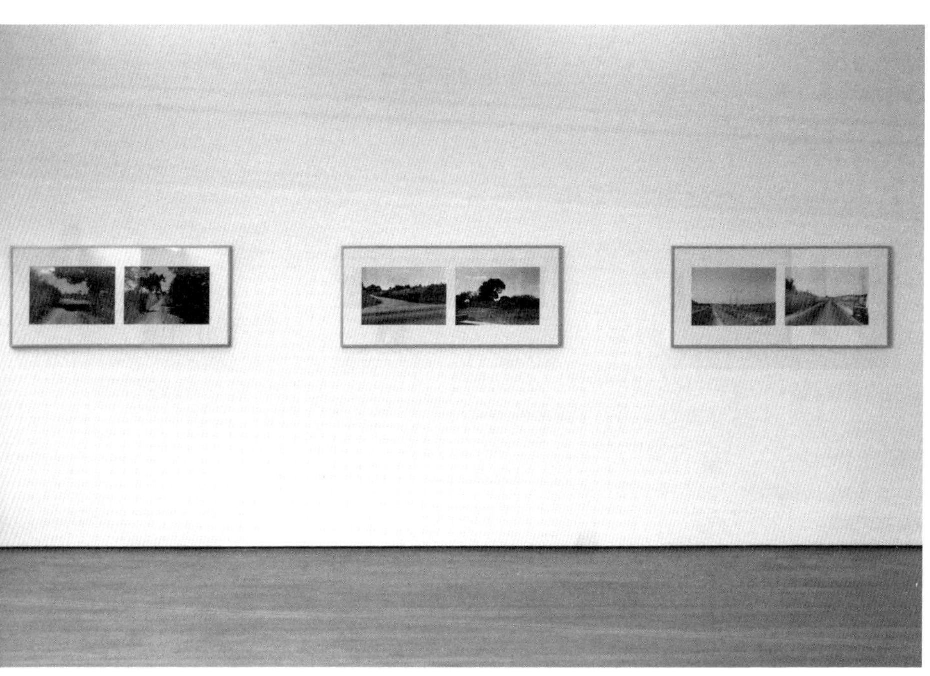

Exhibition view; Sven Augustijnen, "Spectres," WIELS, Brussels, 2011

Yet clearly Brassinne is not the only one concerned with these events. The fraught history, or rather controversial historiography, of Belgium's relationship to the Congo has repeatedly appeared in—as if also haunting—Augustijnen's recent work. For the journal *A Prior* in 2007, for instance, the artist presented a series of historical articles and covers from the old French magazine *Pourquoi Pas?*, addressing how the passage to Congolese independence, as well as the shady circumstances around the alleged Belgian complicity in the death of Tshombe, was covered—and covered up—with anxiety in the Belgian press. Continuing this line of research, Augustijnen's *Les Demoiselles de Bruxelles* (2008) consisted of an installation of photographs and texts that interlink the lives of Karl Marx, Leopold II, and several African prostitutes who work on Avenue Louise, a major thoroughfare in the Belgian capital—a grouping, the artist explains, brought together by a shared relation to the city of Brussels. There, Marx wrote *The Communist Manifesto*; today, former colonialists gather at the equestrian statue of Leopold II at Place du Trône and Congolese women ply their trade, their presence owed to Belgium's colonial history.[9] For Marx, of course, the specter haunting Europe was "the spectre of communism," as he declared famously in his manifesto; for Augustijnen, it is the specter of colonialism, as he claimed when he announced his plans to make *Spectres* in the context of *Les Demoiselles de Bruxelles*: "We will go on a journey to the heart of contemporary Europe, where a number of archetypal personages are haunted by the premises of colonial history and the trauma it has caused."[10]

If *Spectres* offers an account of one man's relationship to an event of world-historical significance, insofar as Lumumba's assassination would presage the general tendency of African nations to move from independence to neocolonial servitude (seventeen gained independence in 1960 alone), the film is not merely a documentary of Brassinne and his archive. Rather, *Spectres* proposes an innovative modeling of what we could term the research film, one that draws on essayistic inquiry, ethnographic analysis, and philosophical and political investigation, connecting to a history of filmmaking over the last few decades including the work of Jean Rouch, Claude Lanzmann, Chantal Akerman, Chris Marker, Harun Farocki, Raoul Peck, and Marcel Ophüls. The tendency of Augustijnen's film to blur the boundaries between fact and fiction, thereby avoiding the documentary traps of objectivity, truthfulness, and authority, connects his practice further to those experimental film precedents, and brings it into constellation with likeminded contemporaries, such as the Otolith Group, Hito Steyerl, and Deimantas Narkevicius, as well as his collaborators in the Brussels-based Auguste Orts platform, Herman Asselberghs, Manon de Boer, and Anouk De Clercq.[11] Yet the performative quality of Augustijnen's investigation, coupled with its focus on the discourse of a single figure implicated in (post)colonial history, brings

9   See Sven Augustijnen, interview by Ronald van de Sompel, "What a Day for a Daydream," *Mousse*, no. 27 (February–March 2011). Augustijnen also mentions that "the eminent historian Jean Stengers lived up until his death only a hundred meters from my house on the Avenue de la Couronne. His masterpiece *Congo: mythes et réalités* (1989) impelled me to scrutinize the boundaries between the legitimization and the historiography of our colonial past." See "Roundtable on Sven Augustijnen's *Spectres* (2011) with Sven Augustijnen, Filip De Boeck, Dirk Snauwaert, and Françoise Vergès, moderated by T. J. Demos and Hilde Van Gelder," in *In and Out of Brussels: Figuring Postcolonial Africa and Europe*, eds. T. J. Demos and Hilde Van Gelder (Leuven: Leuven University Press, 2012), 35.

10   "Nous y suivrons le périple, au cœur de l'Europe actuelle, d'une foule de personnages archétypaux, 'hantés' par les prémices de l'histoire coloniale et les traumatismes qu'elle a causés." Sven Augustijnen, preface to *Les Demoiselles de Bruxelles* (Amsterdam: de Appel, 2008), 6; my translation.

11   See T. J. Demos, "Auguste Orts: Sensing Politics," in *Auguste Orts: Correspondence* (Antwerp: MuHKA, 2010). For further analysis of the work of the Otolith Group and Steyerl, see Demos, *The Migrant Image*. Augustijnen invited Narkevicius to participate in the special issue of *A Prior*, no. 14 (2007), which he coedited. On the essay film, see Timothy Corrigan, *The Essay Film: From Montaigne, After Marker* (Oxford: Oxford University Press, 2011); and Alter, "Translating the Essay into Film and Installation."

to mind other notable contemporaries such as Wendelien van Oldenborgh and her video work *Maurits Script* (2006). Filmed in the Mauritshuis Museum in The Hague, the artist choreographs eight young people who are shown speaking the words of the seventeenth-century Dutch governor of colonial Brazil, Johan Maurits van Nassau, who attempted to modernize the New World. Taking its discourse from various sources, including historical council reports and personal letters, the film materializes the words of van Nassau on topics such as the economic benefits of slavery, the practice of colonial government, and the supposed "nature" of the native population—but it does so disjunctively in the contemporary voices of a racially and ethnically diverse group of Dutch actors. Exemplifying a contemporary slice of the Netherlands' heterogeneous population, the group's discussion allows still unresolved historical conflicts to emerge in relation to present policies regarding immigration, economic inequality, racism, and segregation, particularly in the second part of the video where the actors tackle these thorny issues directly.[12]

By offering a critical perspective on Belgium's imperial history and creatively intervening into how images and sounds are organized in documentary film, Augustijnen's film contributes to this paradigm shift in terms of bringing forth the history of cultural representations of power and particularly that of colonial history. (Of course Augustijnen's focus on Brassinne—as a contemporary apologist for a past colonialism—differs markedly from van Oldenborgh's focus on the dramatic reanimation of a historical exemplar of colonial practice.)[13] More specifically, *Spectres* advances Augustijnen's aesthetic of what we might call "performative documentary," wherein the dramatization and direct transmission of reality intertwine (as with *Maurits Script* and, as we'll see, with Vincent Meessen's *Vita Nova*). Proposing a specific version of what Jacques Rancière usefully calls "documentary fiction,"[14] the speaking subjects of Augustijnen's films tell stories at the same time as they are shown dramatizing their roles—such as the thieves who share the secrets of their trade in *L'École des Pickpockets* (2000); or the insider who divulges the codes of the gay cruising scene taking place under the cover of trees in the Parc de Bruxelles in *Le Guide du Parc* (2001); or, again, the pseudo-journalist who interviews various members of the financial-political establishment, in-

12   Yet, like Augustijnen's practice, van Oldenborgh's is one "that can only be productive if concepts are pushed to the point where the antinomies they constitute are exposed as *historical contradictions* that are themselves seen as traces of history to be explored and exploited, rather than as logical paradoxes to be removed," as writes Sven Lütticken in "Interzone: On Three Works by Wendelien van Oldenborgh," *Afterall* 29 (Spring 2012): 55; also see Emily Pethick, "Wendelien van Oldenborgh: 'The past is never dead. It's not even past,'" *Afterall* 29 (Spring 2012).

13   For an example of the mythologizing forces of cinema brought to bear on royal power in the colonial context, consider the filmic precedent of André Cauvin's portrayal of King Baudouin's visit to the Congo in his 1955 documentary, *Bwana Kitoko (Noble Seigneur)*.

14   See Rancière, "Documentary Fiction," in *Film Fables*.

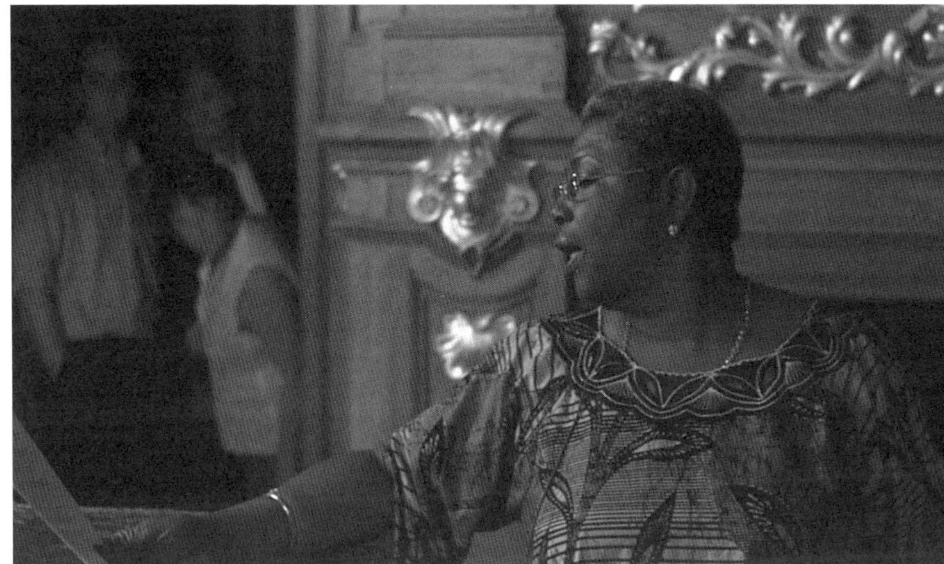

Wendelien van Oldenborgh, still from *Maurits Script*, 2006

cluding one female real-estate magnate, involved in the early
planning stages of the contemporary art center that would later
become WIELS, in *Une Femme Entreprenante* (2005). These figures perform the conventions of the documentary mode, while
Augustijnen documents their performances. The result dissolves
the clear divisions between fact and fiction, documentary truth
and subjective dramatization.[15] Documentary and fiction—normally opposed—are here made to intertwine such that fiction
is shown to be a way of recreating the world through inspired
narration, and documentary becomes a contingent, subjective act
that is equally an imaginative construction. That said, Augustijnen
diversifies his use of this format, each film being its own singular
experiment (for instance, there is no figure of the pseudo-journalist in *Spectres*), though there is one important continuity:
in each the filmmaker remains a nonspeaking
and hidden witness.

According to Augustijnen's longstanding deconstruction of documentary practice,
the object is not to record speech as a transparent medium of reality or to reveal some
faithful transcription of a social and political truth, but instead to investigate how his
subjects construct one version of reality. As

15   In his book *Blurred Boundaries:
Questions of Meaning in Contemporary
Culture* (Bloomington: Indiana University Press, 1994), Bill Nichols details
five modes of documentary practice:
expository, observational, interactive,
reflexive, and performative. Augustijnen
provides a further development of
this last category, where documentary
records a performance that reveals
documentary's constructive aspects.

the artist acknowledges: "Aren't journalists and documentary filmmakers always the first to manipulate reality? Aren't they constantly lying to get the images and testimonies they want? The ones that best sell the story?"[16] That documentaries are in some sense fictions is of course not a new realization—the fact goes back to documentary's very origins with pioneers like Robert Flaherty—and Augustijnen has acknowledged an interest in the work of filmmaker Marcel Ophüls on this basis. In his 1994 film *Veillées d'armes: Histoire du journalisme en temps de guerre*, Ophüls called attention to the famous journalist and critic Phillip Knightley, whose observation that "the first victim of war is the truth" Augustijnen mentioned in a recent interview.[17] The motto—Ophüls's as much as Knightley's—could also serve as the underlying principle in *Spectres*, which has as much to do with the war for truth as it does with the sacrifice of truth in war. That is to say, *Spectres* is far from a fly-on-the-wall recording of the real; rather, it represents a determined organization of movements and sounds that produces a multivalent construction of its subject.

More precisely, *Spectres* investigates the way discourse releases the ghosts of history *despite*—and no doubt *because of*—its speakers' intentions, as they try but inevitably fail to bury the traumatic episodes of the past that continue to haunt them in the present. In this regard, the film and the installation take up the fundamental problem that the spectral poses to representation: how to take the seen and the spoken and allow the normally silent and invisible elements that shadow them to be visible and heard. What would an aesthetics of the ghostly be? How can we bring about an "apparition of the inapparent" and a conjuring of "the untimely," as Derrida describes it insightfully in his own investigation of "spectropoetics"—designating the aesthetic conditions of specters and their challenge to representation? It is the artistic and specifically *filmic* relation to the aesthetics of the ghostly, and further, its potential for a critical history of the postcolonial that Augustijnen explores, which I will analyze in greater detail in what follows.

—

16   Augustijnen, "Interview with Braeckman," n.p.

17   Ibid. See Phillip Knightley, *The First Casualty: The War Correspondent as Hero, Propagandist, and Myth Maker from the Crimea to Kosovo* (London: Prion, 2000).

Not surprisingly for a story about one man's haunting, *Spectres* is set within the mise-en-scènes of the ghostly—a cemetery, an execution site, a church crypt, the grounds of a museum filled with fallen monuments—which provide the setting for a film that includes shots of old photographs and audio recordings from the history in question, all connected in one way or another to Brassinne. We follow Brassinne, for instance, to the Etterbeek cemetery and the grave of Tshombe, who oversaw Lumumba's execution by firing squad, only to be later exiled by the dictator Joseph-Désiré Mobutu, dying under mysterious circumstances in Algiers—again with alleged secret Belgian involvement.[18] Additionally, an eight-minute passage in the film documents the royal commemoration of the sixteenth anniversary of the death of King Baudouin on July 31, 2009, at the Church of Notre Dame of Laeken, attended by Baudouin's surviving widow, Queen Fabiola. The ceremony, at once religious, nationalist, and aristocratic, offers a glimpse at how some among the Belgian elite—including Brassinne—remain faithful to their ancestors and celebrate what they imagine to be their glorious historical achievements. A nostalgic undertone competes with the mourning of the colonial era they helped realize, one that is clearly at odds with the dark revelations of the film.

Spectres also shows Brassinne at his home amid his historical archive and carefully hand-drawn maps, where at one point he is seen listening to recordings of the famous speeches King Baudouin and Lumumba made on that fateful day, June 30, 1960, at the Palais de la Nation in Leopoldville during the country's independence ceremony. Whereas the king marked the occasion in paternalistic tones, paying homage to the genius of Leopold II, who purportedly delivered the country to this triumphal moment, Lumumba responded with an impassioned, confrontational rebuttal in which he recalled the Congolese experience of Belgian rule as one of "cruel and inhuman" inequalities, of being "mocked, insulted, beaten, morning, noon, and night," and submitted to "injustice, oppression and exploitation." In his speech, Lumumba made it clear that if "the Congo's independence […] is being proclaimed by Belgium […] no Congolese worthy of that name should ever forget that *we* gained it by fighting for it."[19] By showing Brassinne listening to the speeches while sitting on his couch a half century later, the notorious affront to the king's honor replaying, the film suggests that men like Brassinne will never forget that perceived insult, and indeed that their life's work is in one way or another a desperate and endless defense mechanism.

Spectres also takes us to the DRC, where Brassinne visits the National Museum's garden in Kinshasa and sits amid the rusting bronze statues of Leopold II and Henry Morton

18   For this history of Belgian involvement in Tshombe's neutralization, see Sven Augustijnen, "Qu'en pensez-vous Bwana Kitoko?," *A Prior*, no. 14 (2007).

19   See Lumumba, "Speech at Proclamation of Independence," in *Lumumba Speaks*, 221.

Stanley (the Welsh explorer who claimed the Congo for Leopold II), resting as cast-off ruins from a bygone age. Like relics, they appear still redolent of past colonial energies, still happy to lord over the territory they once believed to have "discovered," even if lying on their sides. He later joins Lumumba's widow Opango and her family for an awkward visit at their house in the DRC's capital, where Lumumba's life-size portrait looms forlornly in the background, propped against the wall just behind where Brassinne clumsily sits, offering us an uncanny and sudden materialization of Lumumba's ghostly presence. Brassinne also retraces the ruins of the Brouwez house in Katanga, where Lumumba was held and savagely beaten during his final hours, and lastly the savannah nearby where he faced a firing squad.

Yet more than this staging of ruins, relics, and spaces that continue to resonate with the presence of irrepressible revenants of the past, the film offers a poetics of the spectral, an aesthetics of the ghostly, achieved through multiple means. It does so discursively (in terms of the film's presentation of speech); textually (by the information presented in the intertitles, which throws the discourse into a new light); sonically (by the use of Bach's *St. John Passion* on the soundtrack); and visually (in relation to the way shadowy appearances figure in the film). By interlinking these diverse strands, *Spectres* constructs a complex hauntology that leaves us engrossed in the story, as well as shaken in its aftermath. By no means a mere aestheticization of the historical past, Augustijnen's film shows how living with ghosts and registering their presence can be a critical project of social justice today.

—

The film begins with Brassinne visiting Arnoud d'Aspremont Lynden's opulent château—the twenty-six minute conversation between the two is the film's longest. The exchange commences with reference to an open letter published in the Belgian newspaper *Le Soir* in 2009 by the collective Mémoires Coloniales, which holds Belgium accountable for the murder of Lumumba and names Harold d'Aspremont Lynden among those responsible. As proof, the group quotes the now-famous telex written by the minister on October 6, 1960, which states, "The main goal to pursue—in the interests of the Congo, Katanga and Belgium—is, obviously, the definitive elimination of Lumumba."[20] When Brassinne brings up this charge in the film, d'Aspremont Lynden

20   "L'objectif principal à poursuivre dans l'intérêt du Congo, du Katanga et de la Belgique est évidemment l'élimination définitive de Lumumba." Cited in Imbach, "Patrice Lumumba," as it appears in Tallon et al., *Sven Augustijnen: Spectres*, 118; and in d'Aspremont Lynden, "Patrice Lumumba," reprinted in ibid., 122.

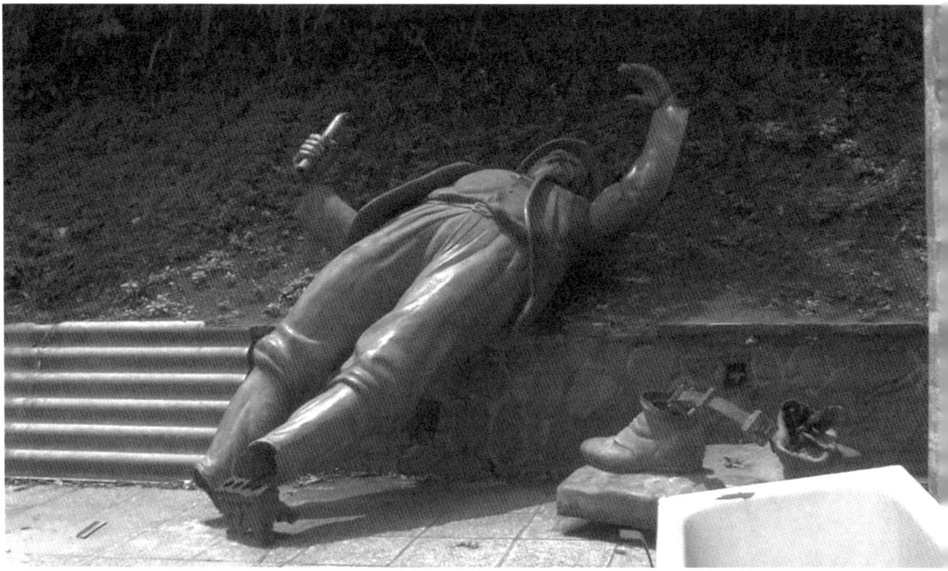

Sven Augustijnen, still from *Spectres*, 2011

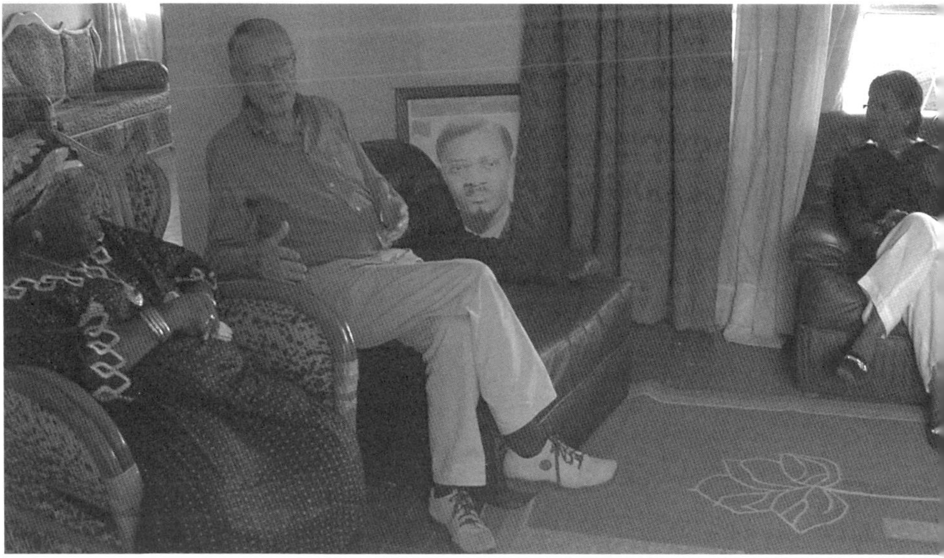

Sven Augustijnen, still from *Spectres*, 2011

responds disdainfully that his father was no "idiot" and that "if he had really intended to have Patrice Lumumba killed, he wouldn't have put it in black and white in a telex to a diplomat, with a copy to another diplomat and the minister of foreign affairs, which was then Pierre Wigny, who was an extremely cautious man."[21] Situated among a larger series of refutations, the passage is extraordinary because it represents a curious moment when d'Aspremont Lynden's defensive logic can be seen to surprisingly flip sides. Whereas he attempts to discredit his adversaries' accusation by pointing to its internal contradictions, he also imagines on what plausible terms his father *could* have been involved in the affair. By including this scene, *Spectres* shows d'Aspremont Lynden's words getting the better of him and unwittingly illuminating the dark shadows that surround his statements.

As the two continue their conversation, Augustijnen's handheld camera roves around the figures, surveying them from a distance, zooming in on details such as their shoes, panning toward peripheral areas. These visual elements bring about a disjunction between the seen and the heard, imagery and discourse, whereby the camera's unsettled mobility parallels the dislodging of the speakers' words. Things do not appear to be what they seem, as the camera anxiously searches the offscreen for the presence of the unsaid and unseen. At one point, when the figures transition to the living room to continue the discussion, the camera pans past an old photograph of Harold d'Aspremont Lynden, who peers into the interior of his son's château, an intruding ghostly presence still bearing on the living, shown as if to point out the origin of the visual and auditory idiosyncrasies that disturb this house.

Arnoud d'Aspremont Lynden's defense—even if it includes a semi-acknowledgment cloaked in denial of his father's complicity in the affair—is in fact a familiar motif from a longstanding argument, one that, as *Spectres* shows, connects with Belgium's official narrative since 1961. Most recently, that argument reprises a similar exchange that arose from the publication in 1999 of Ludo De Witte's book, *The Assassination of Lumumba*. Cited numerous times in the film, the book charges Harold d'Aspremont Lynden with assuming a leading role in the elimination of Lumumba, even if several other representatives of Belgium, the United Nations, and the United States, together with Congolese leaders Tshombe and Mobutu, are also named as responsible. As the collective Mémoires Coloniales quotes De Witte, "It was Belgian advice,

21   "Si son intention était vraiment de faire assassiner Patrice Lumumba, il n'aurait évidemment pas écrit ça noir sur blanc dans un télex envoyé à un diplomate, avec copie à un autre diplomate, avec copie au ministre des affaires étrangères qui se trouvait être Pierre Wigny à l'époque et dont tout le monde connait l'extrême prudence." As with all subsequent quotes, I use the English translation as it appears in the film's subtitles.

Belgian orders and finally Belgian hands that killed Lumumba on that 17 January 1961."[22] In fact, De Witte's argument was a direct rebuttal of Brassinne's 1991 doctoral thesis, which argued that Belgium was innocent of such charges, the assassination being a "Bantu affair." It is for this reason that Brassinne exclaimed to Augustijnen that "Ludo De Witte is my spectre!" when he was first approached about the possibility of appearing in the film.[23]

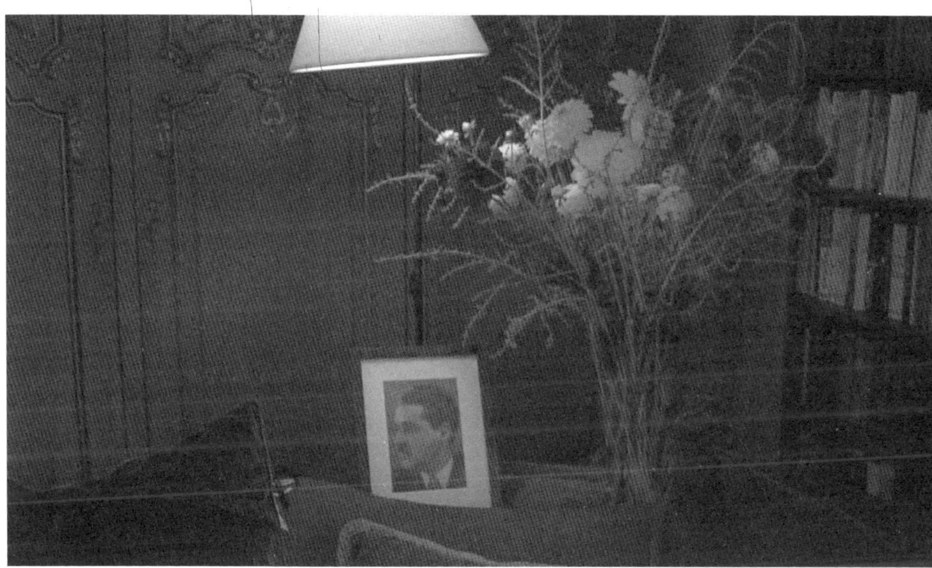

Sven Augustijnen, still from *Spectres*, 2011

22   De Witte, *The Assassination of Lumumba*, xxii; cited in Imbach, "Patrice Lumumba," in Tallon et al., *Sven Augustijnen: Spectres*, 118.

23   See Augustijnen, "What a Day for a Daydream," n.p. Also see Augustijnen, "Every Evening, We Wired News to Brussels: An Interview with Jacques Brassinne," in Tallon et al., *Sven Augustijnen: Spectres*, esp. 102, where Brassinne discusses his relation to De Witte at length.

24   "Dans un rapport extrêmement fouillé de 988 pages avec une collection incroyable d'autres documents, elle a, à mon avis, prouvé le contraire à savoir il s'agit d'une élimination de la scène politique et non pas d'une élimination physique."

A more significant accomplishment of De Witte's book was its role in bringing about Belgium's 1999–2001 parliamentary commission (established to investigate the circumstances of the assassination of Lumumba), and which responded officially to De Witte's damning thesis. Arnoud d'Aspremont Lynden refers to its conclusions in the film, claiming that "in an extremely detailed report of 988 pages with an incredible collection of other documents, it proved the opposite, in my view. Namely that [the telex] was referring to [Lumumba's] elimination from the political scene and not his physical elimination."[24] Whereas d'Aspremont

Lynden found reprieve for his father in the commission's findings, the latter's conclusions in fact established that Belgium bore a "moral responsibility" for events surrounding Lumumba's assassination, which others took to heart. Reflecting on the commission, Belgian Foreign Minister Louis Michel, for instance, denounced "the general attitude of disinterest and apathy towards the fate of Patrice Lumumba" as "a serious lapse in good government and respect for a sovereign state," and recognized that "certain members of the then government and certain other Belgian protagonists at the time bear an irrefutable measure of responsibility for the events leading up to Patrice Lumumba's death."[25]

Nevertheless, it is clear that d'Aspremont Lynden has drawn his own conclusions, and Brassinne shows himself in agreement during the conversation in the film when he claims, "The commission went too far when it says that the Belgians knew and are morally responsible. That's not true. The Belgians aren't morally responsible. The Belgians were used as an instrument. That's completely clear."[26] He proceeds to blame various Katangan government officials, such as Tshombe, and those from Leopoldville, such as Justin Bomboko and Victor Nendaka, for the murder. Which is not at all surprising coming from the author of the "Enquête sur la mort de Patrice Lumumba" (Inquiry into the Death of Patrice Lumumba), the unpublished doctoral dissertation he defended at the Université Libre de Bruxelles in 1991 and dedicated to Harold d'Aspremont Lynden (as *Spectres* points out in its intertitles). Brassinne wrote that even the Belgians who took part in the actual shooting of Lumumba were "disciplined subalterns" who "bear no responsibility for what happened."[27] Yet not only does De Witte contradict this thesis, but so does Brassinne himself when he appeared in Raoul Peck's documentary film *Lumumba: Death of a Prophet* (1992) as one of several witnesses to the events of the early 1960s. There he explained that "in my mind the term 'neutralize' can mean house arrest, for others expatriation, for others physical liquidation," and went on to acknowledge sinisterly that because the Congolese had no custom (or, in the French original, *mœurs*) for "political crime," "it was necessary to find a solution."[28]

What we have in *Spectres* is the unfolding of Brassinne's narrative, which includes reference to the charges—and countercharges—

25   Louis Michel in a speech delivered at the Belgian Federal Parliament, Brussels, February 5, 2002, as cited in De Witte, afterword to the paperback edition of *The Assassination of Lumumba*, 187, and in the open letter of Mémoires Coloniales, as reprinted in Tallon et al., *Sven Augustijnen: Spectres*, 117. See De Witte's description of the flaws of the commission's report and its conservative historical basis (where murder is effectively relegated to "cultural difference"), *Assassination of Lumumba*, 186–87.

26   "Quelque part la commission va au-delà de la vérité, à mon avis, quand elle dit que les Belges étaient conscients. Et qu'à la limite ils ont une responsabilité morale. Mais ce n'est pas vraie. Les Belges n'ont pas de responsabilité morale. Les Belges ont été un instrument, ça c'est tout à fait clair."

27   Cited in De Witte, *Assassination of Lumumba*, xxi.

28   Brassinne in Raoul Peck, dir., *Lumumba: Death of a Prophet* (Paris: Velvet Film, 1992).

and presentations of contradictions from earlier statements, where the subject takes us through the defense of his position, reconstructing his story of the events of 1960–61 some fifty years after the fact. Why, one might wonder, would Brassinne participate in Augustijnen's film in the first place? Augustijnen explained that "by releasing his doctoral thesis, [Brassinne] himself set the ghost free"—an unleashing that De Witte's book also encouraged in condemning Belgium's complicity. Brassinne apparently felt compelled to respond, and agreed to appear in the film. "To him," Augustijnen expanded, "the movie is in a certain way a means to recapture the ghost by showing that it was a 'Bantu affair' and that at present historians cannot grasp the spirit of that age."[29] Certainly that is also the argument put forth by d'Aspremont Lynden, who, in one shocking moment of Augustijnen's film, mimics the Congolese to make the point: "We are Africans. We are Bantus, not Westerners. Let us keep our traditions, our customs, our morals. That's how we solve problems."[30] Laughing smugly, Brassinne adds in agreement, "My opinion is certain, but others don't have to share it. One is free." To which d'Aspremont Lynden replies, "Ah yes, and on that little ray of sunlight, I propose an aperitif." With this seemingly enlightened exchange, the two wrap up their denial of responsibility in a cynical and patronizing "respect" for Congolese cultural traditions—the "tradition" in question being the custom of the Bantus to murder their democratically elected prime ministers. Brassinne's and d'Aspremont Lynden's excuses, diversions, and disclaimers, presented by the two figures as reasonable and well-researched knowledge, in fact replicate Belgium's strategy of responding to the events of the early 1960s by mounting a campaign of disinformation that took decades to unravel, the history of which is today still subject to controversy—or rather the manufacture of controversy.

In other words, the film invites us to witness the workings of a defense mechanism, constituted by Brassinne's and d'Aspremont Lynden's admission to the seriousness of an event (Lumumba's execution), but denying all responsibility on behalf of Belgium and its representatives.[31] The symptoms include their focusing on insignificant historical details, repeating lines from books and essays for the nth time, repeatedly expressing their blame-

29 Augustijnen, "What a Day for a Daydream," n.p. Furthermore, Augustijnen notes that "both the son of d'Aspremont and Brassinne were motivated to refute the thesis of De Witte on camera," which helps to explain their willingness and motivation to appear in *Spectres*. In addition, Brassinne, notes the artist, was also motivated to make the trip to Katanga to have the execution site documented and filmed, which had not been done before.

30 "Nous sommes des Africains, nous sommes des Bantous. Nous ne sommes pas des Occidentaux, donc laissez nous avec nos traditions, nos habitudes, nos mœurs ... Nos manières de régler les problèmes."

31 On "defense mechanisms," see Anna Freud, *Ego and Mechanisms of Defense*, trans. Cecil Baines (London: Hogarth Press, 1968), where she discusses various forms, including denial, displacement, intellectualization, projection, rationalization, reaction formation, regression, repression, sublimation, and suppression. Also see Phebe Cramer, *Protecting the Self: Defense Mechanisms in Action* (New York: Guilford Press, 2006).

less position, performing the role of self-righteous authority, and assuming a unique access to the truth. Yet by focusing on the shakiness of the defense—translated into a disorienting visual effect by Augustijnen's handheld camera—and bringing attention to various contradictions in the statements as well as the considerable energy the speakers invest in repeating their claims, *Spectres* elicits the uncertainty, mobility, and overdetermined nature of speech. It demonstrates how one can say one thing while unwittingly revealing another.

Ultimately, the defense misses the larger issue and functions as a smoke screen. For it's not so much the precise circumstances of one man's murder that is ultimately at stake—though clearly it remains important to establish who is responsible and to question why the "political elimination" of a democratically elected leader would ever have been acceptable as a goal of Belgian diplomacy. The point is that Brassinne and d'Aspremont Lynden fail to condemn, let alone say anything about, the long-standing Belgian colonial control of the Congo, and more broadly how it connects to the long history of European colonial activities in the Global South, with all of the brutality, slave labor, and mass killings that went along with it, among which Lumumba's murder was only one of many such violations.[32] In other words, it's not a matter of the mere individual responsibility of Harold d'Aspremont Lynden and Brassinne, but rather of their involvement in the larger collective project of Belgium's direct intervention into all levels of the Congo's government, economy, military, industry, and culture. In *Spectres*, they are shown seeking individual ethical exception to what was a structural, political, and economic intervention. But it is the injustice of the larger political, economic, and military involvement—and the entire history of the brutal and murderous colonization of the Congo—that Brassinne implicitly denies, fixed as he is on an isolated event. Pointing out this larger framework, Mémoires Coloniales states, "Beyond the question of responsibility, Lumumba's assassination raises questions concerning the West's political interference in Africa, and concerning the pursuit of the colonial project by retaining a strong-hold on Africa's natural resources. [...] The danger, for the Belgian government, of Lumumba's vision for independence, lay in his stress on political and economic sovereignty, an evident threat to Belgium's economic interests."[33] The stakes are geopolitical, global, and current.

[32]   For an accounting of the brutality of Belgian colonialism, see Adam Hochschild, *King Leopold's Ghost: A Story of Greed, Terror, and Heroism in Colonial Africa* (London: Macmillan, 1999); David Renton, David Seddon, and Leo Zeilig, *The Congo: Plunder and Resistance* (London: Zed Books, 2007); and Martin Ewans, *European Atrocity, African Catastrophe: Leopold II, the Congo Free State and its Aftermath* (London: Routledge, 2002).

[33]   Imbach, "Patrice Lumumba," in Tallon et al., *Sven Augustijnen: Spectres*, 118–20.

Midway through the film's portrayal of the discussion between Brassinne and d'Aspremont Lynden, the camera drifts away from the two and shows the grounds before the opulent château. A Belgian flag flutters in the light wind above the formal garden. This passage implicates the symbolic meaning and honor of Belgian national identity and the justness of the country's accumulated wealth, which Brassinne's regime of justification ultimately serves, and which stands accused by this history. Yet Brassinne never offers any sign of a critical consciousness.[34] Driving away from d'Aspremont Lynden's château, Brassinne nearly runs over the count's dog accidentally, exclaiming with relief that had he done so, he'd never be allowed to set foot in the house again. Augustijnen's inclusion of this small detail, wherein Brassinne's emotional response is strikingly greater than any other to the fate of the Congo or that of Lumumba, speaks volumes.

—

If there was any ambiguity about the meaning of the word "elimination" and the precise circumstances of Belgium's involvement in the neutralization of Lumumba, it has been further clarified in the evidence submitted to the Belgian parliamentary commission, as indicated in *Spectres*. The film's intertitles—scrolling paragraphs appearing at several junctions   provide important historical background for its subject, including contextual information about Lumumba's assassination and Belgium's involvement, and details about key figures including Brassinne. Intriguingly, at times the texts demonstrate conflicts with Brassinne's and d'Aspremont Lynden's narratives. At one point, for instance, the text draws on the commission's evidence by quoting a letter of Guy Weber, major in the Belgian military based in the Congo and military advisor to President Tshombe, dated October 19, 1960, and addressed to the head of the cabinet of the king, which reads: "Tshombe met Mobutu. Excellent talks. In exchange for financial support, Mobutu is following advice: status quo until 31 December—wait until the situation looks brighter—Lumumba will be completely neutralised (if possible physically...)."[35] Also mentioned is the proposal of Jules Loos, right-hand man of Harold d'Aspremont Lynden, that the Belgians hire a "crocodile hunter" to take care of Lumumba. The film shows that

34   In this regard, Brassinne is typical of former officials of the Belgian Congo who commonly remain unrepentant decades later about their role in the colonial past. See, for instance, Marie-Bénédicte Demobour, *Recalling the Belgian Congo: Conversations and Introspections* (Oxford: Berghahn Books, 2000).

35   "Tshombe a rencontré Mobutu. Excellente entrevue. En échange d'un certain appui financier, Mobutu suit les conseils: statu quo jusqu'au 31 décembre—on attend que la situation s'éclaircisse—on neutralise complètement (et si possible physiquement...) Lumumba." See Document Parlementaire, "DOC 50 0312/007" (report published November 16, 2001, Brussels); Tallon et al., *Sven Augustijnen: Spectres*, 138.

Arnoud d'Aspremont Lynden's explanation—that "elimination" was meant politically, not physically—is, clearly, not historically accurate.

    Spectres' use of intertitles is crucial in that it provides a corrective to Brassinne's narrative. The film thereby creates a friction between the subject's spoken words and the artist's researched historical text. This is based in part on Augustijnen's careful reading of the report of the parliamentary commission, which connects to the methodological questions that inform the film: "What does historiography stand for? What is the value of a testimony, of the memory of the past and what is the value of the written word, of the document?"[36] These are questions that viewers are meant to ask in relation to a film that puts written text and oral testimony in critical juxtaposition. Yet this friction does not work to reveal "the truth" of what happened, nor does *Spectres* offer a definitive account that puts to rest all controversy and dissenting views—for there are no footnotes in the film, no archive of evidence, no presumption of scholarly authority. The fact that the film and installation re-present Brassinne's research further suggests there will be no convincing one way or another, only the likelihood of a mimetic battle of archives without end. Yet the intertitles do function to indicate that Brassinne's narrative is his own construction and not the definitive truth. Moreover, the presence of the film's intervening text adds support to the suspicion that Brassinne is in the grip of denial, which problematizes the documentary as it demonstrates that the more evidence is presented, the more complex the defense mechanism becomes. In this regard, Brassinne emerges not so much as a tragic figure, but as a pathetic one, unable to see the truth of his own haunting.[37]

    The point brings up a further line of continuity with Augustijnen's past work. Analyzing the earlier films of the artist, critic Jan Verwoert has argued that the artist's speaking subjects evoke Michel Foucault's reflection on "discourse's ambiguous power to deny and to redouble," as in *Le Guide du Parc* and *L'École des Pickpockets*, where speech is paradoxically coded as revelatory and secretive at once: "Like the thief who protects his identity by exposing it, the open secret is hidden in plain sight."[38] Brassinne offers a similar cover, claiming "no one has anything to hide," even as he builds his dubious defense. Yet, while Verwoert's reading is not inaccurate, I would argue the conclusion that Augustijnen's work exists beyond the logic of documentary—where

36   Augustijnen, "What a Day for a Daydream," n.p.

37   As Françoise Vergès observed at the WIELS symposium. See Demos et al., *In and Out of Brussels*, 45.

38   Jan Verwoert, "The Practical Surrealism of Power," *A Prior*, no. 14 (2007): 149, 155. Verwoert refers to Foucault's 1968 essay on the Belgian surrealist René Magritte, "This Is Not a Pipe."

"it would be pointless to question whether the people tell the truth or whether they are truly the people they say they are"[39]— does not apply in the same way to *Spectres*, as it *is* historically and politically crucial to come to terms with the historical truth of Belgium's interventions in the Congo. Still, the significance of the film is not to provide that guarantee, but rather to explore how one man's regime of justification covers up the truth even as he reveals it.[40] The result is uncanny: Brassinne shows himself to be possessed by the ghosts of his colonialist masters— d'Aspremont Lynden, King Baudouin—whose cause he continues to serve as a loyal foot soldier, his duty being to beat down Lumumba's spirit, which still yearns for a decolonized history.

The film's soundtrack, comprised of excerpts from Bach's *St. John Passion*, brings out a further dimension of its spectropoetics. It does so most immediately by granting the images and speech a sense of weighty seriousness that goes beyond their literal meanings. Perhaps most obviously, given the religious content of the oratorio, the use of the music works to liken the suffering and death of Lumumba to that of Christ, as critic Ronald Van de Sompel has suggested.[41] Yet that reading doesn't seem quite right, as Lumumba hardly figures in the film. (The analogy has been made, by contrast, in Peck's *Lumumba: Death of a Prophet*, which does focus on and mythologize the Congolese leader as a modern-day savior.) Yet the artist declined this reading in a recent interview, explaining instead that the use of the Bach was motivated by the racism of the colonial context, exemplified in the Belgians' code names for Tshombe (the "Jew") and Lumumba ("Satan") when it came to the latter's transfer to Katanga (as in the telex that reads, "Demand accord du Juif de recevoir Satan"—"request permission from the Jew to receive Satan"). "Conceptually," Augustijnen explains, "I found an association with the most anti-Semitic Passion, namely the Passion of John, for which the Jews were held responsible after the death of Christ, thus connecting to the themes of justification, condemnation, denial and betrayal in the film."[42]

Still, I would suggest that, as with the film's other elements, the soundtrack possesses no univocal meaning; instead it operates in multiple ways. More than a single metaphor, the music also communicates a sense of Brassinne's own suffering, who clearly feels himself the victim at times, exiled as he was by Mobutu, but unable to acknowledge the real crime of Belgian complicity in the neocolonialist

39   Ibid., 151.

40   As Eyal Sivan points out, "Although there is a great tradition of documenting, collecting, and archiving images and stories of victims, documentary cinema and archival work have rarely dealt with representations of perpetrators." "Archive Images: Truth or Memory? The Case of Adolf Eichmann's Trial," in Enwezor et al., *Experiments with Truth*, 284.

41   Augustijnen, "What a Day for a Daydream," n.p.

42   Ibid.

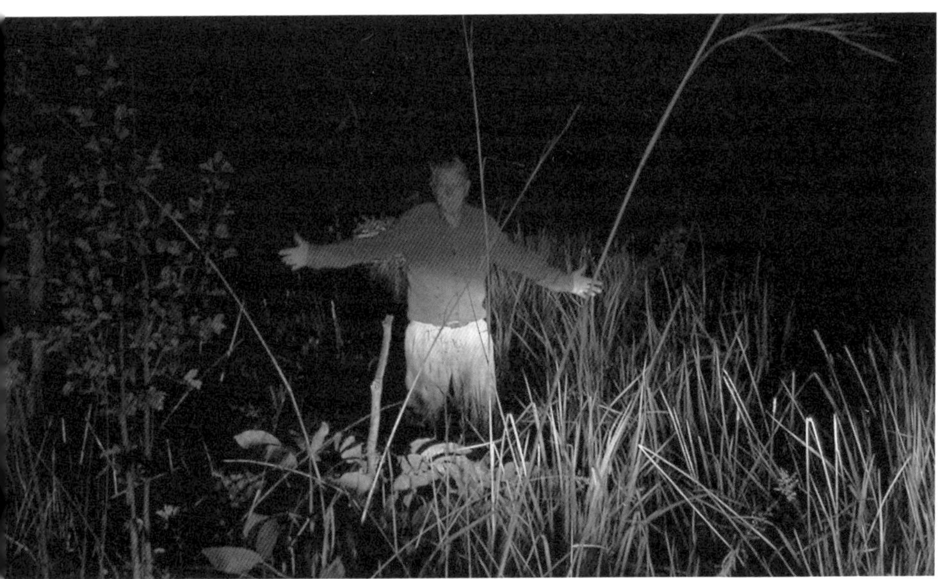

Sven Augustijnen, still from *Spectres*, 2011

project. The music also serves to slyly condemn Brassinne at certain moments, as during his meeting with the Lumumba family when the words "Crucify! Crucify!" are sung.[43] In this sense, the music places us in the realm of a judgment that is quasi-religious, where Brassinne's discourse is revealed to be a betrayal of the past, for which the film rebukes him. More allegorically so when the *Passion* lends a sense of the tragic to the entire historical episode—the tragedy of Lumumba as well as of the Congo. It also suggests, given the focus on Brassinne, the tragedy of history's nonavailability to the present as plain, transparent truth. This is perhaps another dimension of the ghostly as repressed historical presence: to appear only as nonappearance, the apparition of the non-apparent, as a negative rupture in the continuity of the seen and the heard in relation to the past and the present. One such moment of rupture occurs, for instance, when the soundtrack drowns out the speech of Brassinne, as if to indicate the irrelevance of his words, to signify that we've heard enough (the negation of his own negation). At other times, the music acts like an accompaniment to Brassinne's discourse, turning his speech into a tragic song and the documentary suddenly into an operetta. In this light, the film emerges not so much as a documentary, but as an imaginative and otherworldly choreography of movement

43 Augustijnen pointed this out at the WIELS symposium.

and sound, which situates Brassinne as the performer of his own pathetic dramatic act.

The most powerful moment of the apparition of the inapparent is the film's last scene, in which Brassinne searches for the execution site in the Katangan savannah, looking for the tree against which Lumumba was shot. He is shown searching during the day, and then, shockingly, again at night.[44] In the dark he wanders around the trees and bushes, illuminated only by the headlights of an automobile, in the same way that Lumumba was reportedly spotlit the night he was executed. The film records Brassinne mapping out the likely location of those involved in the execution—based on his years of research and diagrams—and feeling for bullet holes in one tree trunk. The film's visual conditions subtly derealize the boundaries between past and present, factual and imaginary, specular and spectral. As Brassinne realizes his morbid choreography, the film reveals his mania. He is shown in the grips of an irrational drive to discover the truth of an event from which he was excluded, as if it somehow holds the key to his innocence. Yet it only convicts him further; his desire to release the ghosts only sets them free.[45] The soundtrack intervenes, rising above his words, throwing him into dramatic light. With this uncanny reconstruction, it's as if he himself becomes a ghost, reanimating the execution, moving through the gestures of the historical players, replaying the tragic drama. Meanwhile, the handheld camera elicits a sickening viewing sensation and disorienting effect, making for a powerful and upsetting conclusion to a film that remarkably both allows Brassinne to present his defensive narrative, and conjures the shadowy realm that hovers around his speech, and shows him to be haunted by a crime he cannot acknowledge. As a result, he is allowed to condemn himself.

—

One important question remains: is it not a risk for the film to give a platform to an apologist for Belgian intervention in the Congo, intervention that included criminal activity?[46] By offering the opportunity for Brassinne to tell his story, does *Spectres* not also offer the audience a potential pathway to identification, thereby

44   Augustijnen notes that "Brassinne himself wanted to go back at night because the facts had occurred at night," in "What a Day for a Daydream," n.p.

45   As Augustijnen explains, "Georges Didi-Huberman, in his book *Images in Spite of All*, writes: 'Doesn't he who, too violently, conjures the spectres give the best indication that he is subjected to their haunting.'" See Augustijnen, in Demos et al., *In and Out of Brussels*, 39. The actual English translation reads, "Doesn't exorcising ghosts suggest that one might be haunted by them?" See Georges Didi-Huberman, *Images in Spite of All: Four Photographs from Auschwitz*, trans. Shane B. Lillis (Chicago: University of Chicago Press, 2008), 65.

46   This was a problem, for instance, for Bambi Ceuppens, who made an objection to the film at the symposium that I organized with Hilde Van Gelder at WIELS on May 21, 2011, as part of our ongoing research project. She explained: "My main problem with the film is that I think that Sven actually colludes with him in ways that he may not be aware of. And this is an argument that I often make when Belgians show themselves critical of colonization. I say: 'You think that you're critical but you're actually enforcing a colonial discourse.'" See the edited transcript of the conversation in Demos et al., *In and Out of Brussels*, 50.

negating the critical history that is ostensibly its goal, even publicizing the perpetrator's account? Similarly, what are the risks in reproducing material from Brassinne's family photo albums that shows him with members of the military in Katanga, the same military that was committing atrocities at the time? Facing a similar dilemma, the filmmaker Eyal Sivan—director of *The Specialist* (1999), which is about the trial of Nazi SS officer Adolf Eichmann—observes that "to focus on the perpetrator is to risk making us identify with him; as he explains and justifies himself, tells us about his work, his joys, his sorrows, he looks like anyone else and we grant him our understanding."[47] Yet the alternative, Sivan notes, is to center on the suffering of victims, which repeats a cliché of documentarism in substituting the spectacle of misery for the analysis of the causes and conditions of horror. The advantage in exploring the perpetrator's side is that we can learn something new about the past, think through the horror, see how it was and is normalized, and therefore learn how better to negotiate the present and future.[48]

It is exactly for these reasons that, in my view, *Spectres* opens up the prospect of the audience's identification with the main character. In fact, Augustijnen has spoken openly of his own identification with Brassinne, which is not surprising given the artist's intensive work and travel with his subject during the preparation and making of the film.[49] And this prospective identification is also extended to the spectators, who are placed in the position of viewing Brassinne in the starring role of the film, appearing as a monumental image on the screen. This risk may represent the film's very ambition and complexity: for it is through the process of granting the perpetrator space for self-expression that we can learn something new about neocolonial violence and how it is justified by those originally responsible and by subsequent generations. *Spectres* does not offer a simple condemnation or moralistic judgment of an object of pure evil, which would put viewers in the conventional role of identifying with the mythologized heroism of Lumumba as opposed to the despised and murderous colonizers (as does, for instance, Peck's *Lumumba: Death of a Prophet*). Rather, viewers are invited to consider their own subtle complicity in this history, how we may have participated through so many small acts in everyday life, moments of inattention, and the negligence of nonintervention within dominant narratives. These contributions form part of the larger system that allows violence

47   Sivan, "Archive Images," 285.

48   Sivan quotes Tzvetan Todorov, *Les Abus de la mémoire* (Paris: Alréa, 1995), 31–32: "Exemplary use of memory [...] allows the past to be used in view of the present. Memory can be used as a lesson about injustices acquired in the past and to help fight those taking place in the present, to help us live ourselves and to advance toward the other." Sivan, "Archive Images," 288.

49   Augustijnen discussed this identification at the WIELS symposium. See Demos et al., *In and Out of Brussels*, 52.

to occur on an institutional and national level, even if we didn't participate in the spectacularized acts of brutality that are only the most visible symptoms of that larger state of affairs. Will we as viewers accept Brassinne's narrative and the official position of Belgium, the film asks us, and thereby join the ranks of the many who overlook the history of neocolonial violence? Will we forget the crimes of colonialism in order to enjoy its rewards, including a good part of European wealth? In what ways have we already been complicit without realization? In relation to these questions, the film challenges us to a politics of memory, which implicates us all, and especially those in countries that once colonized Africa.

In *Specters of Marx*, Derrida speaks of a "politics of memory, of inheritance, and of generations," which presents us, we recall, with the imperative not only "to learn to live *with* ghosts" but to live with them "justly."[50] As he argues, "No justice seems possible or thinkable without the principle of some *responsibility*, beyond all living present, within that which disjoins the living present, before the ghosts of those who are not yet born or who are already dead, be they victims of wars, political or other kinds of violence, nationalist, racist, colonialist, sexist, or other kinds of exterminations, victims of the oppressions of capitalist imperialism or any of the forms of totalitarianism." The problem is, he continues, that "without this *non-contemporaneity with itself of the living present*"—a non-contemporaneity that Brassinne is shown to live within, unconsciously—"without that which secretly unhinges it, without this responsibility and this respect for justice concerning those who *are not there*, of those who are no longer or who are not yet *present and living*, what sense would there be to ask the question 'where?' 'where tomorrow?' 'whither?'"[51]

In regards to *Spectres*, Augustijnen explains that "the movie is in a certain sense a reflection or a shadow from another angle; the movie was a process that was meant to exorcize the ghost. However, it's in the nature of the ghost—*un spectre, un revenant*—to keep coming back."[52] He thereby provides an important response to Derrida's questions: when one attempts to singlehandedly bring to a conclusion traumatic events of world-historical significance—as if to pay one's debt to the injustice of the past—the ghosts inevitably return. *Spectres* reveals this complex hauntology by developing a spectropoetics that helps us to begin to live more justly with the ghosts of the past, and which refuses to accept the culture of amnesia, one of irresponsibility to the past. One impending return of the specters is that on June 23, 2011—more than a month after the film's release on May 7, 2011—Lumumba's sons

50   Derrida, exordium to *Specters of Marx*, xviii.

51   Ibid., xix.

52   Augustijnen, "What a Day for a Daydream," n.p

François, Roland, and Guy filed legal proceedings against eleven unnamed Belgians (of which Brassinne is likely one) for "passive or active complicity and participation in the arrest, transfer to Elisabethville and torture in the Brouwez house of Lumumba, as well as his confinement and assassination in the savannah," as pointed out in the film's titles.[53] Will we join the plaintiffs in opposing the ongoing violence of neocolonialism, with its systems of economic, social, and political inequality? *Spectres* asks about our future responsibility to this history, conjuring our own existence as yet another untimely ghost hovering about the film.

53 See Colette Braeckman, "Dix noms remis à la justice," *Le Soir*, June 24, 2011, 10. A year later, the Belgian court, operating at a snail's pace, ruled that since the charge concerns the "physical elimination" of Lumumba, it constitutes a "war crime" and as such carries no statute of limitation according to Belgian law. The case can thus continue as an "affaire criminelle." Meanwhile, two of the eleven defendants have died and Brassinne has reached the age of eighty-two. See Gilbert Dupont, "L'assassinat de Lumumba n'est pas prescript," *La Dernière Heure*, June 21, 2012. At the time of this book's editing in November 2012, the trial is pending.

2. A Colonial Hauntology: **Vincent Meessen's** *Vita Nova*

In *Vita Nova*, a thirty-minute video from 2009, Vincent Meessen takes up the iconic 1955 cover image of the French magazine *Paris Match*, which features a close-up of a young African cadet giving a military salute. The image is the same one that Roland Barthes referred to in his book *Mythologies* as an example of visual culture that defines an ideological operation in support of French colonialism: "I see very well what it signifies to me," wrote Barthes, "that France is a great Empire, that all her sons, without any colour discrimination, faithfully serve under her flag, and that there is no better answer to the detractors of an alleged colonialism than the zeal shown by this Negro in serving his so-called oppressors."[1] While he went on to criticize that logic, Barthes investigated the image no further. Meessen did. After performing research on the image and its historical context, in 2006 he embarked on a search for Diouf Birane, the one-time African cadet named in the *Paris Match* issue, hoping to track down the subject of the photograph who would now be an old man possibly living in Ouagadougou, Burkina Faso, his country of origin listed in the magazine. The resulting video records moments of that journey and its unexpected discoveries, weaving together a provocative meditation on the philosophy of history, its repressed narratives, and the spectral nature of photography.

Thanks to Meessen's efforts, *Vita Nova* gives "new life" to that image. Just as the camera slowly pans out from an initial close-up shot of the boy's eyes—as if asking insistently what did *he* see in 1955 and experience thereafter?—the film makes the magazine cover, which is visually revealed in full only gradually over several passages throughout the video, into a platform for an investigation into wider and interlinking histories that have come to light only recently. The filmmaker did not find Birane, who died in Senegal in the 1980s, but his old schoolmate Issa Kaboré, who appeared in other photographs in the same issue of *Paris Match*. The magazine publicized Les Nuits de l'Armée, the televised 1955 military pageant featuring a spectacle of more than four thousand participants, including the Garde Noire de Dakar, the French Foreign Legion, the Paris Fire Brigade, and the Republican Guard, all appearing at the Palais des Sports in Paris to celebrate France's colonial empire.[2] It was for this event that Birane and Kaboré had come to Paris. The film opens with shots of a recording session to which Meessen invited Kaboré to sing the French national anthem. Once a common ritual of France's extended national

1   Roland Barthes, "Myth Today," in *Mythologies*, trans. Annette Lavers (New York: Noonday, 1972), 116.

2   The caption for the cover image reads: "Les Nuits de l'Armée: Le petit Diouf venu de Ouagadougou avec son comarades, enfants de troupes d'A.O.F. [Afrique Occidentale Française], pour ouvrir le fantastique spectacle que l'Armée française presente au Palais des Sports cette semaine." (The Nights of the Army: Little Diouf came from Ouagadougou with his comrades, children of the troops of French West Africa, to open the fantastic spectacle presented by the French Army this week at the Sports Palace.)

community—it would have been sung that day in Paris in 1955—Kaboré no longer fully remembers its words. (He recalls the opening, "Allons enfants," but strikingly has forgotten the various parts of the revolutionary anthem that condemn "blood tyranny," "vile despots," and the battle cry for the victory of liberty.) The pain that this experience elicits for Kaboré is palpable. If, as Barthes argued in *Mythologies*, the *Paris Match* image represents the perfect rejoinder to the critics of France's colonial empire, then the memory of such acts of native patriotism is shown to be on the verge of oblivion following the intervening years of decolonization and independence.

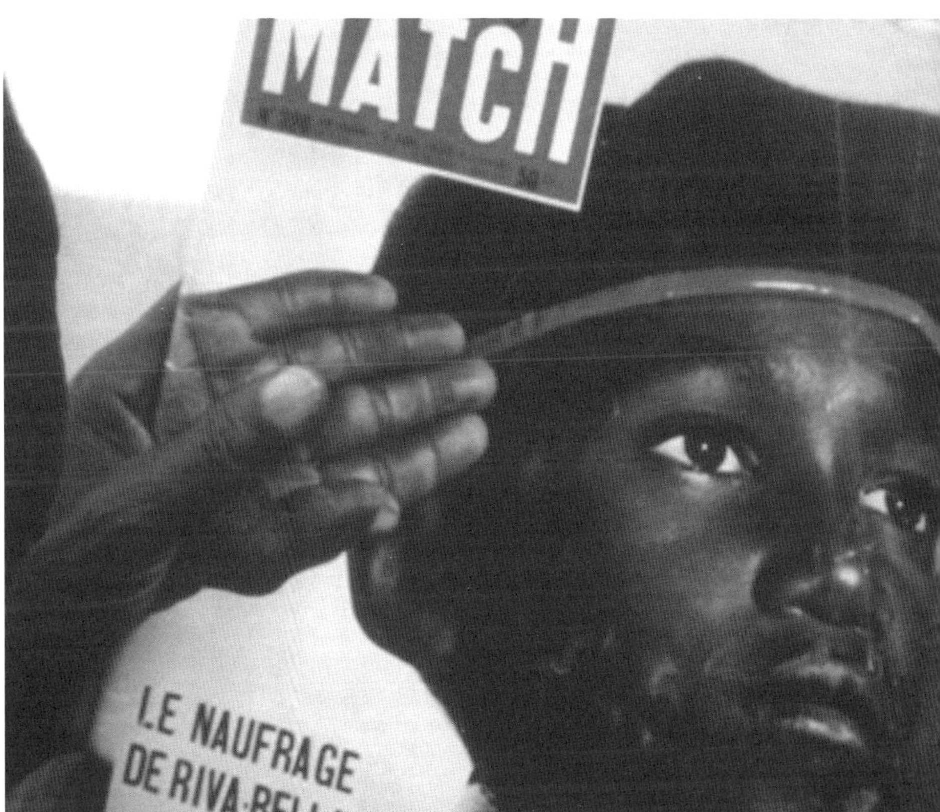

Vincent Meessen, still from *Vita Nova*, 2009

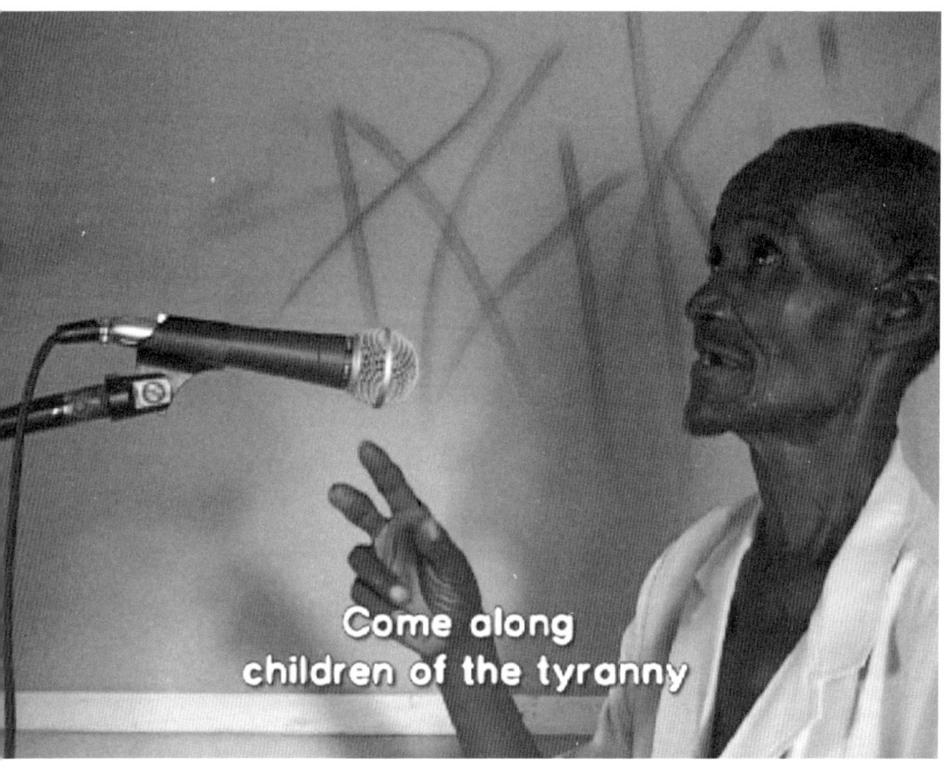

Vincent Meessen, still from *Vita Nova*, 2009

Yet, as the film goes on to observe, Barthes's celebrated analysis of the image was not quite as complete as it might now seem. In fact, his critical performance had its own moments of forgetting, or at least selective remembrance. For, as Meessen discovered in his research—in an astonishing historical revelation that has hitherto gone unremarked in the scholarship— Barthes's own maternal grandfather was none other than Louis Gustave Binger, the French explorer and colonial officer who claimed Ivory Coast for France in the 1880s, served for a time as the colony's governor, and lent his name to Bingerville, the city that remains named in his honor to this day. We learn about that history in a scene where Kaboré is shown sitting in a reconstructed classroom in a former military academy in Ouagadougou and is presented with the story of Binger's life in Africa by an unseen narrator. Born in Strasbourg in 1856, Binger traveled to West Africa in 1887, when he visited Niger and the coast of Guinea, making his way from Bamako to Kong in 1888. He cre-

   A Colonial Hauntology: Vincent Meessen's *Vita Nova*

ated friends and enemies with Africans along the way. (As related in the video, the Dyerma, who "couldn't stand the sight of his white skin," wanted to kill Binger, which he explained to a chief in Tiakéné, who offered him protection and hospitality before he left for Ghana and Ivory Coast.) He died in 1936 in the French town of L'Isle Adam.

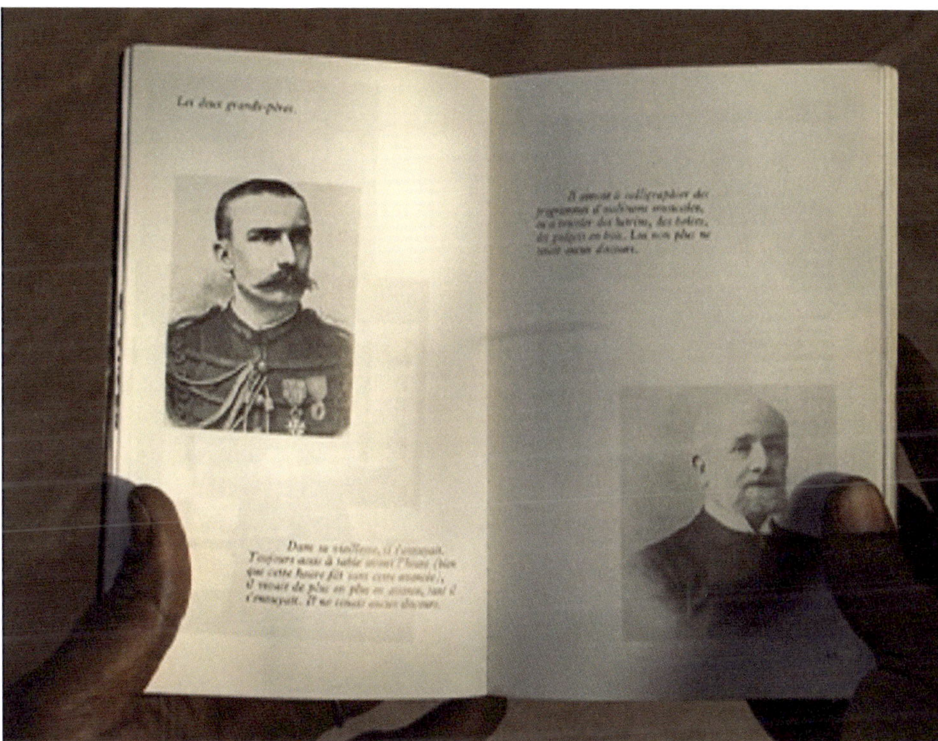

Vincent Meessen, still from *Vita Nova*, 2009

The sequence displays documentary photographs to visually supplement the lesson, including a shot of a copy of *Roland Barthes by Roland Barthes* open to the pages with photographs of the author's grandfathers (but with the most generic of identifications: "Les deux grand-pères"). It leads to a pair of hands flipping through a photo album, coming across old photos of marching troops, Africans in military uniforms, and a final black-and-white photo of two white colonists—identified as "Capitain Louis Gustve [*sic*] Binger and Lieutenant Braulot"—clad in white uniforms, sitting under a tent at a camp in the jungle, and attended by two shirtless Africans. The film thereby opens the colonial visual archive, but does so from a position attentive to the African perspective. In one image depicting Binger's funeral, the young Barthes appears looming in the corner looking on, offering visual evidence of the genealogical relation, and thus of his own familial connection to the colonial context. It is striking that Barthes declined to discuss his relationship to his grandfather in *Roland Barthes by Roland Barthes*, his later autobiographical account. By opening up that history, the film offers a tale of forgetting—yet a forgetting that is itself diversified according to disparate contexts: Kaboré's perhaps welcomed transcendence of the colonial past appears quite different from Barthes's implicit disavowal of his family's involvement in it. This tale of colonizer and colonized becomes the basis of Meessen's historical reanimation—in particular, one that conjures equally the ghost of Barthes and the histories that may have haunted him.

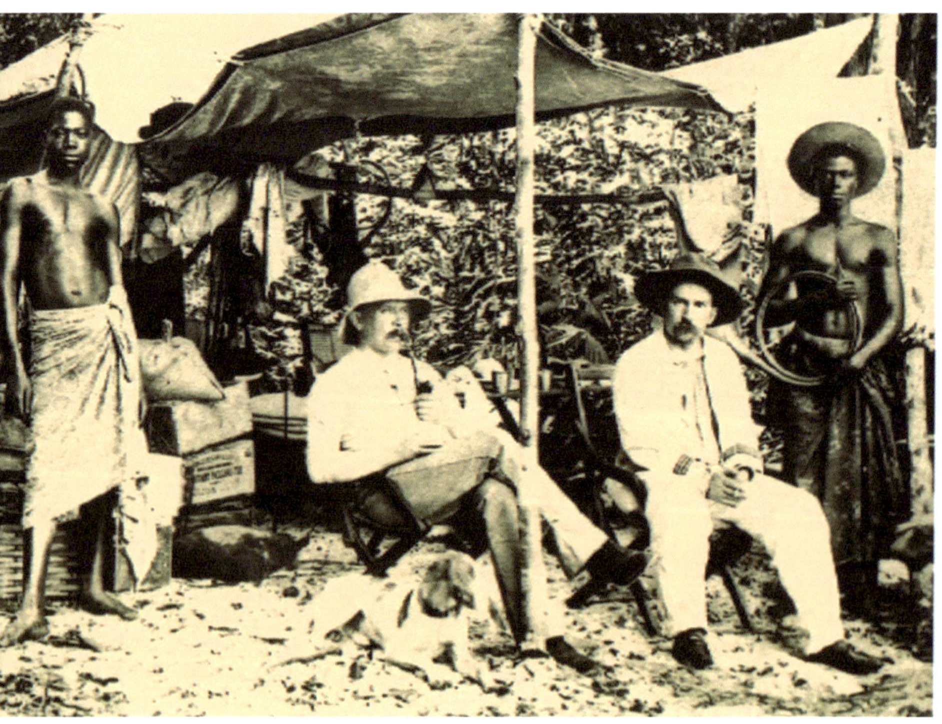

Vincent Meessen, still from *Vita Nova*, 2009

For this reason, *Vita Nova* can be said to constitute a colonial hauntology, insofar as it conjures the ghosts that have hovered around this *Paris Match* image—a key exemplar of late colonial visual culture—which links diverse peoples, geographies, and political histories via France's colonial past. The term proposes a methodology of interpretation that attempts to uncover both the ontology of a haunting (the being, effects, and affects of possession) and the haunting of being (the way presence is shadowed by unacknowledged histories and suppressed relationships that disturb the present's complete severance from the past). For Derrida, writing after the fall of the Berlin Wall in 1989, calling up the world of ghosts meant to contest the claim that the post-socialist world had entered a triumphalist period of globalization, one of the universal rule of free market capitalism, as if it had put all other economic models safely to rest.

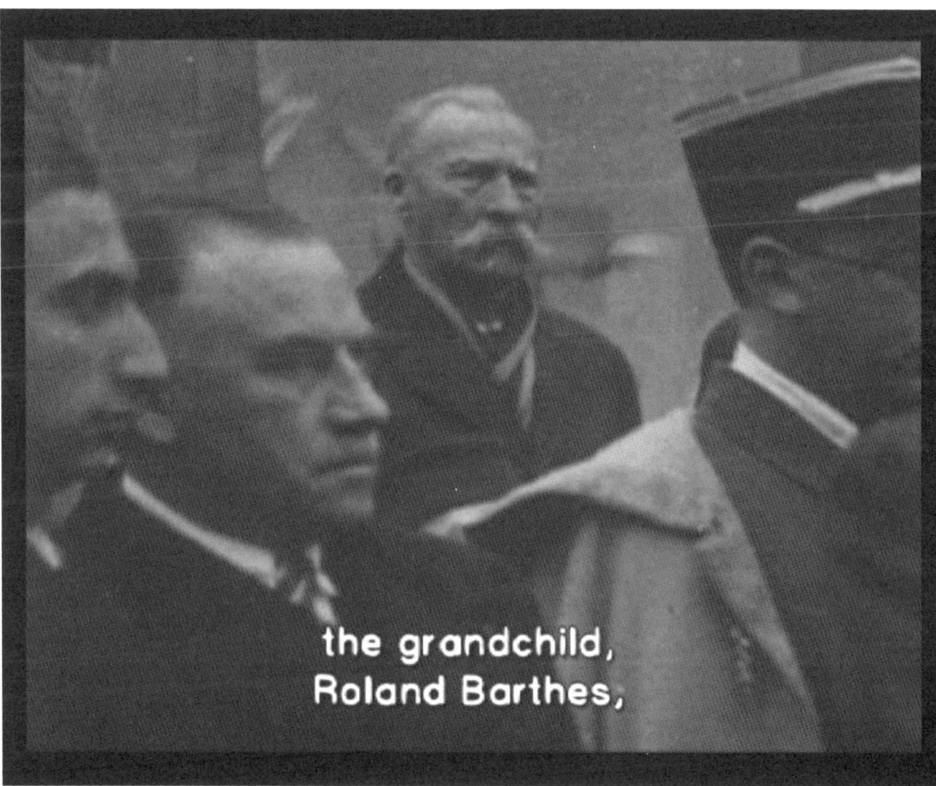

Vincent Meessen, still from *Vita Nova*, 2009

Countering such amnesiac and partially blind glorifications of the present, and responding to the conflicts and failures of modernity that continue to inspire alternative politics of equality, inclusivity, and justice, the spirit of communism remains, for Derrida, irrepressible, even if it is not simply or easily available in the present. "Let us call it a *hauntology*," Derrida writes, designating "the virtual space of spectrality" that operates in the otherwise "sharp distinction between the real and the unreal, the actual and the inactual, the living and the non-living, being and non-being."[3] The question is how Meessen wields this hauntology today.[4] What are its singular aesthetic conditions, the particular "spectropoetics" of *Vita Nova*, and what does the video's conjuring of ghosts have to teach us?

—

Hauntology is in fact a longstanding concern in Meessen's work, for which the artist has undertaken numerous visits to postcolonial places, exploring the ruins of modernity and the aftermath of colonial-era utopias. His projects frequently enact performative scenarios, where visitations to distant lands bring about the sudden collapse of geographical and temporal separations, giving way to fraught and uncanny proximities. In 2005, for instance, Meessen created *The Intruder*, a video and public intervention set in Ouagadougou for which he dressed up in a bizarre outfit of white cotton, covering his figure from top to bottom, and silently walked the streets unannounced. Captured by a camera that recorded his stroll, *le blanc*—as he was called—became a source of fascination and anxiety, as well as a site of spectral doubling, as Meessen's hands remained uncovered and thus the figure presented a specter of white skin under a white mask (ambiguously inverting Franz Fanon's famous book title).[5] The performance created a screen for spontaneous responses by locals as the drama suggested an imagined precolonial encounter with racial difference set in postcolonial Burkina Faso. However, this interpretation was never expressed by any bystander over the course of the video's seven-and-a-half minutes—rather, the public teased the figure by calling him Santa Claus and Osama bin Laden. The performance bore no clear meaning, and without voice-over or narrative framework, the figure appeared haunting as a result of its very lack of clear significance or obvious allusion.

3   Derrida, *Specters of Marx*, 10–11.

4   The term was also mobilized by Meessen's organization, Normal, which organized a series of contemporary and historical films and discussions under the title "Hantologie des colonies," between October 8 and November 18, 2011, in coordination with Khiasma in Paris. Meessen, along with Pablo Martínez, also organized the related symposium, "A Bewitched System: The Exorcising Role of Images," at CA2M Centro de Arte Dos de Mayo, Madrid, June 18–20, 2012.

5   For a discussion of the "spectral dizziness" of the whiteness of the anthropologist, with which Meessen's figure resonates, see Pinney, *Photography and Anthropology*, 59; and Michael Taussig, *What Color Is the Sacred?* (Chicago: University of Chicago Press, 2009), 81–82.

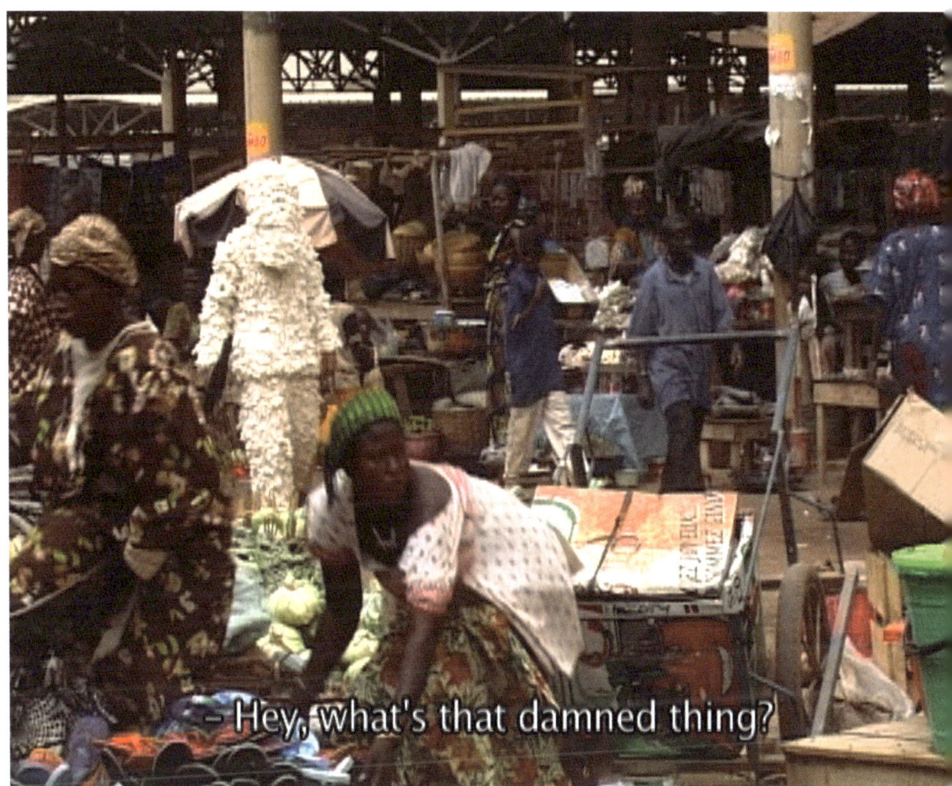

Vincent Meessen, still from *The Intruder*, 2005

Another visitation occurs in *Dear Adviser* (2009), a short video documenting a man wearing a business suit who walks amid a semi-urban landscape of dirt mounds and roads and modernist concrete buildings, which appear mysteriously as both unfinished and in ruins. In fact, the work is set in Chandigarh, the city planned by Le Corbusier in the 1950s as a shining example of Nehruvian modernization in newly independent India and marking the shared capital of the Punjab and Haryana states. Haunted by the ghosts of modernity, as much as by the architectural phantasm of centralized political power transplanted from the West to the Indian subcontinent, the images trace the figure walking among shadows. At the same time, the voice-over relates a favorite fable of Le Corbusier's—who wished to be addressed as "adviser," even as he functioned as a kind of legislator during the project—about a crow wanting to imitate an eagle (playing on the French, where *corbeau*, crow, mirrors "Corbu"). Intimating

53   Return to the Postcolony

a tale of postcolonial mimicry—for how could Prime Minister Jawaharlal Nehru turn to the architecture of international modernism to represent the new Indian state in the first place, was it not a continuation of the cultural logic of Western hegemony?—the scene appears to be affected by its metaphysical disturbances today. "The capital shall be haunted [...] the living shall call, the dead shall call," the voice-over intones repeatedly.

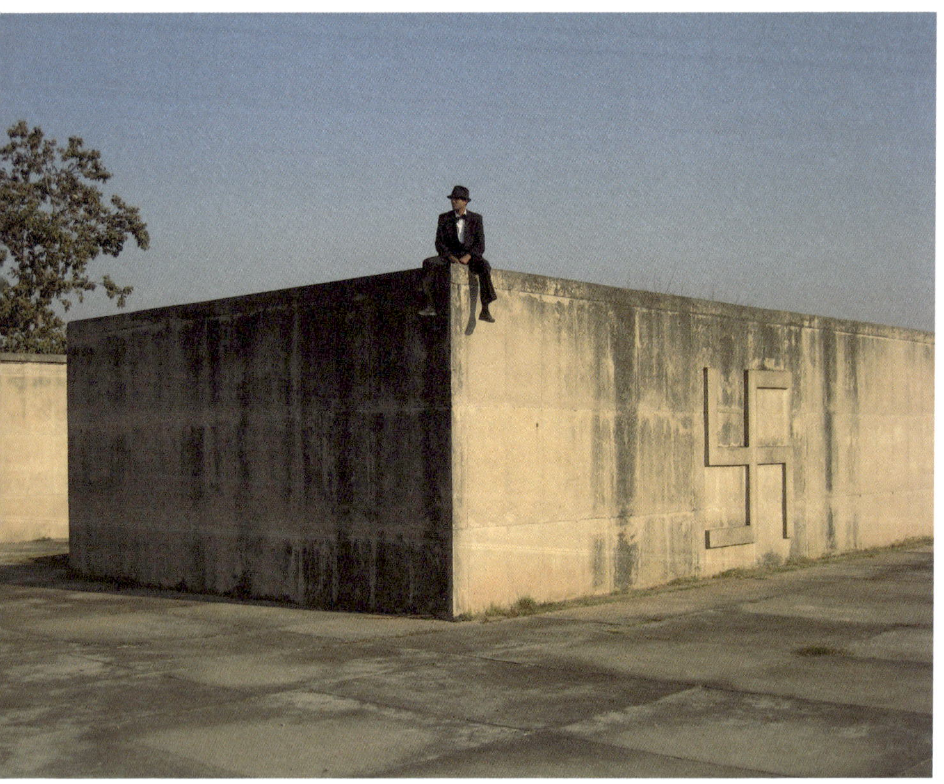

Vincent Meessen, still from *Dear Adviser*, 2009

In both *Dear Adviser* and *The Intruder*, Meessen models his own version of performative documentary in which the recording of an action performed in situ delivers unscripted results. As such, the two works depart from conventional documentary approaches in that they don't record events that are subsequently given narrative explanation; rather, they produce new events by showing how the past subsists as an irrepressible

   A Colonial Hauntology: Vincent Meessen's *Vita Nova*

force in the present, which is always in the process of becoming. The performances featured therein are characteristically left open to interpretation, even as they sometimes appear overlaid with poetic voice-overs alluding to the world of ghosts and hauntings. The result, as with Sven Augustijnen's work, fractures the now into past and present and proposes unsuspected correspondences between otherwise discrete temporalities (though Meessen's dramatic personae, appearing as if visitors from elsewhere, depart from Augustijnen's talking heads, lodged in everyday life).

Vita Nova continues this hauntological structuring, deepening the essayistic component of *Dear Adviser* and intensifying the historical insight of *The Intruder*, even as the video develops further the performative aspect of both. The video is also organized around the spectral figure of Etienne Minoungou, a Burkinabé actor and theater director who plays the role of narrator and is occasionally seen in the film visiting select locations in Ouagadougou, such as the governor's mansion where Binger once resided.[6] For his script, Meessen draws largely from Barthes's own writings—interweaving excerpts from *Mythologies*, *Camera Lucida*, and *Roland Barthes by Roland Barthes*—yet in doing so the narration performs a significant shift in temporal, geographical, and subjective registers. Not only does Barthes's voice appear to speak disjunctively in the present tense, as if he were talking to us today, it also finds itself spatially estranged in its relocation in an African context and embodiment in the enunciative particularities of another man's speech. The result crystallizes the meanings of Barthes's texts, throwing them in unexpected directions whereby they generate new narrative lines of flight. In effect, by relocating Barthes's speech in an African's voice, *Vita Nova* grants language to the formerly colonized, animating beings that then come to haunt Barthes's words from within.

As the film makes clear, such a *détournement* is mandated by Barthes's own aesthetico-political analysis presented in *Mythologies*, especially where the author explains that myth is a form of "stolen language," one diverted from its original intended meaning.[7] In fact, Barthes goes so far as to liken myth to "robbery by colonization."[8] If so, what would it mean to steal back Barthes's text, to mythologize *Mythologies* in turn? Would it constitute a belated decolonization of sorts? As the narrator of *Vita Nova* explains, "Words will never die because they aren't beings but functions. They only undergo changes, avatars, reincarnations." If "words undergo reincarnations" then "what would happen if Roland Barthes's words would reincarnate?" Meessen's narrator asks. This

6   Minoungou also collaborated on Meessen's film *Les Sociétaires/De Venoten* (2006) by providing a voice-over.

7   Barthes, "Myth Today," 131.

8   Ibid., 132.

reanimation is exactly what *Vita Nova* performs, and the results bring about new critical insights—despite the fact that the appropriation of myth is no guarantee of criticality.[9] On the one hand, it entails showing how the magisterial act of semiological decoding performed in *Mythologies* was also simultaneously a gesture of veiling—hiding Barthes's own familial investment and complicity in the very colonial project he critically analyzed so brilliantly. On the other hand, it grants the author a new life, albeit one that remains as ghostly as the specters that haunt Barthes's own texts (such as his grandfather), insofar as Meessen opts to position historical facts within new narratives of speculative fabulation.[10]

Of course Barthes himself—whom Jean-Michel Rabaté terms "the ghostwriter of modernity"—wrote frequently about death.[11] For him, death was "the *eidos*"—or most distinguished expression—of photography, and he likened his own experience of being photographed to that of becoming a "specter."[12] As Eduardo Cadava writes: "There can be no photograph without the withdrawal of what is photographed. [...] The conjunction of death and the photographed is in fact the very principle of photographic certitude: the photograph is a cemetery. A small funerary monument, the photograph is a grave for the living dead. It tells their history—a history of ghosts and shadows—and it does so because it *is* this history."[13] In *Camera Lucida*, Barthes's later meditation on photography, he also performed a spectralization of sorts by displacing the *studium* (the symbolic meaning of an image) from his analysis in order to focus on what he terms the *punctum* (the subjective "prick" that resists signification, the shadowy detail that escapes and thereby haunts the image's conventional coding). For instance, consider his discussion of Félix Nadar's 1882 photograph of Pierre Paul François Camille Savorgnan de Brazza. In the image, the famous explorer who claimed western Congo for France is shown seated against a naturalistic backdrop of a seascape and is accompanied by two young black boys dressed up as sailors, one with his hand resting on de Brazza's thigh in a gesture of peculiar intimacy. "This inconspicuous gesture is bound to arrest

9   Indeed, Sven Lütticken points out, "Some appropriations may end up reinforcing myths. Second-degree mythology may indeed become a pseudo-critical, impotent pretension, still dominated by the myths it claims to debunk. It can also become its own myth: the myth of appropriation as intrinsically radical, or productive of radical difference." "The Feathers of the Eagle," *New Left Review* 36 (November–December 2005): 124–25. In this essay, he provides a useful genealogy of modern art and myth, including discussion of Marcel Broodthaers's Barthes-influenced strategies of appropriation, which will be relevant, as we shall see, to Meessen's project.

10   The notion of "speculative narration"—a form of construction that resists probability in order to create a new world—was discussed by filmmaker Fabrizio Terranova at the conference organized by Meessen on February 7, 2012, at Netwerk, Center for Contemporary Art, Aalst, Belgium, on the occasion of his exhibition there.

11   Jean-Michel Rabaté, "Roland Barthes, Ghostwriter of Modernity," in *The Ghosts of Modernity* (Gainesville: University Press of Florida, 1996).

12   See Roland Barthes, *Camera Lucida: Reflections on Photography*, trans. Richard Howard (London: Vintage, 1993), 14–15. When photographed, Barthes explained, "I am neither subject nor object but a subject who feels he is becoming an object: I then experience a micro-version of death (of parenthesis): I am truly becoming a specter."

13   Eduardo Cadava, *Words of Light: Theses on the Photography of History* (Princeton, NJ: Princeton University Press, 1997), 10.

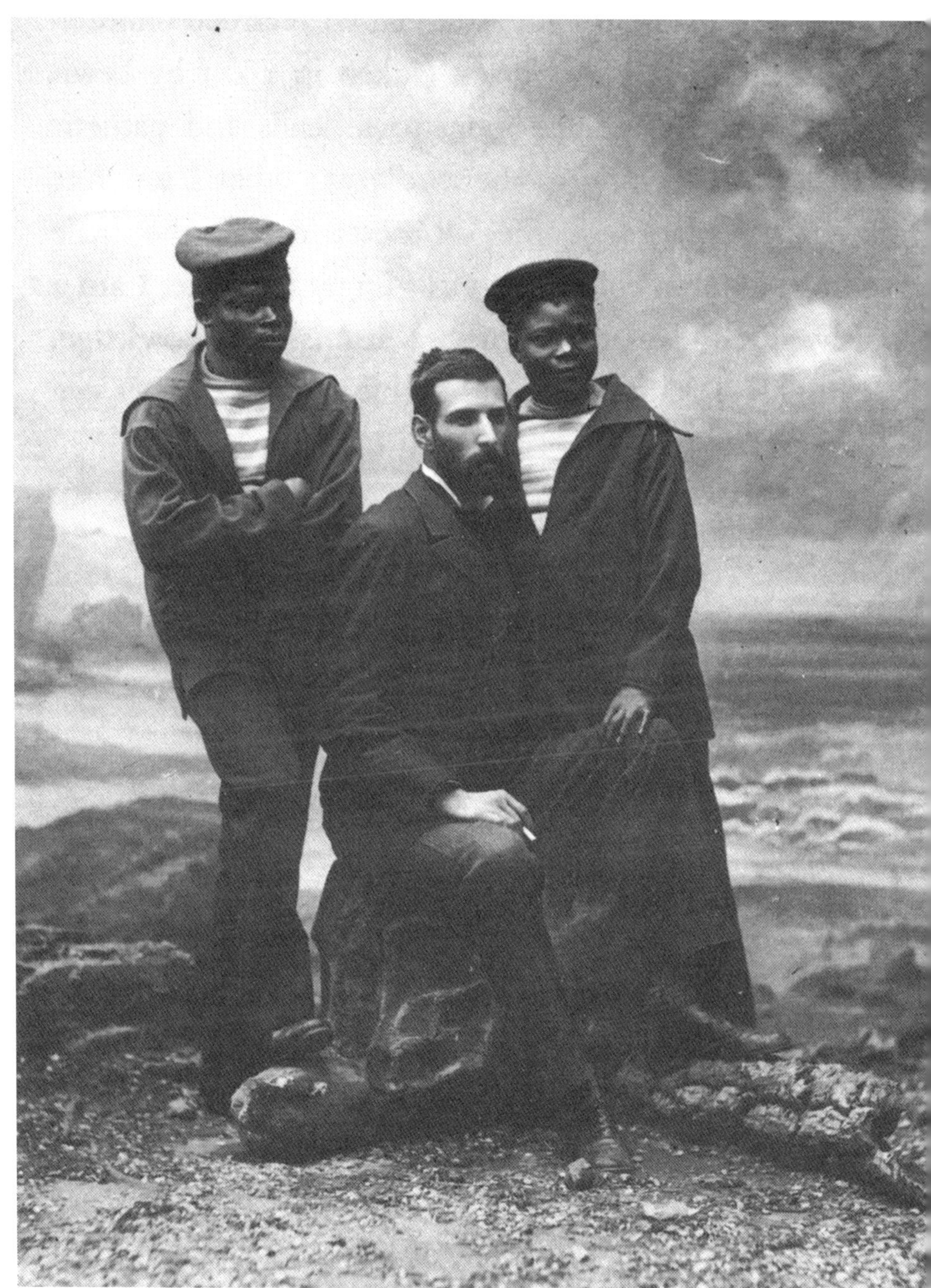

Félix Nadar, 1882

my gaze, to constitute a *punctum*," Barthes confessed, even as he determinedly ignored the image's obvious ideological construction of colonial paternalism. "And yet it is not one," he continued, "for I immediately code the posture, whether I want to or not, as 'aberrant' (for me, the *punctum* is the other boy's crossed arms). What I can name cannot really prick me. The incapacity to name is a good symptom of disturbance."[14]

Yet one wonders why he can't name this disturbing gesture (of crossed arms), one of seeming subtle subversion, offering an opaque hint of self-possession that appears to reject the drama of colonial relations in which he's apparently made to take part. Surely the Barthes of *Mythologies* would have seized on the opportunity to identify this construction. Is it because "the *punctum* is what haunts," as Avery Gordon suggests, but cannot be openly discussed? For her, "it is the detail, the little but heavily freighted thing that sparks the moment of arresting animation, that enlivens the world of ghosts."[15] In this case, is the spectralization a matter of the bizarre transference that places Barthes's father in the role of de Brazza, and splinters Barthes's own subjective positioning into the double parts of the two boys, one faithful to colonial paternalism, the other a distanced critic of it? Yet if the *punctum* enlivens the world of ghosts, then it can also cover up, shroud, and conceal insofar as it punctuates "the incapacity to name." Whereas Barthes was concerned in *Mythologies* with the decoding of the ideological message, and therefore with the as-yet-unnamed *studium*, then Meessen responds in *Vita Nova* by identifying and opening up the *punctum* of that *Paris Match* image, making it into a grave for the living dead—in this case, the subjective but unspoken meaning that that colonial image may have held for Barthes. In other words, the film explores Barthes's personal and familial connections to the colonization of West Africa that likely informed his relation and interest in that image, connections that were then suppressed by "the incapacity to name."

Of course others have taken Barthes to task for his photographic aesthetics as well. For theorist Ariella Azoulay, Barthes's position—as presented in *Camera Lucida*—constitutes a renunciation of what she sees as the ethico-political responsibility to what is represented. In effect, Barthes "reduce[s] the role of the spectator to the act of judgment, eliminating his or her responsibility for what is seen in the photograph. That judgment assumes a passive attitude toward the image and is primarily interested in questioning the extent to which the photograph succeeds in arousing a desired effect or experience."[16]

14   Barthes, *Camera Lucida*, 51.

15   Gordon, *Ghostly Matters*, 106–8. She writes further: "The enchanting detail cannot be predicted in advance or calculated for methodological rigor. It is without doubt, and despite Barthes's desire to create a science of it, a highly particularized, if also fully social, phenomenon."

16   Ariella Azoulay, *The Civil Contract of Photography*, trans. Rela Mazali and Ruvik Danieli (New York: Zone Books, 2008), 130.

What were the circumstances of Barthes's transformation from the 1950s to the 1980s, one that ended with the embrace of this very act of subjective judgment? Was it a matter of increasing age and the shifting of subjective and political preferences? (As critics have observed, with the passing of the 1970s, Barthes turned increasingly to the exploration of textual pleasures that amounted to a withdrawal from political engagement toward subjectivist aesthetics.)[17] Or was it rather determined by the shifting historical context—for France in the 1950s was in the midst of intense conflicts over the politics and militancy of anticolonial struggles, particularly in Indochina and Algeria. For instance, it was this context that led Jean-Paul Sartre to publish "Le colonialisme est un système" in the review *Les Temps Modernes* in April 1956—at exactly the same time when Barthes was writing the short texts of *Mythologies*—in which he claimed: "We, the People of Mainland France, have only one lesson to draw from these facts: Colonialism is in a process of destroying itself. But it still fouls the atmosphere. It is our shame; it mocks our laws or caricatures them. It infects us with its racism. [...] It obliges our young men to fight despite themselves and die for Nazi principles that we fought against ten years ago; it attempts to defend itself by arousing fascism even here in France. Our role is to help it to die. Not only in Algeria but wherever it exists."[18] In relating colonialism to Nazism, Sartre was invoking the leading voices of radical black opposition to France's and Europe's colonial politics, including those of W. E. B. Du Bois, C. L. R. James, George Padmore, and Aimé Césaire.[19] Undoubtedly this anticolonial politics *within* France was what was behind the defense of the colonial project mounted by *Paris Match* in the mid-1950s, even while French West Africa had long been the site of anticolonial resistance, particularly following World War II, and continued as such intermittently until Ivory Coast received self-government status in the late 1950s and full independence in 1960. By 1980, when *Camera Lucida* was published, the colonial question was clearly no longer present in the same way, and it was in parallel with that historical development that Barthes turned to other non-colonial matters.

—

If Barthes's transformation entailed a spectralization of sorts—a rendering ghostly of the historical and political meanings and significances

17   On this transition of Barthes, see Alec G. Hargreaves, "A Neglected Precursor: Roland Barthes and the Origins of Postcolonialism," in *Postcolonial Theory and Francophone Literary Studies,* eds. H. Adlai Murdoch and Anne Donadey (Gainesville: University Press of Florida, 2005), 56; Diana Knight, *Barthes and Utopia: Space, Travel and Writing* (Oxford: Clarendon Press, 1997), esp. 93; Chela Sandoval, *Methodology of the Oppressed* (Minneapolis: University of Minnesota Press, 2000), esp. 113; and Rabaté, "Roland Barthes."

18   Jean-Paul Sartre, *Colonialism and Neocolonialism*, trans. Steve Brewer, Azzedine Haddour, and Terry McWilliams (London: Routledge, 2001), 47.

19   See, for instance, Aimé Césaire's *Discourse on Colonialism*, trans. Joan Pinkham (New York: Monthly Review Press, 2000), which is quite explicit on the count.

of the colonial past, which were excavated in *Mythologies*—then this became the source of further reanimations and conjuring tricks in Meessen's exhibition project, "My Last Life," at Khiasma in Paris in 2011, and at Netwerk in Aalst, Belgium, in 2011/12. "My Last Life" extended the thematic and structural engagements in *Vita Nova*. The series of installations and visual presentations further investigated the hauntings of Barthes, whom Meessen transformed into a spirit that hovered around the exhibition's objects and displays, their fictional constructions revealing their own historically meaningful truths. Decorated with potted palm trees, the display called up the spirit of Barthes's mother, Henriette Binger, whose Winter Garden Photograph the author famously contemplated without reproducing it in *Camera Lucida*.[20] As well, the palm-tree installation also conjured Belgian conceptual artist Marcel Broodthaers and his archival model of the "museum fiction," the presentations of which were similarly decorated in order to reproduce the genteel but nature-dominating institutional environment resonating with colonial Belgium. Meessen's exhibition is a similarly poetic and historically generative model of institutional critique, but here it expands the focus to the artist's construction of a surprising imaginary archive of Barthes. The assembly drew together documents and inventive constructions that turn fiction into the building blocks of a newly revealed historical reality of the cultural and visual institutions of the colonial past. Within the display, the visitor encountered various magazines such as *Paris Match*, *National Geographic*, *La Quinzaine*, and travelogues from the colonial period—including one hardcover, *Le serment de l'explorateur*, authored by Louis Gustave Binger. These were dispersed on the floor along the edges of the gallery. Custom-crafted wooden vitrines, which exhibited the documents in the earlier Paris installation, lay empty and legless on the ground at Netwerk—a shift in display suggesting the possibilities of narrative reconfiguration from one engagement to the next and thus the impossibility of a single definitive history. In objectifying these documents and transforming them into sculptural forms, the installation emphasized their plasticity in relation to historical accounts, which themselves seem endlessly mutable.

The exhibition thereby threw its inclusions—discursive markers of various historical trajectories—into new constellations, partly indicated in the expansiveness of the large "cosmograph" on one wall: a complex linear interlinking of diverse names connecting people, characters, works, and historical periods, including Binger, Barthes, *Paris Match*,

20   As Barthes explained, "I cannot reproduce the Winter Garden Photograph. It exists only for me. For you, it would be nothing but an indifferent picture, one of the thousand manifestations of the 'ordinary.'" *Camera Lucida*, 73.

Stéphane Mallarmé, Alfred Stieglitz, and Philip Sollers. The map's
hundreds of references (produced using an open-source computer
program for genealogy construction) far exceeded the exhibition's
main content in scope, and opened up seemingly infinite potential
narrative plots. A pile of reprinted issues of *Paris Match* appeared
in the opposite corner, reedited to highlight all the material from
the July 1955 issue related to colonial endeavors, which now
seems so clichéd in its portrayal of Africa. It included a short pho-
to-essay documenting the visit of Diouf and his comrades Issa and
Santoura (referred to familiarly by the magazine editors) to the
Eiffel Tower in Paris and La fête à Neu-Neu in Neuilly-sur-Seine in
the week before Les Nuits de l'Armée; a report on King Baudouin's
visit to the Congo; an article on the alleged existence of slavery
in Mali; an illustrated essay on the "last survivors of prehistory"
found in New Guinea; and a four-page small-scale reproduction of
all the pages of the original magazine.

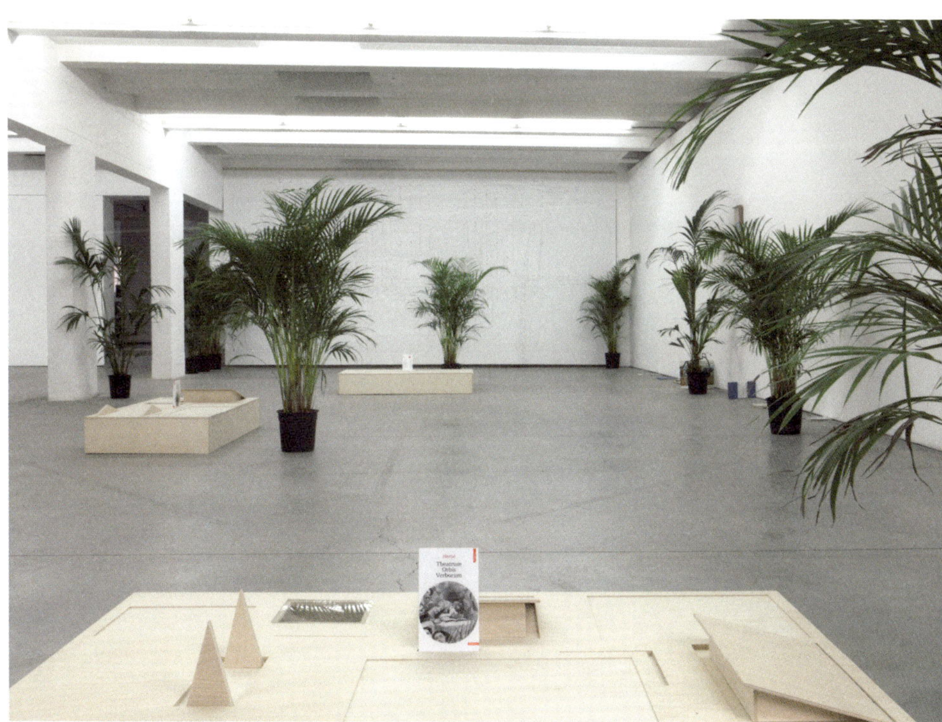

Exhibition view; Vincent Meessen, "My Last Life," Netwerk, Aalst, 2011/12

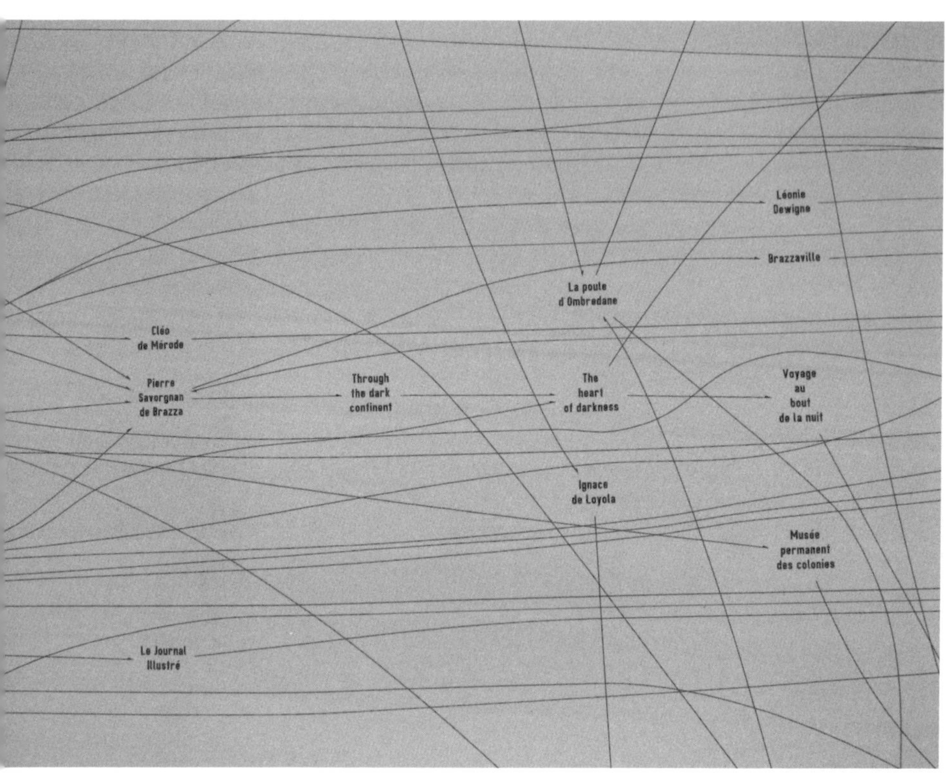

Vincent Meessen, detail of cosmograph, 2011

These romantic and exotic narratives of colonial exploration surprisingly parallel Barthes's own fictional wanderings as imagined in and by the exhibition. For instance, Meessen presented mock-ups of three unrealized books by Herbé—a French homophonic equivalent of the initials "R. B.," as Barthes sometimes referred to himself in print. The titles, based on Barthes's own whimsical indications of possible subjects found in his writings, offer a speculative glimpse of the author's dream to be a novelist. These include: *Psychanalyse istorique des imageries tronquées* (Historical Psychoanalysis of Truncated Images), *Theatrum Orbis Verborum* (The World Theater of Words), and *Mathesis Singularis* (Singular Science), the last one based on Barthes's provocative suggestion in *Camera Lucida* that each text or image deserves its own singular interpretive

21 See Barthes, *Camera Lucida*, 8.

22 See Roland Barthes, *The Preparation of the Novel: Lecture, Courses and Seminars at the Collège de France (1978–1979 and 1979–1980)*, trans. Kate Briggs (New York: Columbia University Press, 2010), 5. The author writes: "Now, for someone who writes, who has chosen to write, that is to say, for someone who has *experienced the jouissance, the joy of writing* (not unlike the 'first pleasure'), there can be no other *Vita Nova* (or so it seems to me) than the discovery of a new writing practice."

methodology.[21] It is such a methodology that *Vita Nova* invents for the *Paris Match* image: the video and exhibition play off of Barthes's desire for a "new life"—one for which he referenced Dante's *La Vita Nuova* in imagining the necessarily different form of existence entailed in becoming a novelist—which, at the same time, would also put to death an old life.[22]

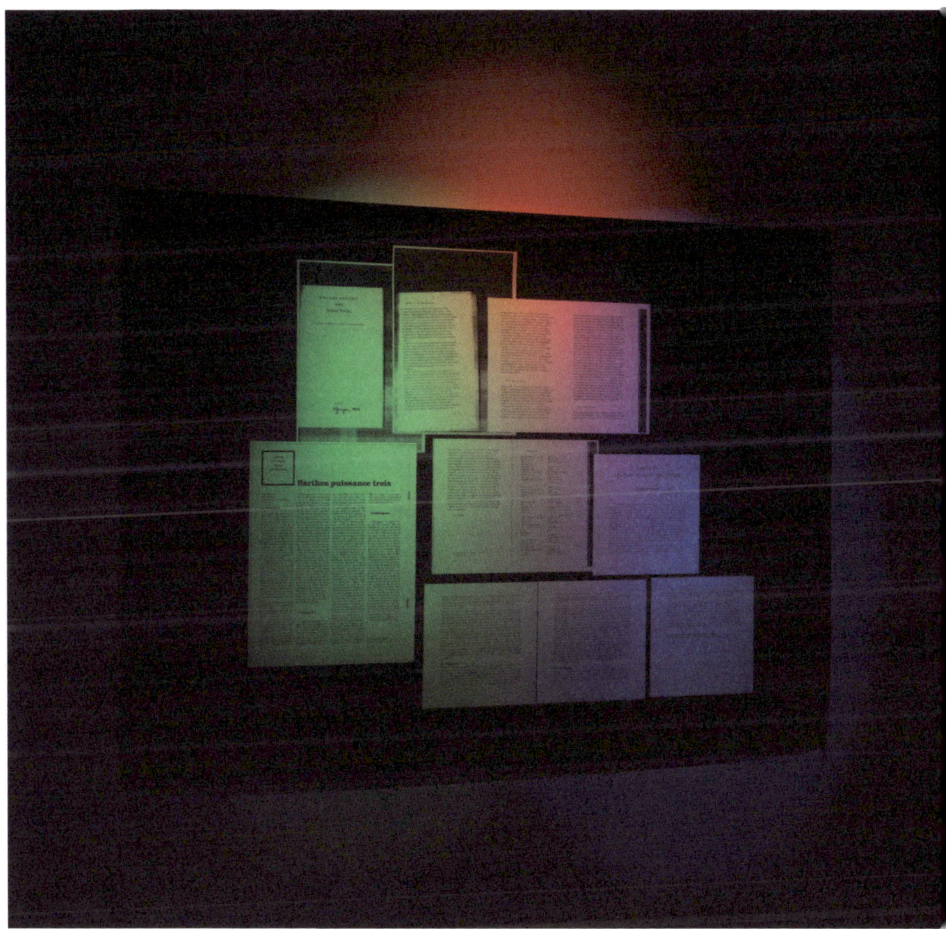

Installation view; Vincent Meessen, *Third Text*, 2011

Taking Barthes's lead, Meessen's projects play on the multiplication of identity at work in Barthes's own writings, particularly in *Third Text* (2011), in which Meessen hung one of the author's short articles on the wall, reproduced it in three languages, and illuminated it with spotlights in primary colors. The text, "Barthes to the Power of Three," was originally published in the magazine *La Quinzaine* in 1975 (also presented in the Khiasma/Netwerk exhibition), for which the author reviewed his own autobiography *Roland Barthes by Roland Barthes*. The playful result brought about a triadic division of the writer's identity, who appeared simultaneously as author, subject, and critic of his work. The distribution realizes some unexpected implications of Barthes's earlier discussion of the fragmentations of authorship in his classic essay "The Death of the Author," leading to the author(s) that Meessen brings back to life.

The significance of these creative sleights of hand is that Meessen doesn't use Barthes's purportedly disavowed family history as context for a corrective, truthful, and more definitive documentary account of the past. Rather, Barthes is shown to have carried out his own "auto-mythologization" when performing his critical decoding of colonial mythology and elaborating his own numerous identities, a mythologizing revealed subsequently by Meessen as the ultimate truth of documentary representation, historical construction, archival assembly, and semiological criticism.[23] That is to say, no "truth" is certain; no narrative, objective or definitive—neither exists beyond the author's interpretive point-of-view, the reader's subjective understanding, and the workings of disavowal and repression. In addition, this mythologizing can function as a way to attack myth itself. As Barthes himself professed in "Myth Today": "Truth to tell, the best weapon against myth is perhaps to mythify it in its turn, and to produce an *artificial myth*: and this reconstituted myth will in fact be a mythology. Since myth robs language of something, why not rob myth?"[24] Such is the significance of *Factitius* (2011), Meessen's realistic sculptural bronze rendition of "bananas," which rested on the documents dispersed throughout the exhibition space. The title draws on the Latin term, meaning "fabricated," which, as Meessen observes, also serves as the origin of the etymologically related but opposite-meaning words such as "fact," "fiction," and "fetish." In this regard, there can be no simple opposition between fact and fiction; rather, the one produces the other.[25]

23   This aspect resonates with the wider developments in contemporary art's "archival impulse" and the "artist as historian," where recent practice—which acknowledges subjective contingency and narrative openness—differs from earlier versions of documentary practice that pursued the goal of an objective and definitive truth. See Hal Foster, "An Archival Impulse," *October*, no. 110 (Fall 2004); and Mark Godfrey, "The Artist as Historian," *October*, no. 120 (Spring 2007).

24   Barthes, "Myth Today," 135.

It is the slipperiness between these significations, and the embracing of a certain "ontological anarchy," that facilitates Meessen's unleashing of ghosts without pretending to capture them in a subsequent narration.[26] As he explains:

> I try to make History legible as a stratification of competing regimes of enunciation: the History of a defeated person whose memory temporarily fails him, the written History of names and dates recited at school, the oral and legendary History told in the village, all of this is a little bit the lost time of narrative. But in parallel, another history is slowly constructed, which functions as the elucidation of the *punctum* of the *Paris Match* photo. Yet for Barthes, this *punctum* is always personal and intimate because it is the thing that moves you so in certain photos, which you cannot put a name to.[27]

Here it is important to be clear: proposing a *punctum* for the *Paris Match* image is far from a simple matter of recovering a repressed history; rather, it entails pointing to the impossibility of Barthes's negation of that history. It involves calling attention to its lingering presence, the way that history lived on in Barthes's work, even as he failed to acknowledge it directly. It means identifying the disconcerting presence of an absence. In other words, such a hauntology exposes the presence of a "radical non-negativity," in the words Steven Shaviro uses to point out that which refuses to be put to rest. For Shaviro, the ghostly trace becomes "a kind of residual, quasi-material insistence, that disrupts and ruins every movement of negation or negativity. That's what the ghost is, after all: something that is gone, or dead, but that refuses to be altogether absent; something that is not here, not now, but that continues to stain or contaminate or affect or impinge upon the here and now."[28] In other words, this radical non-negativity points to the way photography, as a ghostly non-presence, or as the disturbing presence of an absence, repeatedly calls attention to the colonial past in Barthes's work—from the image of de Brazza in *Camera Lucida*, to the portrait of his colonist grandfather in *Roland Barthes by Roland Barthes*—yet in a way that could not be directly addressed or historically elaborated. We are left with the traces of a disavowal, one that will not quite go away.

—

25 This refers to Jacques Rancière's repositioning of the role of fiction, as in his essay "Documentary Fiction," 158: "'Fiction' is not a pretty story or evil lie, the flipside of reality that people try to pass off for it. Originally, *fingere* doesn't mean 'to feign' but 'to forge.' Fiction means using the means of art to construct a 'system' of represented actions, assembled forms, and internally coherent signs."

26 As part of his "Animism" project, Anselm Franke speaks of an "ontological anarchy—where exclusions become increasingly intelligible through their symptomatic displacements in the economy of desires, in the genres of fiction, in psychopathologies, and so forth." Franke, "Introduction—'Animism,'" *e-flux journal*, no. 36 (July 2012): 2.

27 Cited in Katrin Mundt, "A Conversation with Vincent Meessen," *A Prior*, no. 20 (2010): 25.

28 See Shaviro's blog entry on this subject, "Specters of Marx," *The Pinocchio Theory*, February 8, 2006

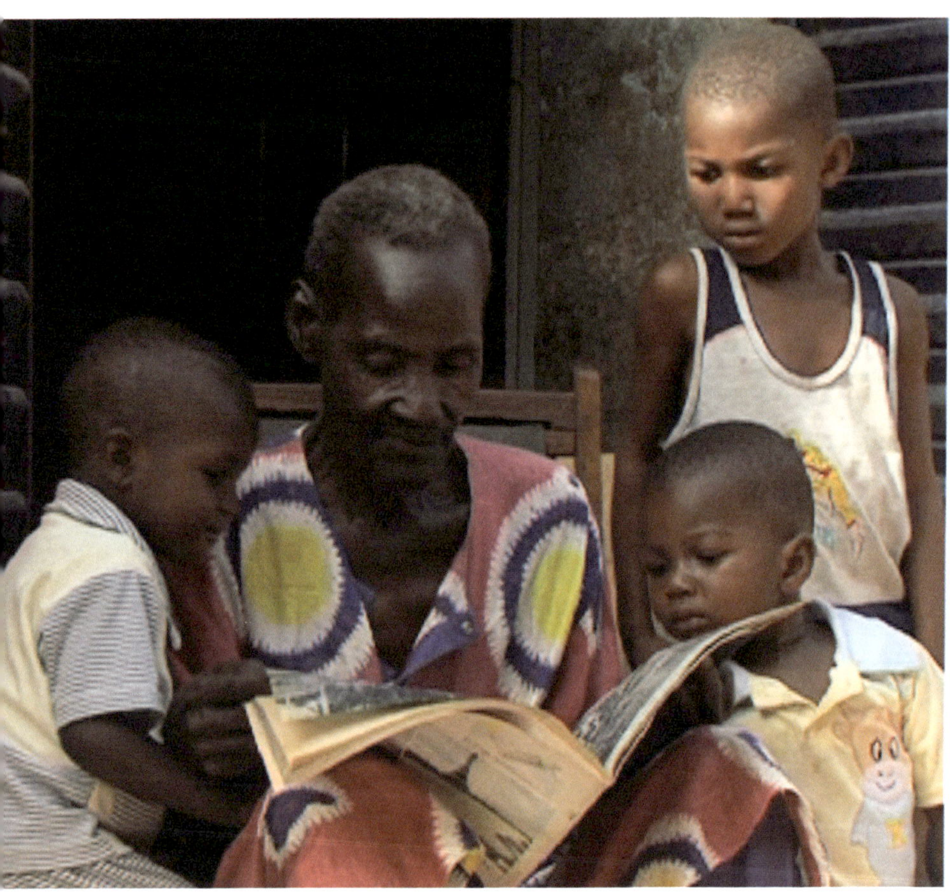

Vincent Meessen, still from *Vita Nova*, 2009

From here we can reassess the significance of *Vita Nova*: if it offers a new life to historical documents, like the cover of *Paris Match*, then this life is open, transformative, and partly unnamed. This aspect is exemplified when the video, toward its end, shows Kaboré receiving a copy of the magazine—the first time he has ever seen the issue—fifty years after the photographs taken of him appeared in it (and the first time we see the whole cover). The moving encounter enables a certain remembrance to occur, experienced by Kaboré and shared with his grandchildren, as shown in the video. These figures become caught in the swirl of a cyclical history that is mutually estranging: the old man returns to his own image, which is given a second life, but it is one that renders him unrecognizable from age. Similarly, his grandsons

     A Colonial Hauntology: Vincent Meessen's *Vita Nova*

recognize themselves uncannily in the image of their grandfather as a boy, but the historical context is completely different.
Rather than reconstructing past events *retrospectively*, then,
Meessen's work provokes new and future events *prospectively*.
Its modeling of performative documentary thus offers a mixture
of historical documents, storytelling and fabulation, and unscripted social situations, all of which converge in a transformative moment in the present and construct a creative pedagogy
for the future. Kobena Mercer points out the redemptive aspect
of this gesture: "Giving a new life or a second life to images
of colonised subjects who would otherwise be unnamed and
unknown, Meessen's film enacts a postcolonial gesture of 'redemptive return' whereby archival material, instead of being
dead and buried in the past, flashes up into contemporary
time in a critical moment of delayed awakening that reveals
the unfinished afterlife of the colonial relation."[29] Yet if it does
so, then *Vita Nova* reveals that the historical image's meaning
will remain forever unfinished, ever capable of producing
new mythologies, ever holding the potential to animate
new ghosts.

This modeling of performative documentary is demonstrated in the film's scenes portraying an outdoor cinema that
Meessen reconstructed at the former Ouagadougou cadets' barracks (which today has become a high school). Burkinabés are
shown watching passages from *La force noire*, a 2007 film by
Eric Deroo, which offers an official account of the colonized African people's participation in France's wars, with footage drawn
from the French Ministry of Defense's archives. A spiraling history unfolds in Meessen's filmic montage that joins these distinct
events. For instance, the film shows African troops parading
in the Palais des Sports—as the Vel' d'Hiv, the old indoor cycle
track, was renamed after the war, in part to distance the site
from its notorious past when it had been used as an assembly
point for those deported to the death camps during World War
II.[30] In this sense, the fact that Les Nuits de L'Armée took place
there in 1955 proposes an appalling connection between the
history of anti-Semitism and the Holocaust and French colonialism. Yet now, it is the Africans who appear as the spectators,
owing to the intercutting of shots in *Vita Nova*:
they watch their earlier selves and observe the
original French audience a half century later.
Do they now sit in judgment of that colonial
spectacle, of that celebration of militarism
and French patriotism against the backdrop
of complicity in racism and genocide? Are its

29   Kobena Mercer, "Vincent Meessen,"
in *Ars 11* (Helsinki: Museum of Contemporary Art Kiasma, 2011), 150.

30   The 1955 Palais des Sports is
distinct from the stadium built in 1960
after the Vel' d'Hiv burned down in
1959.

menacing ghosts finally put to rest when this history of oppression and domination is brought to a measure of historiographic justice? While this conclusion may be one we can never verify—and thus only speculate upon—we do witness a transgenerational transmission, where the now-grandfather-aged men share their nearly forgotten experiences of those earlier colonial days with their grandchildren, some of whom serve in the military of independent Burkina Faso. History becomes a medium of repetition and difference—recalling, according to Barthes, the *punctum* of the "lacerating of time"; for Derrida, that which "de-synchronizes" and "recalls us to anachrony."[31] As *Vita Nova*'s narrator explains, reincarnating the words of Barthes: "History is a spiral. Time brings back previous states, but the spiral's circles expand, none ever produces its exact copy. History is as a polyphonic of strokes of light and mist that answer each other constantly. On the spiral's trajectory, everything recurs, but in another higher place, it is the return of difference, the movement of metaphor, it is Fiction."[32]

While *Vita Nova* constructs an educational exercise that catalyzes remembrance in the postcolonial present, it simultaneously offers a critical history of French literary discourse from the 1950s, when authors such as Barthes contributed to the exposure and critique of imperialist visual culture. Yet even as Barthes's pathbreaking analysis contributed to the delegitimation of colonial mythology, his writings also disavow the complicities and responsibilities that were closer to home. It is in this disavowal that *Vita Nova* intervenes. First, in addressing Barthes's early semio-critique of colonial ideology, the video speculates about the *punctum* that implicates the personal history haunting Barthes's texts, which enacted an erasure that also uncannily revealed the repressed. Here, hauntology finds its definition in the negative ontology of representation: "The spectral *is* not," Derrida writes. It is "neither substance, nor essence, nor existence. [It] *is never present as such*." [33] Second, the film exposes and rejects the subjective phenomenology of *Camera Lucida*, which typifies Barthes's move away from ideological critique and, more specifically, his disavowal of the political image economy of colonialism, which as we have seen was intertwined with his family history. In the end, we are led to conclude that Barthes's later analytical tendencies corresponded to a revealing repression, one that reappeared in Barthes's work in its very non-negativity; in its ghostly presence, as magnified in Meessen's art. As

31   Barthes, *Camera Lucida*, 96; and Derrida, *Specters of Marx*, 6–7.

32   As is typical of the film, these quotes are worked into the film's narrative without citation—and thereby demonstrate a further act of creative reinvention of Barthes's voice. This one is from Roland Barthes, *Essais critiques* (Paris: Éditions du Seuil, 1981), 89.

33   Derrida, exordium to *Specters of Marx*, xix.

such, *Vita Nova* contributes to the work of historical recovery. For its hauntology, furthermore, serves as a model for how the *punctum* and *studium* might find some reconnection, if not reconciliation, in an experimental historiography both subjectively implicative, historically and politically aware, and sensitive to representational complexity.[34] Such a historiography would be founded not on the easy availability of historical presence, but rather on the impossibility of history's totalizing impulse, on the insistence of the radical non-negativity that haunts historical consciousness and representation. It would thereby challenge all historicism that is founded upon a strict sense of chronology or that conceptually solidifies the past.[35]

Finally, these points identify the particular significance of Meessen's work in the present, in a context where French culture, education, and politics—like much of European discourse from the Netherlands to Italy, Belgium to Germany—have been moving toward a neo-revisionist "imperial winter," one defined by a growing historical amnesia matched, not surprisingly, by a colonial nostalgia.[36] Indeed, postcolonial studies has received a conspicuously delayed reception in France, coming to light only in the last decade (despite the rich history of resistance movements in the colonies, and the theoretical analyses by writers such as Fanon, Césaire, and Albert Memmi), and remains at best a continually embattled discipline there. It is one whose belated appearance corresponds to right-wing efforts to renounce inherited traditions of internationalism and anticolonialism and, likewise, to rid the country of its complex legacy of Marxism and the memory of the social and political struggles of 1968—including the solidarity movement with the Third World.[37] Such cannot be unrelated to the politics of anti-multiculturalism, which, in denying the violence and negative legacy of the colonial past, makes it all the easier to continue its logic—whether in relation to the attacks on immigration or in terms of the neocolonial maintenance of relations of inequality between the North and South as exploited by Western political and economic elites. Not that Barthes's political position is continuous with this conservative turn, but his overdetermined silence does testify to the hidden depths of colonialism's immersion even in

34   In some ways this latter proposal offers a redemptive possibility for art history, which has frequently opted to follow Barthes's own turn away from the *studium* to a concern with the *punctum*, but one elevated to the level of structural necessity—often understood as a function of trauma—rather than subjective preference as it was with Barthes. The result is that historical subject matter is altogether sacrificed. For example, consider Benjamin H. D. Buchloh's reading of Gerhard Richter in "The Anomic Archive," *October*, no. 88 (Spring 1999); and Hal Foster's reading of Warhol in "Death in America," *October*, no. 75 (Winter 1996); which risk such a sacrifice of history in favor of the historicity of the *punctum*'s formal determinations.

35   On the historiographic implications of ghosts, see Peter Buse and Andrew Scott, eds., *Ghosts: Deconstruction, Psychoanalysis, History* (London: Macmillan, 1999).

36   Achille Mbembe, "Provincializing France?," *Public Culture* 23, no. 1 (2011): 87.

37   On the cultural and intellectual disavowals of the radical lessons of May '68, see Kristin Ross, *May '68 and Its Afterlives* (Chicago: University of Chicago Press, 2002).

the past of its own critique. To investigate that past today, as *Vita Nova* does, is all the more urgent in the reinvention of a different future—a future beyond colonialism.

3. Ghostly Affect: **Zarina Bhimji's** *Yellow Patch*

Yellow Patch, the 2011 film by Zarina Bhimji, includes a slow zoom onto the crumbling facade of an old palace in Kutch, India. With its focus on a site that is seemingly abandoned from a distant time and filled with untold complexity and depth—visible in its layered textures and material embeddedness in its environment—the film builds on a signature trope of the London-based artist: in particular her meditative and careful approach to what I will call her "cinema of affect." Bhimji's films strike a poignant emotional level, mobilizing cinema's ability to correlate moving images and carefully selected sounds with subjective sensation. Her films thereby define a post-documentary aesthetic that relinquishes information and factual presentation in order to probe poetic and aesthetic elements of color, texture, and rhythm. Yet, these films nonetheless connect with postcolonial history and the difficult mobility and displacement of Indians to Africa in the early twentieth century and, later, to Britain in the early 1970s, including Bhimji's own family. It is the links between aesthetics and politics, between affective sensations and the historical developed in Bhimji's films that I will explore here.

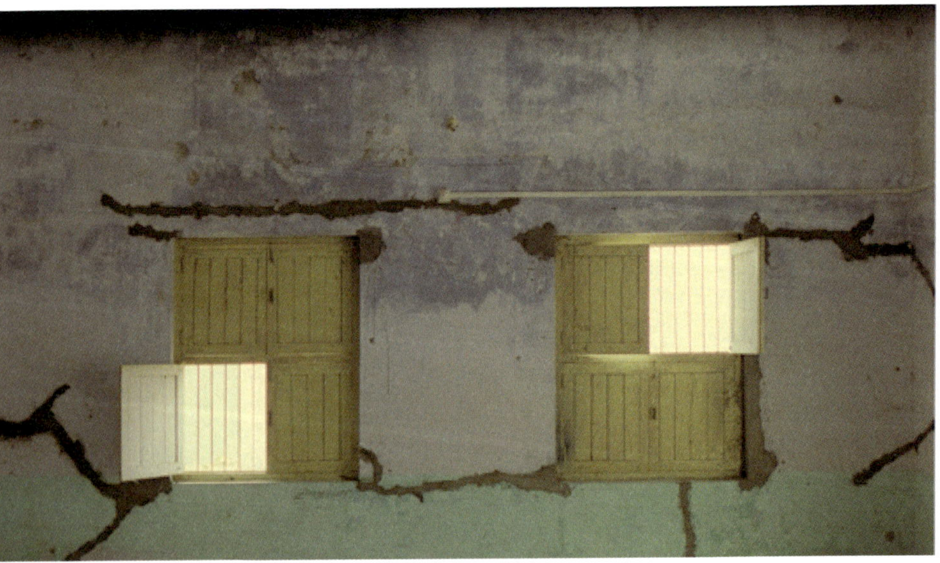

Zarina Bhimji, still from *Yellow Patch*, 2011

The three-story palace in *Yellow Patch*, a *haveli* house—the crafted, historic mansions found in India and Pakistan, and Persian for "enclosed space"—first appears at an oblique angle. Its state of disrepair is immediately evident, as are the unkempt grounds that surround it. Dating from the late eighteenth century, it is exemplary of an eclectic colonial Indian architecture, which is slowly revealed in Bhimji's approaching camera. The steady advance and smooth pan produce a disembodied viewing experience, even as the physicality of the building and the world around it is also foregrounded.[1] She focuses acutely on the environment's material sensuousness and interaction with the subtle effects of light and wind. This sensitivity is also characteristic of Bhimji's longstanding aesthetic, as it has unfolded over several of her earlier works, including *Out of Blue* (2002) and *Waiting* (2007). Drawn to the imagery of old abandoned buildings, frayed textiles, and spiderwebs, the artist assembles a repertoire of recurring visual tropes. Here, the buildings perform as characters, thematizing Bhimji's relationship to the India of her parents' early life. The filmic exploration of these buildings is thus deeply personal, even while the work is not concerned immediately with the artist's biography.

Throughout the film's nearly thirty minutes, viewers gradually come to witness several such resonant sites in Gujarat and Bombay, which speak to the many attachments and desertions of the past that connect to Bhimji's family history. Growing up in a small town near Jamnagar in the Indian state of Gujarat, her father moved to East Africa in the late 1920s at the age of eleven, traveling to the frontiers of Britain's expanding colonial empire. The film loosely retraces the geography of that journey, which includes several locations. It begins with shots of the Princess Dock in Bombay, constructed by the British in 1885, where Bhimji focuses on the old Victorian offices full of ancient files redolent of British colonial bureaucracy and containing the tantalizing traces of stories now forgotten. It moves on to shots of the decaying ornate structures and desolate windswept desert area of the Rann of Kutch, once a princely state, now a remote and culturally unique region of Gujarat that borders Pakistan. And it closes with footage from the Mandvi port on the Indian Ocean in Gujarat, from where many Indians embarked for Africa in the wooden boats called dhows, which are still built today. Overall, the film is cast in moving colors and warm sunlight—the film's title alludes to a lecture Bhimji attended by the

1   My understanding of the film is informed by conversations with the artist during September and November 2011, and by the artist's unpublished treatment—or preproduction conceptualization—for *Yellow Patch*. In this, she wrote further about her use of architecture: "It's not about describing a house or making it picturesque. It is to go beyond the description. It is to reveal attachment, to explore subtle shadings of our attachment. To build up emotional intensity, empty/full, communal/solitary, rational/irrational with sound."

writer Doris Lessing on the color yellow, and suggests, according to the artist, a patch of sunlight and the painterly sensibility it invokes. Color infuses the film: steel gray skies arc over the rippling mirror of the sea, and abstract blue-green compositions emerge on decaying walls. These subtle scenes endow the film with captivating visual allusions to a past that is unavailable to viewers, but nevertheless seems inscribed in the architecture, landscape, and environment.

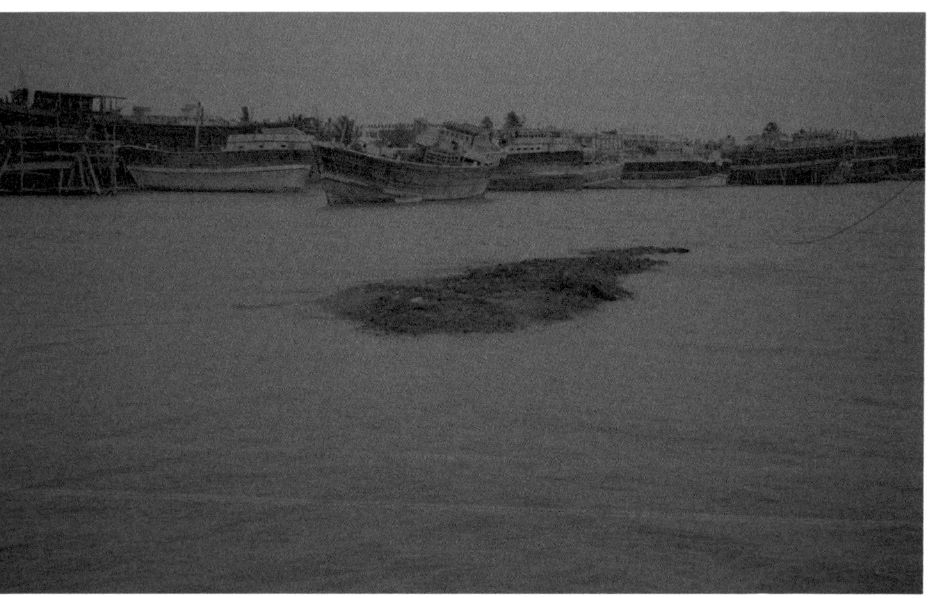

Zarina Bhimji, still from *Yellow Patch*, 2011

Adding to this visual array of geographical sites is a soundtrack of disparate sources. The soundtrack builds on the film's panoply of visual sensations, generating a wide range of affects, including ominous dread and painful loss, as well as the excitement of rediscovery and loving intimacy. There are oceanic sounds of symphonic strings; chattering typewriters and the shuffling of anonymous workers; recordings of the natural elements such as waves, thunder, and birdsong; ghostly voices, barely decipherable, making confessions and proclamations; and lyrical and poetic Sufi songs sung in melismatic and haunting ornament. Short sound clips of what seem to be political speeches echo in a chamber of distant remembrance, with phrases such as "the soul of a nation, long suppressed" emerging from background noise, as one man's voice explains how he was "made by the British." The fact that these and other voices include those of the independence-era leaders Mohandas Gandhi, Muhammad Ali Jinnah, Jawaharlal Nehru, and Louis Mountbatten, recorded both at the time of India's and Pakistan's postcolonial emergence and after, is, however, never made clear in the film; rather, the voices hover in ambiguity and perceptual estrangement.[2] The result is that while the content brings to mind the historical experiences of colonial repression and burgeoning national freedom, the uncertainty of their sources places viewers in the role of investigator, trying to figure out how to relate to these experiences in the present. The film consequently implies that this history continues to resonate with contemporary events. The off-screen sounds and voices also spatialize the image, casting visual sensation into an expanse of past and present reverberations so that the presentation of current-day India takes on momentous significance and temporal breadth, even while the meaning of the images is never entirely clear or univocal. Indeed, through this formal construction Bhimji's film indicates its sensitivity to the formidable complexity and depth of history, but a history where meaning inevitably overflows the grasp of documentation and information and remains open-ended, opaque, and full of potential consequence.

The first of two sequential films that explore the history of Indian migration to East Africa and the contemporary aftermath of that passage, *Yellow Patch* was inspired by Bhimji's father's journey from India to East Africa, the artist explains in a press release for the film. However, it veers away from the biographical, rather opening onto an expansive story about the collective migration that Bhimji's family took part in. "This story is the lived experience of many East African Asians," Bhimji adds.[3] The second part—a yet-to-be-made film—will continue that journey by revisiting places connected to the later part of that migration, focusing on sites in Zanzibar, Kenya, and Uganda, various destinations for some 32,000 Indians in the late nineteenth and early twentieth centuries. Many of them came to work on the construction of the Uganda Railway (now known as the Kenya Railway), which stretches over 582 miles from Mombasa to Lake Victoria, or to pursue related employment opportunities. Built between 1885 and 1905, the railway was part of the colonial conquest of East Africa, an imperial history that came to an end in Uganda with its independence in 1962.

2   The artist explained to me that she collected some of these materials in the British Sound Archive. Bhimji, interview by the author, November 12, 2011.

3   Zarina Bhimji, press release for *Yellow Patch*, 2011, publicized in conjunction with her survey exhibition at Whitechapel Gallery, London.

Yellow Patch thus explores a history prior to those of Bhimji's past films, such as *Out of Blue*, which investigates the psychogeography of postcolonial Africa and Europe—particularly the artist's relation to the collective trauma experienced by Asians expelled from Uganda by the dictator Idi Amin in 1972[4]—and *Waiting*, which depicts old textile factories in Mombasa and Voi, Kenya, and reflects on the production of sisal (used to make sacking and ropes) during the colonial period. The locations portrayed in these films—the architectural ruins of workhouses, factories, military barracks, and police prisons—provide symbolically rich sites for Bhimji's metaphors of painful loss, brutality, and abandonment, as well as mystery and beauty, which complicate the meanings of her works significantly. Similarly characterized by their dreamlike sensibility—owing to the camera's steady drifting around depopulated sites, the material and architectural remainders of the colonial project and its postcolonial transition—these films, like *Yellow Patch*, offer no clear voice-over narration, contextual intertitles, or speaking figures that would otherwise explain the history that informs them.

In *Yellow Patch*, the focus on the materiality of specific locations (for example, the dwelling on architectural details, atmospheric conditions, and interior spaces) comes without information that might otherwise tell us what we're looking at, just as the soundtrack is delivered without interpretive direction or specific contextualization. Slow-paced and meditative, the camera glides through the locations, impersonally, as if making a ghostly visitation to places still possessed by past, unresolved experiences. Unlike the use of a handheld camera that might indicate the filmmaker's subjective viewpoint, Bhimji's sense of visuality is disembodied, as if decontextualized from her own specific personhood, floating over its objects, as if haunted by them. These elements define Bhimji's aesthetics of opacity, a poetics of the image abstracted from background information, which is striking for an artist who researches and confronts such complex postcolonial histories in her work. As Gilane Tawadros observes, we know that "the echoes of 'something that is not there anymore' haunt the works of Zarina Bhimji,"[5] but the explicit identification and elaboration of this "something" is withheld from her films.

Bhimji's participation in the 2008 Guangzhou Triennial, "Farewell to Postcolonialism" (curated by Sarat Maharaj), and "Who Knows Tomorrow" at Hamburger Bahnhof in Berlin in 2010 (curated by Udo Kittelmann, Chika Okeke-Agulu, and Britta Schmitz), marked the beginning of the artist's tendency

4   See Chika Okeke-Agulu, "Conversation with Zarina Bhimji," *Art Journal* 69, no. 4 (Winter 2010): 66.

5   Gilane Tawadros, "The Revolution Stripped Bare," in Tawadros et al., *Fault Lines*, 20.

to present some of her research materials alongside the display
of her films, including her storyboards and treatments—which
emerge out of intense historical and geographical investigations.
For her 2012 Whitechapel Gallery retrospective, she presented
storyboards for *Yellow Patch* and select photocopied excerpts
from her historical research in vitrines. Her preparatory investigations are demonstrably extensive, typically involving site visits
and significant time spent in libraries reviewing historical documents and scholarship regarding the periods and places that
her projects explore. This stage then leads to her construction
of treatments and storyboards (including special storyboards
for the audio track) and finally to the production of the films
themselves. For this reason, it is all the more noteworthy that she
withholds this historical research from her films. If anything, her
work is informed by the very blockage of information that results
from her own collection of historical research. "I am interested
in the tension between lyrical, intense beauty and sociopolitical
language," she explained recently in relation to her film *Waiting*.
"It is important for me to remain allegorical even if I touch the
subject of politics."[6]

Wrapped up in this tension and allegorical quality is
Bhimji's relation to her own experience living in East Africa as
a child, and her family's embroilment in the traumatic episode
when Asians were given ninety days to leave Uganda. From early
on in her career—for instance, at the time of her participation in
Rasheed Araeen's "The Essential Black Art" show at Chisenhale
Gallery in 1988—she made it clear that her work, which has
included photographs, mixed media collages, sculptural installations, and films, concerned this history: "I want to create, communicate new meanings by bringing Indian languages, objects,
memory, dreams, conversations from East Africa and Indian
backgrounds, as well as my experience of Western culture, to play
in between two realities."[7] That said, with the advancement of her
career, Bhimji has taken on an increasingly indi-
rect relation to her biographical history in her
art. While her work on *Yellow Patch* emerged
from her desire to address the circumstances of
her family's migration from India to East Africa,
she also makes it clear that her film's relation
to her family's past is far from explicit and,
moreover, it is not concerned exclusively with
that history. This antihistorical tendency leaves
us with the following questions: Why does her
work reject the historical account, the discursive treatment, the contextualization, and what

6   Okeke-Agulu, "Conversation
with Bhimji," 68. Similarly, the entry
for her Turner Prize reads, "Bhimji's in-
quiries into the past and present of her
chosen sites become intensely personal:
historical fact can only be abandoned,
allowing her image making to begin,
once this level of knowledge and
intimacy has been achieved." Laurence
Sillars and Darren Pih, *Turner Prize 07*
(Liverpool: Tate Liverpool, 2007), n.p.

7   Quoted in Mark Hanworth-Booth,
introduction to *Zarina Bhimji: I Will
Always Be Here* (Birmingham: Ikon
Gallery, 1992), n.p.

is gained by her formal decisions regarding her filmmaking projects? What is behind Bhimji's omission of information and her desire to place "beauty and sociopolitical language" in "tension" in order to make "allegorical" films, and what is achieved by this approach? Alternately, how does her work reflect on that historical narrative, and make it relevant and compelling in ways that circumvent the direct testimonial or documentary account?

—

In 1998 Bhimji made the first of two research trips to Uganda, the country she was forced to leave as an eleven-year-old girl. The experience of visiting her lost homeland led to a series of photographs entitled Love, which portrays various emotionally charged sites in Uganda, and which relates to her first film, *Out of Blue*, commissioned for Okwui Enwezor's documenta 11 in 2002. As she explained: "During my first visit back to Uganda in 1998, I listened to the land, to the sounds in the air, to the smell of guns, and I realised that it had to be a film. So I started doing research, looking through the African and international press from 1972 to 1974—newspaper cuttings on Ugandan Asians leaving Uganda— and from that I put a film narrative together."[8] That period in the early 1970s is key, for the turbulent postcolonial context in Uganda that Bhimji lived through has marked her life and art strongly, and for her to return to Uganda nearly twenty-five years later was to revisit the primal scene of postcolonial violence as well as the site of positive childhood memories of a place suddenly taken away from her.[9]

On August 5, 1972, General Amin announced his decision on national radio that henceforth all Asians with British passports (approximately sixty thousand people) would have to leave the country within three months. It was one year after he assumed power by military coup—a coup largely welcomed by the West, including Britain, as it put an end to Milton Obote's left-leaning government, which was allied with Julius Nyerere's socialist Tanzania. A few days later, Amin amended his statement to include all Asians—Ugandan citizens as well—increasing the number of people who would be expelled within three months to 80,000. The move was part of the dictator's "Africanization" of Uganda, which included the declaration of an "economic war" on those "outsiders"—even though many had lived in Uganda for several generations—who were perceived as owning the majority of the country's resources and businesses. As an act of ethnic cleansing, it formed part of Amin's

8   Quoted in Maite Lorés, interview with Zarina Bhimji, *contemporary*, no. 49 (2003): 60.

9   Bhimji, in conversation with the author, 2011.

strategy for achieving full economic independence, justified as part of the country's process of decolonization. It followed on the heels of other recently emancipated African states, namely Libya, to which Amin turned on behalf of Uganda to replace Britain and Israel as financial donors and suppliers of arms. Indeed, Libya's Colonel Muammar Gaddafi had expelled Italians as soon as he assumed power in 1969, and Amin followed suit by expelling Israelis in 1972 (in order to court the support of Arab governments) before turning to Asians later that year.[10] With his unpredictable shifting policies, Amin's politics exemplify what Mbembe terms the "socialization of arbitrariness," which, joined with the "violence of economics," characterize the extreme authoritarian regimes in postcolonial Africa of the 1970s.[11]

Why had Asians come to Uganda? As historians point out, the African territories that Britain conquered in the late nineteenth century had precapitalist economies—people in East Africa typically lived and worked on the land[12]—and so the colonizers required an external labor source. Following the Berlin Conference in 1885 that divided up African colonies, Britain turned to India, its more advanced colony with a more developed and regimented work force, for resources for its African possessions, and encouraged Indian migration to East Africa, Mauritius, South Africa, the West Indies, and Guinea for indentured servitude. Indians served variously as soldiers in the imperial army, as laborers to build the railways, and as artisans, machine operators, plantation workers, administrative clerks, and small traders in the expanding market.[13] It was this context that Bhimji's father entered when he moved to Uganda in the 1910s, later returning to India to marry and bring his wife, Bhimji's mother, to his new home.

If, in 1972, Amin acted against this "foreign" labor population, then part of his reasoning was that Asians had discriminated against Africans (what Amin called "Asian business malpractices"). Yet, as Mahmood Mamdani points out in *From Citizen to Refugee*, his harrowing firsthand account of the expulsion, "It was not the era of independence, but that of dependence—of colonialism—that politicised race, tribe and religion in Uganda. This was the

10   See Phares Mukasa Mutibwa, "Expulsion of the Asians," in *Uganda Since Independence: A Story of Unfulfilled Hopes* (Trenton, NJ: Africa World Press, 1992).

11   Mbembe, *On the Postcolony*, 32, 67.

12   See Mutibwa, "Expulsion of the Asians."

13   For an extensive account of the passage to East Africa from India, see the historical and contemporary testimonials collected in the three-volume series, Cynthia Salvadori, ed., *We Came in Dhows* (Nairobi: Paperchase Kenya, 1996), which Bhimji also consulted during her research for *Yellow Patch*. Additionally, in her treatment for *Yellow Patch*, Bhimji mentions M. F. Hill, *Permanent Way: The Story of the Kenya and Uganda Railway* (Nairobi: East African Railways and Harbours, 1949) as a further historical source. For an excellent literary account of nineteenth-century Indian migration by sea, see Amitav Ghosh, *Sea of Poppies* (New York: Farrar, Straus and Giroux, 2008).

14   Mahmood Mamdani, *From Citizen to Refugee: Uganda Asians Come to Britain* (London: Frances Pinter, 1973), 15. Also see Mamdani, *Citizen and Subject: Contemporary Africa and the Legacy of Late Colonialism* (Princeton, NJ: Princeton University Press, 1996); and Bhimji's treatment for *Out of Blue*, part of which is published in *Art Journal* 69, no. 4 (Winter 2010), and includes excerpts from newspaper reports of the expulsion from the early 1970s.

kernel of truth in the theory that colonialism rested on the basis of *divide and rule.*"[14] According to Mamdani, Amin extended that colonial logic, which began with the practice of separating tribes and pitting them against one another, formalizing divisions between races and ethnic classes into legal, political, and economic groupings. As Mamdani explains, "There was rigid compartmentalisation in the newly colonial political economy," such that laws prohibited Africans from entering trade and Asians from owning land. In the hierarchical economy that emerged—which Bhimji's family had to negotiate—"Africans were primarily peasants and workers; Asians primarily shopkeepers, artisans and petty bureaucrats; and Europeans bankers, whole-salers and the administrative and political elite."[15] Indeed, the postcolonial government of Obote, the first prime minister of independent Uganda, followed suit by further formalizing this hierarchy. In 1968, a committee was charged with "Africanization in Commerce and Industry" and made far-reaching Indophobic proposals, implementing a system of work permits and trade licenses in 1969 to restrict the role of Indians in economic and professional activities. By the time Amin assumed power, there was an established tendency to segregate and discriminate against Asians, which Amin exploited further with a new intensity.[16] In 1972–73, he continued with his economic war by nationalizing British and other foreign-owned businesses and properties.[17]

Amin's eight-year rule left a wake of brutality and destruction that was foreshadowed early on by his treatment of Asians. Given the order to leave, they could depart with only fifty pounds in cash and minimal baggage. This meant that they were forced to give up their life savings, houses, property, and much of their personal possessions, and were then denationalized and thrown into an uncertain refugee status, all within three months.[18] After Amin's announcement, his forces secured the borders of the country to prevent unregulated flight, and banks were ordered to stop illegal transfers of assets. Many were robbed by troops on their way to the airport, where they endured invasive baggage searches. There would be no compensation for lost property, even though Amin promised it. (Some businesses and

15 Mamdani, *From Citizen to Refugee*, 15.

16 See Hasu H. Patel, "General Amin and the Indian Exodus from Uganda," *Issue: A Journal of Opinion* 2, no. 4 (1972): 12–22. On the fragmenting results of Africanization policies under postcolonial regimes, see Mamdani, *Citizen and Subject*, 20.

17 According to Mamdani, Amin created a "'semi-fascist state'—'fascist' because the object of his policies [was] to organise all of society's resources, human and material, and put them at the service of capital; 'semi' because Uganda's productive resources [were] not sufficiently advanced to permit him the sort of organisation and control that was possible for fascist Japan." *From Citizen to Refugee*, 61. For a film portrait of Idi Amin, see Barbet Schroeder, dir., *General Idi Amin Dada: A Self-Portrait* (Paris: Le Figaro Films, 1974).

18 Mamdani recounts how many Asians nonetheless refused to become refugees: "A refugee is not just a person who has been displaced and has lost all or most of his possessions. A refugee is in fact more akin to a child: helpless, devoid of initiative, somebody on whom any kind of charity can be practised; in short, a totally malleable creature. A part of this book is the story of those who *refused* to become refugees." *From Citizen to Refugee*, 8.

properties were returned by the subsequent Ugandan government in the 1980s.) Because of the strategic lack of clarity about
who must go—Asians with British passports versus those with
Ugandan citizenship—all were rendered uncertain and anxious,
resulting in internal discrimination within the Asian community
and between Africans and Asians. It is difficult to fully comprehend the dire consequences of Amin's order to leave.

Britain accepted the transfer of expelled Asians, including some non-British. About 27,200 went to the UK, while others
went to Canada, India, Kenya, Pakistan, West Germany, and the
United States.[19] Yet the reception was far from smooth—inter-
minable queues, bureaucratic difficulties, discrimination, and the
indignities of emergency refugee housing awaited those who came
to Britain. Moreover, right-wing Members of Parliament argued
against letting Ugandan Asians into the country, contending that
even though they were British citizens, they had no links to the
home country and their immigration would only lead to racial tension, which contributed to an icy welcome. Those who didn't leave
Uganda confronted potential arrest, torture, even death, contributing to the estimated five hundred thousand people who were killed
overall during the course of Amin's reign, which came to an end in
1979 when he was overthrown and sent into exile.[20] Still, Bhimji's
family managed to stay safely—albeit illegally—in Uganda for two
years until 1974, when they left for the UK. Ultimately, Uganda's
Africanization policy represented a massive
theft by Amin's regime and his country's willing
businessmen, who nearly unanimously congratu-
lated Amin on his decision to expel the Asians.[21]
Furthermore, Amin's extremist act of social engineering, stripping Asians of their African identity
and Ugandan nationality, constituted a form of
ethnocide, resonating with what Mbembe calls
postcolonial "necropolitics"—the governance
over life and death—which was realized through
the forced evictions of entire ethnic and racial
populations, who were summarily stripped of
an integral part of their identities.[22] That Britain
didn't intervene on behalf of its citizens—allowing Amin's expulsion decree—meant that Amin
achieved his short-term goals.

—

As indicated earlier, once Bhimji completes her
initial research for a film, she moves away from

19 The fact that Ugandan Asians had
British passports was part of the legacy
of the colonial agreement made decades
earlier, when Britain offered citizenship
to Indians for indentured labor in East
Africa, a deal Britain never thought
would lead to Indians ending up in the
home country.

20 The number of deaths has been
estimated by Amnesty International.
See Patrick Keatley, "Obituary: Idi
Amin," *Guardian*, August 18, 2003.

21 See Mutibwa, *Uganda Since
Independence*, 92–97, 115–20; and
Jan Jelmert Jørgensen, *Uganda: A
Modern History* (London: Taylor &
Francis, 1981), 288–90. As reported in
Jørgensen, 5,655 firms, ranches, farms,
and agricultural estates belonging to
Ugandan Asians were expropriated,
including cars, homes, and household
goods, most of which was reallocated to
individuals, government bodies, and or-
ganizations (including the state-owned
Uganda Development Corporation).

22 Mbembe, "Necropolitics," 34–40.

the informational address of her subject in order to center on an emotional response to the material, one built of rhythmic, aural, and imagistic affects. As she explains in relation to *Out of Blue*: "Originally the research started with wanting to understand the basic history of what happened in Uganda, but then I wanted to understand what the word 'asylum' means, or the word 'state-less,' from a political and personal perspective. From that, I put an idea together about how I could communicate this feeling. And how I could enlarge it through sound and create a rhythm out of it."[23]

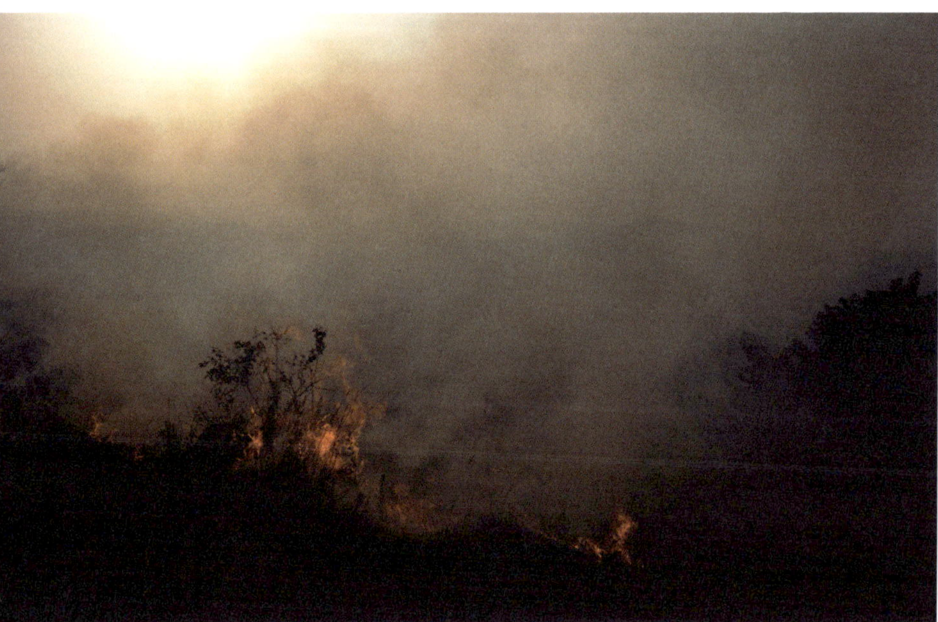

Zarina Bhimji, still from *Out of Blue*, 2002

Out of Blue commences with a panoramic shot of an African countryside, rendered in a slow meditative tempo. Rolling hills appear in the distance, with lush green flora in the middle ground shrouded by a sea of mist. Bhimji's camera then pans left, moving from the cool blue of the early morning to the warm tones infusing the land below the rising sun. We hear the buzzing of insects, as well as the low foreboding murmur of a mysterious string instrument with a distant female voice singing ominously,

23   Quoted in Lorés, interview with Bhimji, 60.

while the camera cuts to a stunning shot of the glaring red sun. Returning to an overview of the misty land, the film introduces a British voice on the soundtrack, heard as if on a radio with an interrupted signal and speaking in largely inaudible tones. In the foreground, smoke begins to rise from the brush beside a tree. Gunshots ring out, as the burning savannah comes into view in a series of close-ups. The ululations of a female voice add to the sense of emergency and to the complex layering of images and sounds, as the fire builds in intensity. Throughout this passage, the fact that the soundtrack was sourced from Ugandan radio is never identified, the landscape is not specified as Uganda, and the meaning of the fire is left a mystery. (Although in her treatment for *Out of Blue*, Bhimji reveals her own associations: "A deep fire would start at 3:45pm when Amin announced on Radio Uganda that all Asians were to leave.")[24]

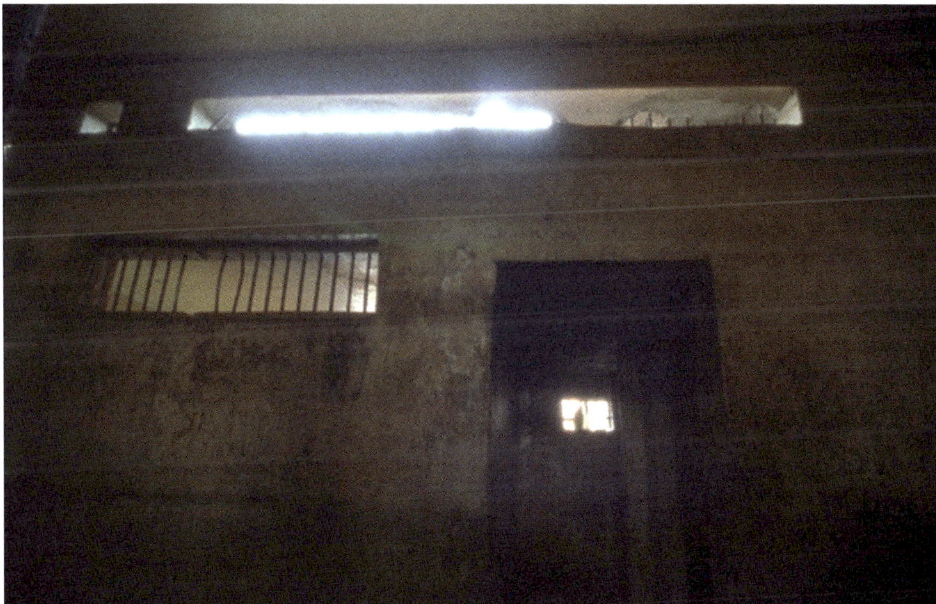

Zarina Bhimji, still from *Out of Blue*, 2002

24   See Zarina Bhimji, "Outline of a Film," *Art Journal* 69, no. 4 (Winter 2010): 74.

Such withholding of details characterizes the film's other passages as well. Later, we see several buildings that look like old military barracks. In the interior, fabrics hang from the ceiling beams

and mats lie on the floor as if a large group of people was stay-
ing there but are no longer present. Other rooms seem to be
one-time prison cells, the walls divulging a palimpsest of graffiti,
bloodstains, and burn marks from untold violence and captivity.
There is a shot of a collection of rifles standing on end and lined
up against a wall; shadows of figures appear unexpectedly in
doorways. An old airport appears toward the end of the film,
its decrepit tower showing the sign "Entebbe, 3,789 feet." The
building, with its broken windows and corroded surfaces, is
decaying, but there is no indication given that it was from this
airport that many Asians (Bhimji's family included) left Uganda
during the expulsion.

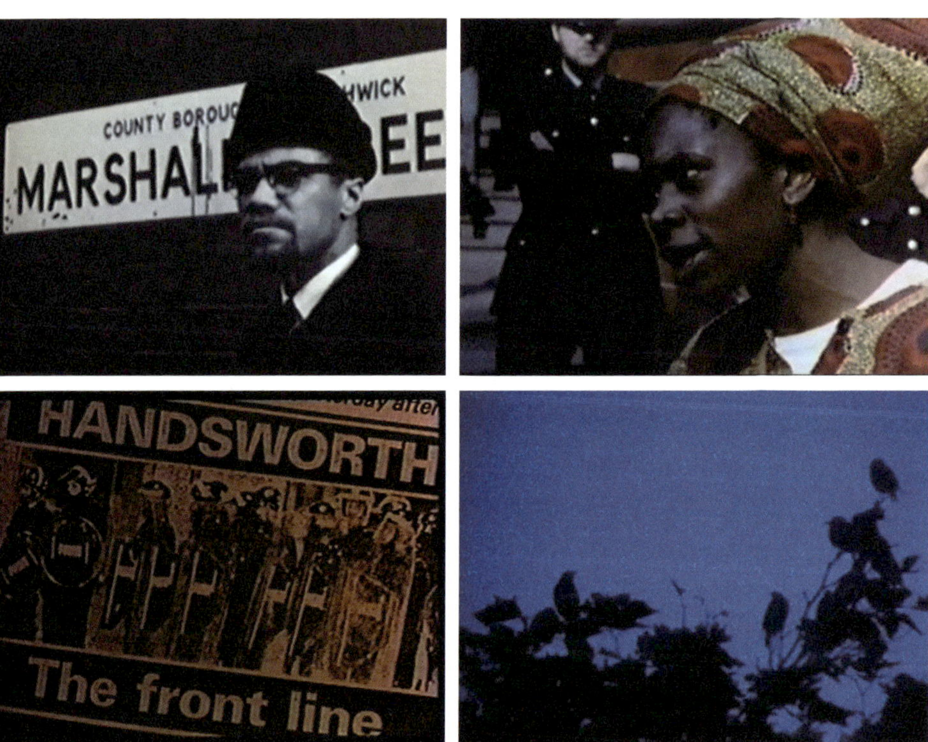

Black Audio Film Collective, stills from *Handsworth Songs*, 1986

The fact that no or few people appear in Bhimji's films does not mean that they are subjectless. Indeed, Bhimji speaks of how the filming of architecture leads to an "architecture of the internal," which is made clear in these passages by the opening up of "imagining" in a way that is "instinctive."[25] "I am interested in the traces of war, its unspeakable horrors and rites of passage and rebuilding," she explains.[26] In this regard, her cinema of affect is partly achieved by negating factual information, motivated in part by the artist's questioning of the presumption that the fullness of the past, including the complexity of its meanings and subjective effects, *could* be adequately captured. Her skepticism has led commentators, such as Deepali Dewan, to observe that her films are built out of "anti-documentary images"[27]—in the sense that they reject the documentary image's association with objectivity, neutrality, factual truthfulness, and evidence.[28] As Bhimji explains: "My work is not an idea of fact or scraps of evidence to support the assertion of history. The process is something about traces as symptoms of strange structural links between history, memory, and fantasy."[29]

In this sense, Bhimji's abstraction constitutes a critical, post-documentary approach. This quality distinguishes her filmmaking from that of other like-minded artists who emerged in the 1980s context of postcolonial British art making, and who were redefining the parameters of documentary at the time. Consider Black Audio Film Collective's *Handsworth Songs* (1986), or Mona Hatoum's *Measures of Distance* (1988), or Isaac Julien's *Territories* (1984): each of these investigates black British diasporic identity and multicultural politics via a reinvented, poetic documentary approach. *Handsworth Songs* probes the history of the riots against the perceived police repression and racist policies during Margaret Thatcher's regime in the mid-1980s, lyrically weaving together a series of stories of Afro-Caribbean British people in the area of Birmingham who disputed the government's claims (mimicked ever faithfully by the mainstream news media) that the uprising's violence was mindless and without legitimate cause. *Measures of Distance* explores the subjective effects of the artist's displacement in London during Lebanon's civil war, explored through a video montage that mediated Hatoum's distanced relation to her mother in Beirut. And *Territories* examines London's Notting Hill carnival as a place of cultural hybridity and an allegory for the diasporic conditions of

25   Okeke-Agulu, "Conversation with Bhimji," 70.

26   Bhimji, unpublished treatment for *Out of Blue*.

27   Deepali Dewan, "Tender Metaphor: The Art of Zarina Bhimji," in Tawadros et al., *Fault Lines*, 136.

28   See, for instance, Frits Gierstberg et al., eds., *Documentary Now! Contemporary Strategies in Photography, Film and the Visual Arts* (Rotterdam: NAi Publishers, 2005).

29   Quoted in Okeke-Agulu, "Conversation with Bhimji," 69.

video's carnivalesque blurrings and transformations of representational codes. Each achieved its ends by using a form of voice-over narration marked by a theoretically informed sophistication in the analysis of race, politics, and postcolonial subjectivity. Bhimji's films clearly possess an affinity to these various modelings of the aesthetics of the diasporic, especially given the artist's ambition to reinvent the creative possibilities of cinematic practice beyond the merely informational, and to endow the image with a lyrical quality opening onto a space of agency beyond the potentially victimizing representations of conventional media's reportage of sociopolitical crises.[30] Yet, unlike these precedents, Bhimji's films are marked by their rejection of such discourse-heavy presentations and, more formally, by the absence of voice-over narration.

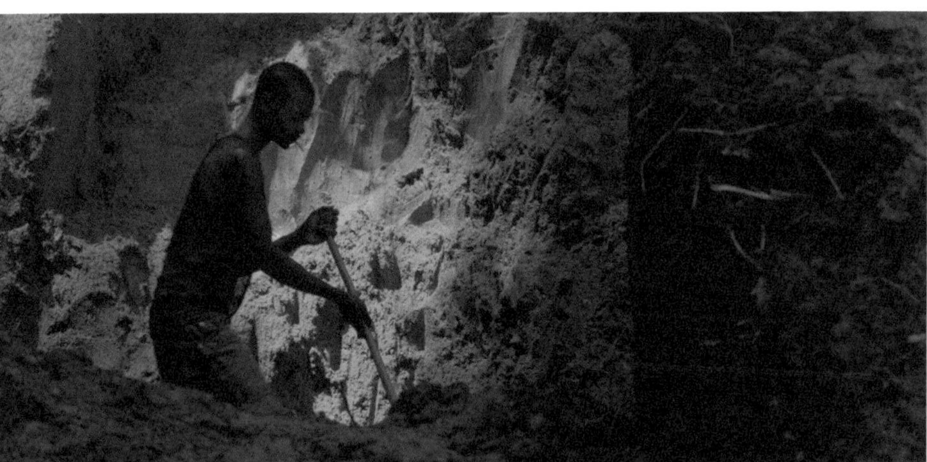

Steve McQueen, still from *Gravesend*, 2007

Still, Bhimji's films are not simply abstract, for they do carry reference and signification, as well as a visual-aural relation to researched historical conditions. There are, as the artist puts it, "traces as symptoms of strange structural links between history, memory and fantasy," which rupture the serenity and abstraction of the white cube environment, bringing her postcolonial history into view, even if she negates that history on another level. In this translation of historical research into aestheticized imagery, her film-

30   Moreover, her early work is indebted to the conceptual context of the politics of representation, such as her mixed-media project, *She Loved to Breathe—Pure Silence* (1987), which investigates the history of the Home Office's "virginity inspections" of immigrants from India during the 1970s, and recalls the work of conceptual artist Mary Kelly (who was Bhimji's tutor at Goldsmiths in the early 1980s).

making bears comparison to other artists of her generation, such as Steve McQueen, insofar as his films also offer a powerful range of cinematic affects in relation to postcolonial histories and do so without narrative contextualization (differing again, for instance, from the essayistic kind of discourse-intense filmmaking that is creatively developed in the work of the Otolith Group).[31] For Bhimji, if things can't be "fixed" through documentary in relation to "facts" (and "it's impossible to get to the truth—ever," as she explained recently to me), then her goal is "how to express the emotional, warmly and deeply."[32]

Bhimji's desire for emotional expression and her negation of informational content are no doubt connected, and one explanation for their intertwinement is Bhimji's sensitivity to the fact that strong emotional events often resist linguistic expression. Particularly with the case of traumatic experience—as is well established in Freudian psychoanalysis and in the post-structuralist philosophy of history[33]—shocking events tend to overflow the language of comprehension, interrupting its ability to communicate. This has been frequently observed in the reception of Bhimji's work from early on, as when one interviewer picked up on the fact that the artist had read Elaine Scarry's book *The Body in Pain: The Making and Unmaking of the World*, and had underlined the point that "physical pain does not simply resist language but actively destroys it."[34] Clearly the sensitivity to the way in which painful experiences resist language informs Bhimji's approach to the expressive image and offers insight into her films, which access and activate the emotional through a cinema of colors and sounds, movements and rhythms, rather than through verbal or written language and description. Indeed, part of the emotional affect of her work is also the anxious, estranging, and haunting transgression of language by psychologically challenging historical events. In other words, her films "speak" with a telling silence.

—

How can we further specify what I have been calling Bhimji's affective cinema? "Affect" designates emotional feeling stimulated by an outside source, such as a filmic image, in contrast to what originates internally; and it is further distinguished as a prestructured bodily

31   See my essays "Indeterminacy and Bare Life in Steve McQueen's *Western Deep*" and "'Sabotaging the Future': The Essay-Films of the Otolith Group," in Demos, *Migrant Image.*

32   Bhimji, interview by the author, August 22, 2011.

33   For example, see Sigmund Freud, "Beyond the Pleasure Principle," in *The Standard Edition of the Complete Psychological Works of Sigmund Freud*, ed. and trans. James Strachey (London: Hogarth Press, 1953), 18:31–32; and Maurice Blanchot, *The Writing of Disaster*, trans. Ann Smock (Lincoln: University of Nebraska Press, 1986). Blanchot also explains, "Writing is not destined to leave traces, but to erase, by traces, all traces, to disappear in the fragmentary space of writing more definitively than one disappears in the tomb, or again, to destroy, to destroy invisibly, without the uproar of destruction." *The Step Not Beyond*, trans. Lycette Nelson (Albany: State University of New York Press, 1992), 50.

34   Cited in *Zarina Bhimji: I Will Always Be Here*, n.p.

sensation prior to its formalization as "emotion."[35] As such, affect designates a flowing and transformative quality that makes it difficult to analyze, structure, or organize via interpretation, and in this sense affect exhibits a similar resistance to language as does physical pain. For Steven Shaviro, affective cinema is both "symptomatic," in that it provides indices of complex social processes, which it transcodes and rearticulates, and "productive," in that it does not simply *represent* social processes and historical meanings, but also participates actively in those processes and meanings, which it partially constitutes.[36] For Sara Ahmed, affects are relational and social, constitutive of subjects and communities.[37] We might relate the affective image to the "crystal-image," as described by Gilles Deleuze in his writings on cinema—that is, one that multiplies distinct temporalities, mixing past and present, as well as joining virtual and actual aspects of the image's historical, mnemonic, subjective, and imaginative values.[38] These various approaches offer helpful ways to describe Bhimji's allusive aesthetic and its associative metaphorics. Building further in this direction, the anthropologist Christopher Pinney, writing about Bhimji's use of photography, points out how the artist's imagery is uncontainable—it always goes beyond its representational significance, which resonates again with Deleuze's theory of the crystallized time-image: "Photography, because of its ineradicable *more-than*, intrinsically constitutes a kind of xeno-epistemics."[39] Pinney further notes, "It will always capture more of the world—its surplus or *xenos*—than the photographer expects or desires."[40] In this sense, Bhimji's is not just a diasporic aesthetic of the postcolonial subject; it is also one that is not easily circumscribed or pinned down, given its transformative nature, ever generating new meanings and sensations.

Part of the implication of this "ineradicable *more-than*" that characterizes Bhimji's aesthetic is that her charging of images always results in a certain multiplicity of meanings. As Stuart Hall observes, "Look at Zarina Bhimji's light boxes, which, like the eerily evacuated Ugandan landscapes of her recent film *Out of Blue*, speak volumes through absence, summoning up the profound sense of emptiness and loss which forced exile produces, and the silent devastation left behind by those who

35   See Brian Massumi, "The Autonomy of Affect," in *Parables for the Virtual: Movement, Affect, Sensation* (Durham, NC: Duke University Press, 2002). Steven Shaviro also explains that "affect is primary, non-conscious, asubjective or presubjective, asignifying, unqualified and intensive; while emotion is derivative, conscious, qualified, and meaningful, a 'content' that can be attributed to an already-constituted subject." *Post-Cinematic Affect* (Winchester: Zero Books, 2010), 3.

36   Ibid., 2.

37   See Sara Ahmed, *The Cultural Politics of Emotion* (Edinburgh: Edinburgh University Press, 2004).

38   See Gilles Deleuze, *Cinema 2: The Time-Image*, trans. Hugh Tomlinson and Robert Galeta (Minneapolis: University of Minnesota Press, 1989).

39   Christopher Pinney, "What is to be done?," *Source*, no. 48 (Autumn 2006): 17.

40   Ibid. Pinney draws on the concept of "xeno-epistemics" as developed by Sarat Maharaj, "Xeno-Epistemics: Makeshift Kit for Sounding Visual Art as Knowledge Production and the Retinal Regimes," *Catalogue*, Documenta11_Platform 5, eds. Okwui Enwezor et al. (Ostfildern: Hatje Cantz, 2002).

wreak a brutal revenge on difference."[41] While Hall's observation is insightful, the point I want to stress is that such metaphors—for instance, Bhimji's landscape of emptiness and loss that Hall describes—are never limited or final in their interpretive possibilities; indeed, the image "speaks volumes." It remains full of virtual potential, ever capable of further crystallizations. Without this sense of indeterminacy, her cinema would risk a collapse into the sentimentality of hackneyed imagery accompanied by a Hollywood-like soundtrack—in fact, I would argue that her films attempt to rescue images of India from exactly that kind of sensationalist fate, and as such express an earnest belief in the power of cinema. That her images are complexly defined is evidenced by the artist's own description of the beginning of *Out of Blue*: "The film starts with a panning shot of a misty romantic landscape. The mist, however, turns out to be smoke from the burning ground. Should that be read as a political statement on a country like Uganda, which has suffered so much destruction, or as poetic evocation of landscape as a metaphor for personal feelings of nostalgia and grief?"[42] It's this relation to surplus and unknowability, as well as indeterminacy and infinitude, that marks Bhimji's cinema of affect.

Perhaps at a fundamental level, this stress on the post-informational affective image, one that is complexly charged and endlessly multivalent, is also related to Bhimji's desire to relocate and reexamine her powerful childhood experiences, defined by the traumatic relation between intense feeling and youthful incomprehension. As she stated in the early 1990s:

> What I am doing is trying to make sense of my own history. To do this I need to project back into the feelings I had as a child, when I was eight, when I first came to England, the clothes I wore, the food I ate with my parents. These things are so relevant to what I do now. The tiniest memory can evoke all kinds of feelings. One strong sensation is that of a sense of loss—almost like death. I remember a line by T. S. Eliot, "We had the experience but missed the meaning." You can never return to what you didn't have but I need to make sense of those moments.[43]

In a certain sense, Bhimji's work reopens emotionally disturbing experiences to produce new meaning retrospectively. In doing so, Bhimji defines a way to work through past traumas: "It is important for me to take charge of my childhood myself, in order to control my adulthood. I need to make light of my childhood experience, to release the pain."[44] In this regard, the

41 Stuart Hall, "Maps of Emergency: Fault Lines and Tectonic Plates," in Tawadros et al., *Fault Lines*, 33.

42 Quoted in Lorés, interview with Bhimji, 61.

43 Quoted in Sonia Boyce, interview with Bhimji, in *Zarina Bhimji: I Will Always Be Here*, n.p.

affective joins with the psychoanalytic working of the image, rendering it subjectively functional in relation to the traumatic past. The films are thereby defined by a certain "belatedness," a term Bhimji has used more recently. It describes the experience of visiting places resonant with her parents' history—specifically, the history of Indians who made their way to East Africa, including sites where Asians in Uganda lived, were arrested, and were deported. With filmic gestures made a generation later, Bhimji's cinema offers a belated reckoning with the past, this time grappling with and apprehending the meaning and feeling that is produced after researched analysis of the historical events in question—a belated affective response informed by retrospective comprehension.

—

As we've seen, *Yellow Patch* adds a new thematic dimension to Bhimji's project by extending back to a migration that connects to an earlier point in her family's history, though is not directly about her childhood experience in the way that her previous film *Out of Blue* was. Rather, the later film concerns the distant history of her parents' generation, a distance translated into the allegorical dimension of the piece, which doesn't carry the same pathos or sense of ominous fear and traumatized experience that is present in her earlier work. The distance also appears between image and reference, proposing a poetic and lyrical disjunction, which again invites a multiplication of meanings. These meanings are not, however, always defined; rather their indecisiveness arouses diverse sensations through evocative scenes: the pinkish glow of the old stone houses set against the blue sky, the blurred yellow streaks of sunlight stretching over an ocher plaster wall, the dusty bone gray of a set of antlers lying strangely on a concrete floor, a spider's silver web appearing against the warm timber of an old wooden dhow.

Pointing to this aesthetically captivating quality of her films, Bhimji has frequently used the term "beauty," which I take as offering a way to describe her complex use of sound and imagery that verges on the transcendental, insofar as their significance moves beyond our own immediate factual and material experience of the world. Her films draw together visual pleasure, affective depth, and historical and psychoanalytic insight—resulting in the beautiful. For instance, consider the *haveli* houses in

44 Ibid.

45 Bhimji, interview by the author, September 2011. On the relations between love, beauty, and the idealizations of the visual gaze, see Kaja Silverman, *The Threshold of the Visible World* (London: Routledge, 1996).

46 See Okwui Enwezor, *Snap Judgments: New Positions in Contemporary African Photography* (New York: International Center of Photography, 2006), 10–19.

Yellow Patch—spaces of "safety and tenderness" that Bhimji has described as "architecturally beautiful." For her, they figure as "parents" or "lovers," indicating an affective investment in their imagery.[45] Beauty is more than visual pleasure for the artist: it designates the act of presenting the unconventional and unexpected in a way that challenges social and political hierarchies. For Bhimji, to present blackness—that of races as much as visual references—in an unforeseen light constitutes a beautiful act. Through the poetic ambience of such figures and their historical spaces and environments, the term takes on an emancipatory capacity, which relates to the freedom of becoming something beyond what cultural norms allow or otherwise control. Seen in this light, the beautiful designates a space of liminality and potentiality without the characteristic stereotypes of identity, or what Enwezor terms the "Afro-pessimism" common to mainstream mass media presentations of African blackness.[46] Not that Bhimji's film portrays specific people; rather, her complex representation of charged spaces deepens our understanding of the history of Indians who migrated to East Africa and Ugandan Asians who were expelled from their adopted homeland.

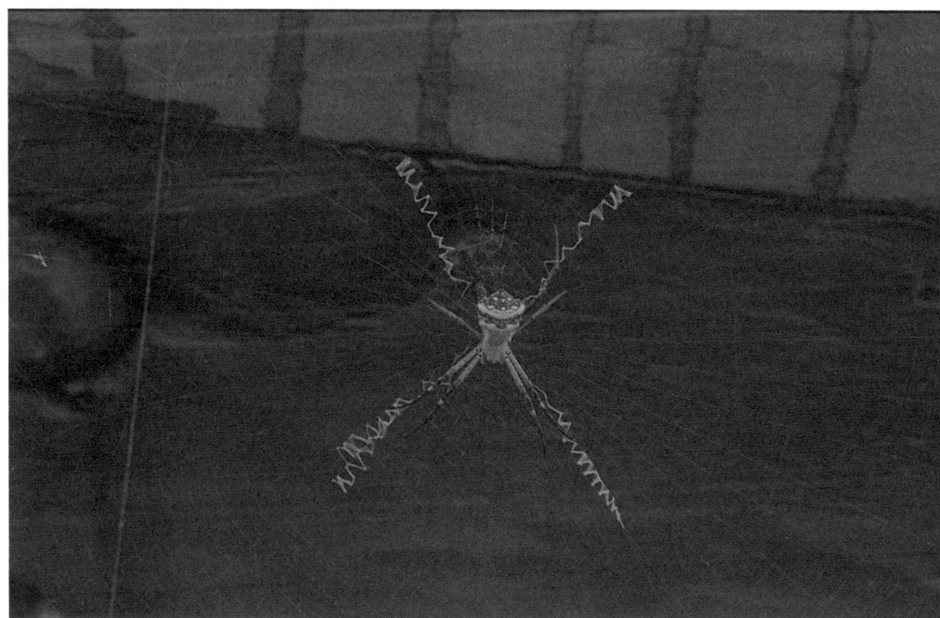

Zarina Bhimji, still from *Yellow Patch*, 2011

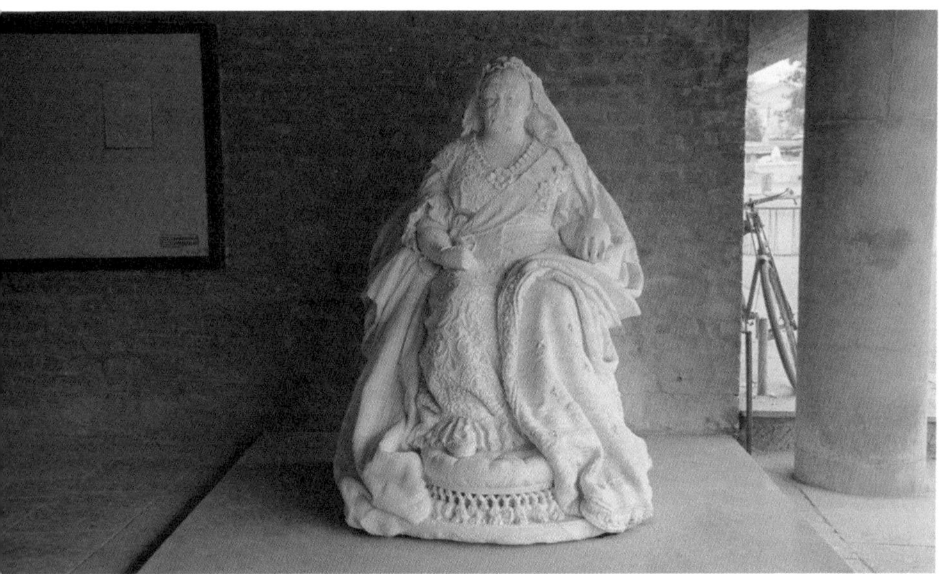

Zarina Bhimji, still from *Yellow Patch*, 2011

Given the transformative and transporting aspects of Bhimji's films, it seems appropriate that she uses the music of Abidi Parveen, first in *Out of Blue* and later in *Yellow Patch*. A Pakistani singer of the Sufi faith, Parveen draws on seventeenth-century Urdu poetry about love and tenderness in her emotive songs. It's not that Bhimji's films are spiritual in the way that Parveen's music is; rather, the connection is that Bhimji's poetic images also take us beyond the mere facticity of things, as does Parveen's singing. Her images crystallize historical significances, which mediates between particularity (the architectural details, say, in *Yellow Patch*) and what she calls her desire that her films gain "universal" significance, where images, sounds, and affects can be diversely interpreted and find specific resonances with distinct viewers (where affect exemplifies its social mobility). As she has explained: "It is essential to find a universal language, to go beyond personal references, yet it can only come out of personal experience. The language I use is related to vulnerability."[47] At the same time, her films express the paradox of representing what resists representation: in relation to *Yellow Patch*, she mentions that "the individual details" of her films "are essential in trying to speak of the unspeakable that wants to be spoken. It is not about capturing an existing thing,

47   Quoted in Boyce, interview with Bhimji, in *Zarina Bhimji: I Will Always Be Here*, n.p.

48   From the artist's unpublished treatment for *Yellow Patch*.

   Ghostly Affect: Zarina Bhimji's *Yellow Patch*

it is about creating a new one."**48** This too might be said to be a universal experience. Between representation of past experiences and production of new meanings lies the transformative capacity of Bhimji's affective cinema. By picturing the beauty of India, we can combat the victimizing images of Asian refugees and thereby open up new ways of relating to the world.

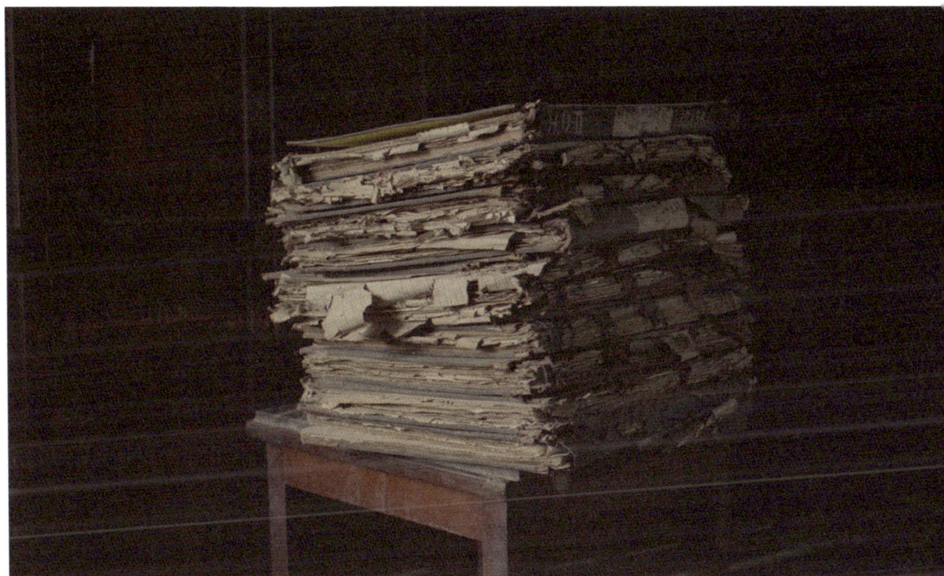

Zarina Bhimji, still from *Yellow Patch*, 2011

Consider in this regard the sense of desertion and emptiness expressed in *Yellow Patch*—the buildings are depopulated, sites appear evacuated, and only wild dogs spot the desert landscape. These images speak to the history of Indians immigrating to East Africa in the early twentieth century. Historical and psychological meanings intertwine, as the evacuated spaces take on a sense of loneliness and subjective loss that also opens onto what we know of the desolate and tragic future awaiting the Asian immigrants who stayed in Uganda, resulting in the postcolonial expulsion and the second loss of home—an exiling of exiles. Yet this loss of home is offset by Bhimji's familial references. For the artist, Kutch is also a place associated with her mother (who was born in Bhadreshwar), a connection mediated in the film, if obliquely, by an unexplained and mysterious scene of an older female figure in a white sari captured from behind, rocking back and forth, and by the use of Parveen's music, some of which is sung in Bhimji's familial language of Kutchi, creating sounds "that absorb the viewer at a primal level."[49] In other words, *Yellow Patch* generates a crystallization of the image, unleashing both melancholy and joyful sensations, such that the painful experiences of transgenerational displacement and the passionate memories of one's homeland collide and diverge. Bhimji's visually striking shots divide and generate multiple meanings, which also proliferate by her withholding of information, avoiding direct interpretation, and relying on the particularities of the biographical.

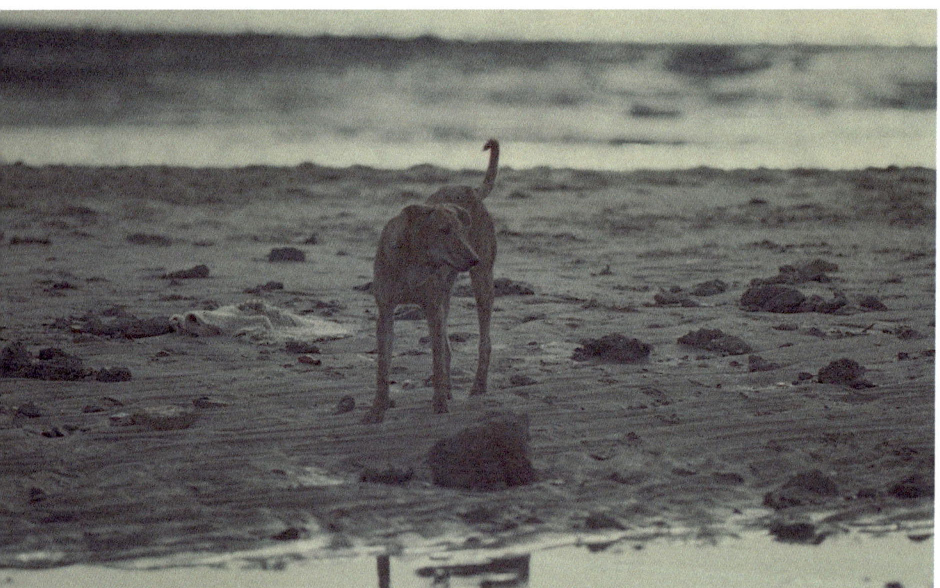

Zarina Bhimji, still from *Yellow Patch*, 2011

Consider one last especially striking scene midway through *Yellow Patch*, which is exemplary of its complex aesthetic. It occurs when the camera reveals an old marble statue by slowly panning upward from the figure's white feet and pausing to focus on the rendering of a richly brocaded gown. The shot frames one of the hands that holds an orb in its lap, one finger broken off, and then ascends past its floral neckline to the face, which is badly disfigured

49   Ibid.

and appears monstrous. The camera eventually zooms out to show what we already suspect: it's a sculpture of Queen Victoria, the so-called Empress of India, whose reign lasted until 1901 and thus oversaw the British Empire's construction of the Princess Dock in Bombay and the initial building of the Uganda railway. Now the sculpture sits in disrepair against an old brick wall, haunting some untold location. Multiple meanings converge in this scene, which characterizes the steady and meditative rhythm of Bhimji's films. We encounter a regal official portrait of the queen, as well as a personification of the British Empire holding the world symbolically in its grip, connecting us to the history of the colonial enterprise and its political-aristocratic image regime. But more, the statue's crumbling intimates the ultimate failure of that otherwise timeless imperial vision of the desire to set British rule in stone. The ruination of the statue speaks to the disintegration of the once glorious colonial project. And, its decomposition reveals the betrayal of Britain's promise to secure modernization, civilization, and progress for its colonial possessions, including its Asian citizens when Amin persecuted them some seventy years later.

Soon after this sequence, the film transitions to a shot of wild dogs resting on a trash-filled street facing a crumbling old building's colonnade. It suggests an image of nature's inevitable victory over culture, showing how the erstwhile grandeur of empire turns into forgotten ruins. Juxtaposed against the image of Queen Victoria, the shot proposes an allegorical picture of wild dogs as the empire's anonymous and pitiful subjects, who have nonetheless outlived their subjection and triumphantly gained their revenge on their one-time imperial masters by retaking their territory. There is no way to finalize the meaning—such potentiality is the truth of Bhimji's generative cinema. What ultimately becomes clear is that *Yellow Patch* is not a fatalistic condemnation of colonial tragedy, a pitiful expression of multi-generational grief, or a film of victimized personal trauma; rather, it is a celebration of the overcoming of difficult historical circumstances, a focusing on the beauty of becoming and survival, of movement forward. This conclusion is also established by the juxtaposition of the Indian-built Mandvi port—a living harbor that still hosts the construction of wooden dhows—and the British port in Bombay, which, with its file cabinets and heaps of papers, appears as a decaying but still intimidating image of the bureaucracy of control. (A premonition, perhaps, of the contemporary state of surveillance, administrative control, and data collection that we confront today in Britain and elsewhere.) By beginning the film with shots of those files, one wonders what amazing stories, or ghosts of stories, lie within the cakes of papers that seem to be turning back into pulp—it is this curiosity and desire for remembrance that Bhimji cultivates and explores throughout the rest of the film. With the Mandvi port—by far the more alluring one—we are left with a symbol of indigenous knowledge, skill, and creative survival, expressed via a critical and experimental cinematic intervention. It is one that goes beyond facts and offers an affective imagery of poetic constructions, which lets us feel the emotional complexity of this lived history and leaves us with a revitalized relation to the present.

4. The Haunting: **Renzo Martens's** *Enjoy Poverty*

Reflecting on the unprecedented flow of contemporary art throughout the world, as new exhibition networks emerge and disparate local contexts are allied and energized, Gerardo Mosquera notes optimistically that "globalisation has certainly improved communications to an extraordinary extent, just as it has dynamised and pluralized cultural circulation while providing a more pluralist consciousness."[1] He may be partly correct, even as he goes on to point out that a dark underside of nationalism, xenophobia, and racism persists. Still, Renzo Martens's film *Episode III (Enjoy Poverty)* (2009),[2] set in the Democratic Republic of the Congo, provides a devastating alternative optic on the brutal nature of North–South relations of inequality and the exploitative image economy that stubbornly mediates it. Martens's portrayal of this image economy belies the optimistic discourse that tends to be uncritically generated in the art context. Despite all its risks—perpetuating stereotypes of Africans as helpless victims, reducing Congolese people to neocolonized servants and neophytes, reproducing a pornography of poverty—and perhaps even because of them, *Enjoy Poverty* bears important lessons. Among them, a reality check for optimistic globalists and a lethal blow to the ambitions of concerned documentarians, especially those that seek to ameliorate suffering by representing abjection in developing countries for sympathetic observers elsewhere. The scandal that is the film puts us squarely before the fault lines of globalization's many crises today, including the disastrous fallout from neoliberal structural adjustment policies implemented in Africa and the Global South since the 1980s, the failures of humanitarian practice and its compromised ethical discourse, and the paradoxes of both politically engaged photojournalism and contemporary political art.

The film focuses on the economy of images that portrays the death and poverty rife in the DRC, centering on the European photojournalists operating there, depicted in *Enjoy Poverty* producing images of dead militiamen for the international media. In one scene, Martens questions an Agence France-Presse photographer about his wages; it turns out he earns fifty euros per shot, plus insurance and travel expenses. This example communicates how famine and war photography flow into a global image industry running on poverty and violence as fuel. As it unleashes a vicious cycle of profit, objectification, and sympathy, this type of conflict photography perpetuates clichés of Africans as helpless victims mired in misery, and reduces spectators to depoliticized charitable donors.

1   Gerardo Mosquera, "Art and Cultural Interactions in a Globalised World," *Stedelijk Bureau Newsletter*, no. 120 (2011): n.p.

2   *Episode III (Enjoy Poverty)* (hereafter: *Enjoy Poverty*) forms the second edition in a planned trilogy of films, including *Episode I* (2003), filmed in war-torn Chechnya. The "main panel" of the triptych, *Episode II*, on the theme of love, is yet to be made.

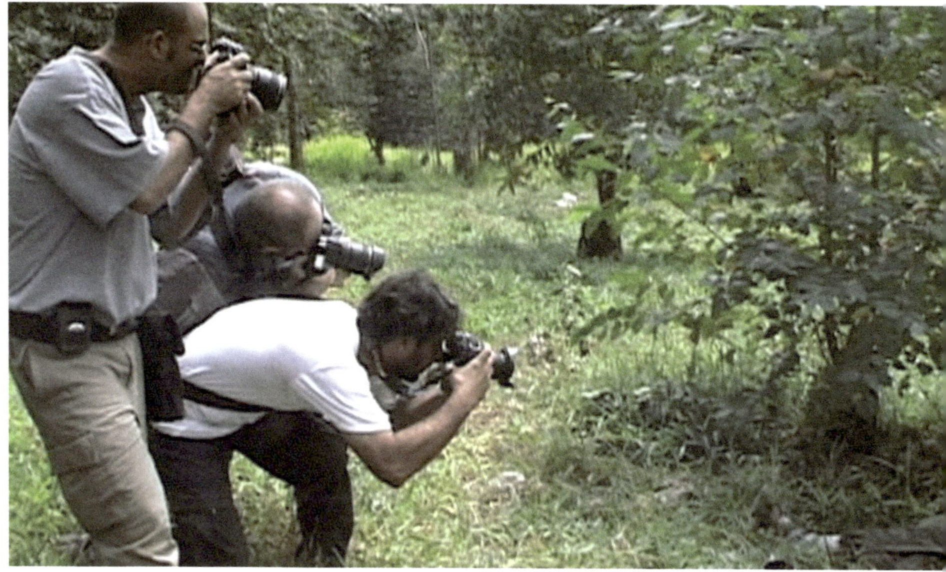

Renzo Martens, still from *Episode III (Enjoy Poverty)*, 2009

It is of course an old story, going back to the food shortages in
Biafra during the 1968 Nigerian civil war when journalists first
produced horrific images of starving children in Africa meant to
encourage relief aid (the images were themselves reminiscent of
the brutal documents of Holocaust camp survivors at the end of
World War II). Soon after, in the 1970s, artists and writers like
Allan Sekula and Martha Rosler articulated some of the most
trenchant critiques of what Sekula termed the "pornography of
the 'direct' representation of misery"—pornographic for presenting a spectacle of poverty while obscuring its social and political
causes and hiding the image's own embeddedness in a system
that commodifies the titillating objectification of others' misfortune.[3] Using a similarly charged metaphor, the filmmakers Luis
Ospina and Carlos Mayolo made *The Vampires of Poverty* in 1978,
shot in Cali and Bogotá, Colombia, reaffirming a similar point.

Their mockumentary, in which an unseen camera records the two artists making a film about
poverty, satirizes documentary portrayals of
the less fortunate. They show themselves going
about their quest to find street kids, prostitutes,
and mentally unstable and homeless people,
and at one point stage a contrived scene of a
destitute family—played by actors—in front of

3   See Allan Sekula, "Dismantling
Modernism, Reinventing Documentary
(Notes on the Politics of Representa-
tion)," *Massachusetts Review* 19, no. 4
(Winter 1978): 867–69; and Martha
Rosler, "In, Around, and Afterthoughts
(on Documentary Photography)," in *The
Contest of Meaning: Critical Histories
of Photography*, ed. Richard Bolton
(Cambridge, MA: MIT Press, 1993).

their broken-down shanty. Through these ploys, the filmmakers self-reflexively critique their own status as "vampires" of poverty, even including seemingly spontaneous interventions by objecting bystanders who take them to task for exploiting their misery.

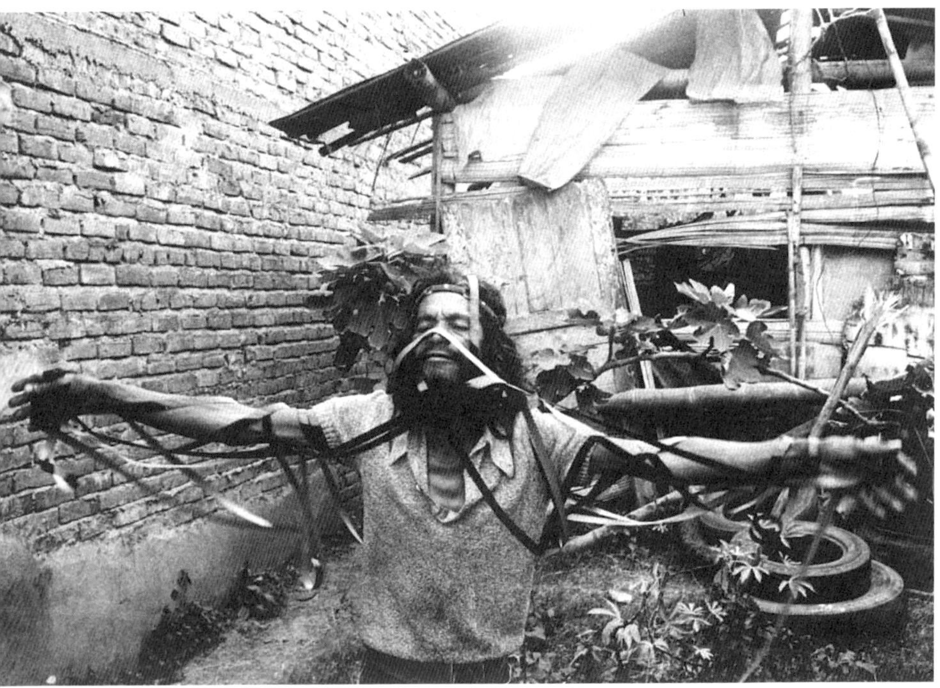

Luis Ospina and Carlos Mayolo, still from *The Vampires of Poverty*, 1978

Invoking such precedents, Martens's film builds on their analyses, but takes an alternate path to recent developments in disaster imagery, both by rejecting the humor and irony of such deconstructions as found in Ospina and Mayolo's film, and by refusing to turn away from the horrible images of media spectacle in a new era of poverty pornography, as Sekula and Rosler did in the 1970s.[4] Indeed, *Enjoy Poverty* portrays the extensive system of humanitarianism, global aid institutions, and the image economy today, which has moved far beyond the modes of vampiric documentarism of the 1960s and '70s, though it simultaneously reinvigorates the meta-critical questions

4　Consider Rosler's *The Bowery in two inadequate descriptive systems* (1974–75), which deconstructed the linguistic and photographic representation of the down and out, in part by refusing to visually represent them. On Rosler's project, see Steve Edwards, *Martha Rosler: The Bowery in two inadequate descriptive systems* (London: Afterall, 2012).

around media economy that were opened up by Sekula and
Rosler—the significance of which remains evident today. Images
of "starving Africans" hawked by mass media, NGOs, and humanitarian organizations continue unabated. Yet charity and aid seem
to be ever inadequate, and so the images return day after day,
leading to a haunting that is more than a cliché in mainstream
media discourse.[5] I'd like to suggest that this haunting—according to which the horrific imagery of countless starving children,
violated women, traumatized people, and victims of violence appears and reappears on the pages and screens of mass media—
emerges from the disconnect between the aesthetics of empathy
and the structural causes for poverty, which fail to add up to any
solution. Without one, the mediatized haunting arises from this
very configuration, where empathy represents an affect that *allows* poverty to continue, even as it creates the conditions for
further media exploitation. In the meantime, viewers all over the
world suffer the unwelcomed visitations of these disturbing images that oscillate uneasily between appalling horror and visual
numbness, inspiring both emergency imperatives and feelings
of insufferable impotency. These are the very tensions that
Marten's film puts to task.

—

Enjoy Poverty reveals a surprising parallel between concerned
image making and the international humanitarian industry,
both of which risk exacerbating conflicts more than mitigating
the contexts they work to alleviate. This owes in large part to
the fact that NGOs, like photojournalists, proclaim to serve
emergency victims (limiting their identity precisely to victim-
hood), yet come to depend on them and importantly on their
sensationalized images—much like vampires
depend on the blood of their victims—to generate the funding streams that guarantee their
continued existence.[6] In this regard, the DRC
is only one flashpoint for many such zones of
conflict—think of Afghanistan, Iraq, Haiti, and
Sudan in recent years. In all of these contexts
we encounter an increasingly common logic of
intervention that joins military response and
humanitarian aid against the backdrop of defunded public institutions and eroding national
infrastructure. Here, ethical imperatives and
political justifications intertwine, challenging ruling concepts of legitimacy and legality.

5   A quick online search yields
the following examples: "'Making the
Invisible, Visible': Haunting Pictures of
America's Most Vulnerable People Shot
by Photojournalists against Poverty,"
Daily Mail, March 21, 2012; Kristin
Davis, "Kenya's Dadaab Refugee Camp
Is a Haunting Place," *Guardian*, July 14,
2011; and "War Haunts Eastern Congo
Voters," *BBC*, August 1, 2006.

6   See Linda Polman, *The Crisis Cara-
van: What's Wrong with Humanitarian
Aid?*, trans. Liz Waters (New York:
Metropolitan, 2010); and Alex De Waal,
*Famine Crimes: Politics & the Disaster
Relief Industry in Africa* (London: Afri-
can Rights & the International African
Institute, 1997).

As social scientist Craig Calhoun points out, "Humanitarianism flourishes as an ethical response to emergencies not just because bad things happen in the world, but also because many people have lost faith in both economic development and political struggle [dominant up until the end of the Cold War] as ways of trying to improve the human lot."[7] This new ethical turn opens onto the wider quandaries of contemporary humanitarianism, including its lack of accountability, its self-perpetuating institutions that prioritize highly visible and mediatized conflicts over non-sensationalized areas of devastation, and its self-declared political "neutrality" that often inadvertently serves the interests of those in power rather than helping victims in need—exactly the problems that *Enjoy Poverty* encounters in the DRC.[8]

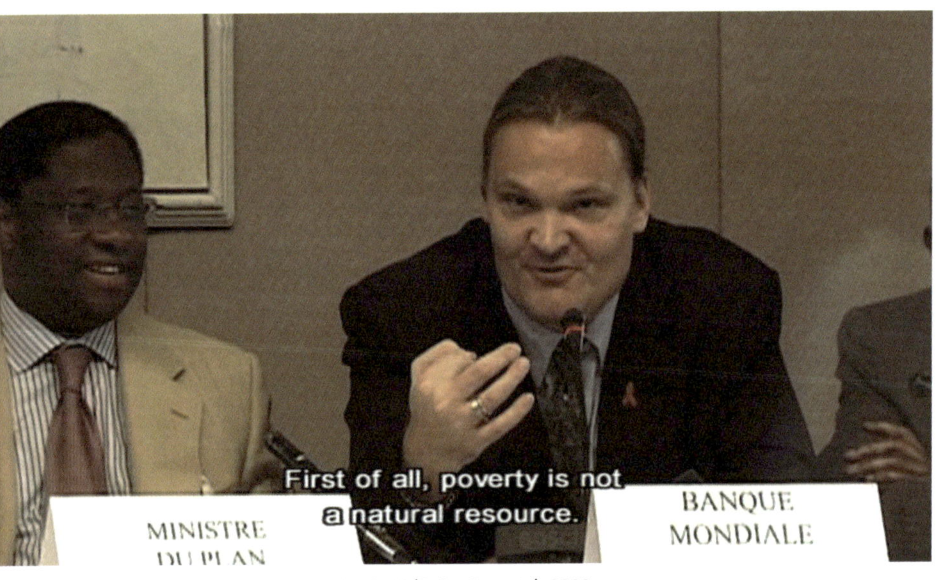

Renzo Martens, still from *Episode III (Enjoy Poverty)*, 2009

In a particularly remarkable scene where Martens poses a question to the representative of the World Bank at a press meeting in Kinshasa, the film reveals the inequality-producing macroeconomic structure behind the "disaster relief industry."[9] Noting that the meeting was being held in part to announce a new grant totaling 1.8 billion US dollars for that year alone, Martens asks, "I'd

7   Craig Calhoun, "The Idea of Emergency: Humanitarian Action and Global (Dis)order," in *Contemporary States of Emergency: The Politics of Military and Humanitarian Interventions*, eds. Didier Fassin and Mariella Pandolfi (New York: Zone Books, 2010), 18.

like to know whether the fight against poverty, for which the money is destined, may be an important natural resource for the Congo, or even the most important?" The spokesman smiles and responds, "Poverty is not a natural resource [... but rather] a shared defeat for the entire international community." He then goes on to acknowledge that "it is true that development aid brings in more money to the Congo than copper or coltan or diamonds. Even if combined. But it's normal. That's how a post-conflict situation develops."

Going further than simply targeting the World Bank, Martens implicates a broad range of international actors—multinational corporations carrying out resource extraction in the DRC, global financial institutions encouraging free trade over social welfare, self-promoting humanitarian and disaster relief organizations cleaning up the civil-war damage, and the media industry sensationalizing the whole carnival.[10] NGOs like the United Nations Children's Fund, United Nations High Commissioner for Refugees, and the European Commission for Humanitarian Aid come under particular fire for their shameless self-promotion, as logos are shown placed on all the clothing, plastic tent sheeting, and supplies they pass out in camps for internally displaced people. (When Martens inquires why, one representative explains, "For visibility.") All are implicated as related players in the massive racket that is neoliberalism, which turns out to be rather continuous with the colonial past in using the language of modernization and development, while in reality wages decrease, poverty grows, and average life expectancy shortens.[11] And indeed Martens's character—shown trekking through the jungle trailed by his retinue of black porters—cannot avoid conjuring the long history of the visual iconography of colonial exploration and plunder, bringing to mind diverse literary and cinematic precedents such as Joseph Conrad's *Heart of Darkness* and Werner Herzog's *Aguirre: The Wrath of God.*

Instead of a more equitable and inclusive New World Order, the present state of

8   See Philip Gourevitch, "Alms Dealers: Can You Provide Humanitarian Aid without Facilitating Conflicts?," *New Yorker*, October 11, 2010; and Linda Polman, *War Games: The Story of Aid and War in Modern Times,* trans. Liz Waters (London: Viking, 2011). For a further critical treatment of humanitarianism, see Eyal Weizman, *The Least of All Possible Evils: Humanitarian Violence from Arendt to Gaza* (London: Verso, 2012).

9   See De Waal, *Famine Crimes.*

10   Thomas Keenan offers a helpful clarification in relation to the possible problematic blurring of humanitarianism, peace keeping, human rights activism, and disaster relief at work here: "Poverty is not a humanitarian question, in the technical sense. Emergencies, refugees, war-induced suffering are what humanitarians respond to. These acute crises are on the margins of [*Enjoy Poverty*], as are the UN peacekeepers and the human rights activist who emerges out of the dark river at the film's end. Those margins are important—they may even be constitutive of the problems at the center of the film—but the film has less to say about them. To those who are engaged in 'poverty alleviation' or development work, though, the film has a lot to say; it poses a direct challenge to its ethical self-certainty and to its standard modes of practice." See Keenan's comments in "Roundtable on Renzo Martens' *Episode III (Enjoy Poverty)*, with Carles Guerra, Thomas Keenan, Toma Muteba Luntumbue, and Renzo Martens, moderated by T. J. Demos and Hilde Van Gelder," in Demos et al., *In and Out of Brussels*, 21.

11   See Harrison, "Neoliberalism in Africa: A Failed Ideology," chap. 2 in *Neoliberal Africa.* For an early European critical response to the humanist-humanitarian argument behind colonialism that remains relevant today, see the collectively written essay by André Breton et al., "Murderous Humanitarianism," trans. Samuel Beckett, in *Negro: An Anthology*, ed. Nancy Cunard (London: Continuum, 2002), 352–53.

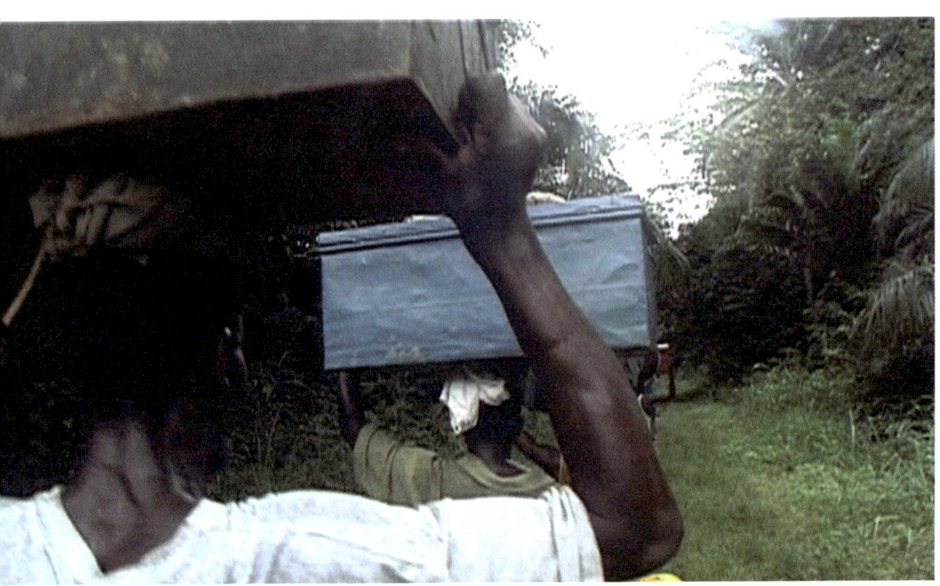

Renzo Martens, still from *Episode III (Enjoy Poverty)*, 2009

things, as witnessed in *Enjoy Poverty*, resembles what the International Forum on Globalization calls "global economic apartheid."[12] According to their argument—counter to the sanguine picture of globalization-boosters like the IMF and World Bank—worldwide environmental devastation has unfolded amid endless brutal wars over precious resources, while a widespread and growing democratic deficit rules and multinational corporations disregard national sovereignty, riding roughshod over their seemingly useless mechanisms of legal and economic accountability. In other words, for these critics, what is happening in the DRC may not be a "failure" at all, but rather an intended outcome—and certainly a cruel one—of avaricious global economic arrangements.[13] "Disaster capitalism" keeps countries in the Global South locked in the position of neocolonialism via debt servitude and neoliberal policies, which provide fodder for the media industry that continues to feed off the spectacle of the negative effects without recognizing the structural causes.[14] If the resulting imagery of

12   See John Cavanagh et al., eds., *Alternatives to Economic Globalization: A Better World Is Possible; A Report of the International Forum on Globalization* (San Francisco: Berrett-Koehler, 2002), 33.

13   For more specific analysis of Congo's complex conflicts, the roles of Congo's neighbors Uganda and Rwanda, mineral resources, government corruption, and ethnic hostilities in the recent wars, see Gérard Prunier, *From Genocide to Continental War: The "Congolese" Conflict and the Crisis of Contemporary Africa* (London: Hurst, 2009); Prunier, "The Eastern DR Congo: Dynamics of Conflict," *Open Democracy*, November 18, 2008; and Pete Jones, "The Material Stakes in the Democratic Republic of the Congo Elections," *Open Democracy*, December 5, 2011.

14   Naomi Klein, *The Shock Doctrine: The Rise of Disaster Capitalism* (London: Penguin, 2007). For Klein, this mode of capitalism began in the 1970s, with government coups (for example, in Chile) and the spreading endorsement of Chicago school economics in the Southern Cone.

the human wreckage continues to haunt Western viewers, it is
because they conveniently misrecognize the dreadful humanitarian outcome of their governments' economic policies as if it were
an accident of nature. Such is the world Martens encounters in
the DRC. And it is the one that he seeks to transform by inverting
the logic of humanitarianism in unexpected ways: "Amidst ethnic
war and relentless economic exploitation," Martens writes, "I
initiated an emancipation program that aims to teach the poor
how to benefit from their biggest resource: poverty."[15]

—

As a documentary set alongside a carefully scripted performance by Martens, *Enjoy Poverty* exposes this system of Congolese poverty, an exposure that is itself a significant act of a new
politics of documentarism. This is especially true as this complex
and international economic structure is most often invisible in
work by artists that deals with social problems in Africa such
as the photographs of Guy Tillim or the films of Mark Boulos.[16]
Martens's film goes further than the work of his contemporaries
in carrying out an attack on the complex image
economy of humanitarianism, at first through a
strategy of critical mimicry, according to which
his character explores the contemporary conditions of poverty, image making, and photojournalism in the DRC. Having learned that the
AFP photographer earns fifty euros per shot,
Martens comes across a run-down photography
stall called Bolingo (meaning "love," as one of its
employees explains). The business specializes
in photos of birthdays, ceremonies, and wed-
dings, for which they charge seventy-five cents
per photo, and advertises its model pictures
taped to a makeshift cardboard display. Martens
proposes the idea of providing "aid" to the Congolese poor—as represented by the workers
at Bolingo—by teaching them Western-style
photojournalism, for when Europeans come to
the DRC, "they don't come to film parties; they
come to film misery" to lucrative ends, explains
Martens. Should the Congolese follow suit, he
suggests, then they too might "enjoy poverty,"
since there's clearly so much money in it.

Cutting to an improvised classroom ar-
ranged in a thatched-roof hut, the film shows a

15   Martens, introduction to Demos
et al., *In and Out of Brussels*, 3.

16   As Martens explains, "There's a
piece by Mark Boulos, *All That Is Solid
Melts into Air* [exhibited near Martens's
Enjoy Poverty in the 2010 Berlin Bien-
nial], it's a two-screen projection: one
shows a group of rebels fighting against
the Shell company in the Niger Delta,
while the other presents a stock market
busy trading the oil. I just use it as an
example, it's an interesting piece. The
problem I see with it, is that it somehow
makes it easy for the spectator to be
critical about the oil industry. You
feel sympathy for the people who are
fighting everyday against a powerful
Goliath. But at the same time, we all
know that we flew here, to Berlin, to
come and see the art shows, on planes
fueled by the same oil companies, with
fuel manufactured in places like the
Niger Delta." Martens argues that the
piece therefore doesn't "have a real
understanding of itself" and loses "its
claim on reality [by] creating an illusion
of criticality." Martens in conversation
with Artur Żmijewski, "Artists Come to
Create Beauty and Kindness," in *Forget
Fear: 7th Berlin Biennale*, eds. Artur
Żmijewski and Joanna Warsza (Cologne:
Verlag der Buchhandlung Walther
König, 2012)

group of young men sitting before Martens, who proceeds to teach them a lesson in the economy of images. As he explains, if Congolese photographers wish to benefit financially from the practice of photography, then they should produce images of starvation, malnutrition, and violence—the country's "natural resources"—which are otherwise monopolized by European photojournalists who supply the global media that pay high prices for such images. Here, Martens performs a mix of the colonial missionary and the motivational speaker: "The fundamental question is to whom belongs poverty? If it can be sold, it's important to know who's the boss, the owner of that poverty. [...] People come to visit you [...] taking pictures, supposedly funding projects. Then they will have the pictures. Let's say they will have freely captured your poverty while you don't benefit too much. It's a resource." He continues with his logic: "You need to make choices based on rationality." As he stands in front of a white board on which he makes a handwritten graph and fills in the numbers, he explains, "There are two options: [...] war, [...] raped women, corpses, and malnourished children," or birthdays and parties. He forms two columns on the board to display the costs, benefits, and profits of each. It turns out that the village photographers earn one dollar per month by making pictures of parties, whereas photographing poverty and starvation, with roughly twenty images per month at fifty dollars a shot, could bring in one thousand dollars.

The logic is worthy of Jonathan Swift—whose satirical eighteenth-century "A Modest Proposal" suggested that the impoverished Irish sell their children as food to the wealthy[17]—and Martens performs its crass immorality without any horror-diffusing wink or knowing nod. The lesson also suggests the realization of a quintessential neoliberal goal: to transform oneself into an entrepreneur, even in this most debasing manner of commodifying the misery of one's own culture. As it turns out, however, Martens's proposal is bound to fail. Global institutions refuse entry to Congolese photographers, as is demonstrated in a scene where Martens brings his troop of photographers to the offices of Doctors Without Borders, who deride their ambitions as a baldly opportunistic and talentless money-making enterprise, even as they acknowledge that the *New York Times*' photojournalists are in the same racket. Indeed, the Congolese cannot "enjoy poverty" in any other way, it seems, than to submit to its irrevocable reality of material destitution. That fatalism is itself transformed into a horrific scene showing poor Congolese plantation workers embracing their fate. Speaking to a large group of people in a backwater village at dusk, Martens prosely-

17   The full title runs, "A Modest Proposal for Preventing the Children of Poor People From Being a Burden on Their Parents or Country, and for Making Them Beneficial to the Publick," published in 1729.

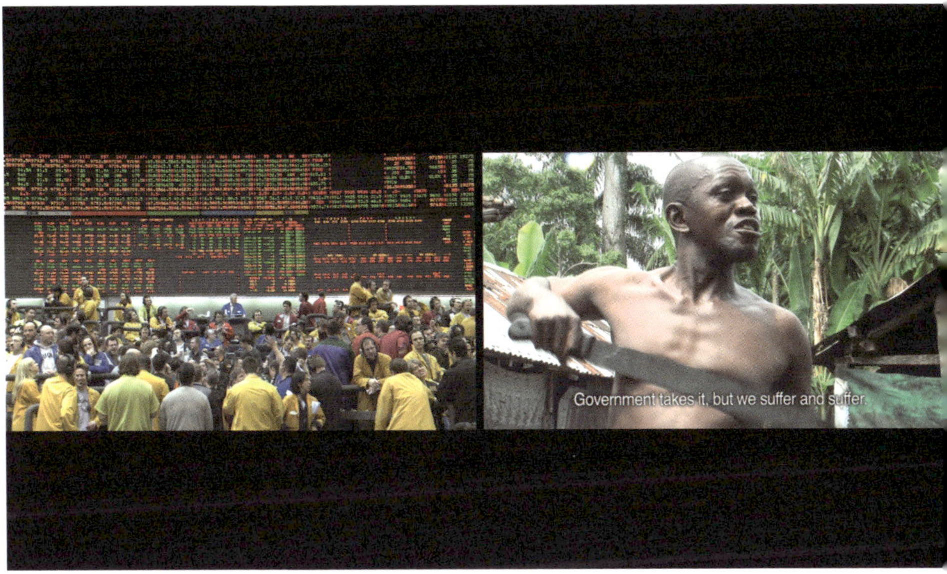

Mark Boulos, still from *All That Is Solid Melts into Air*, 2008

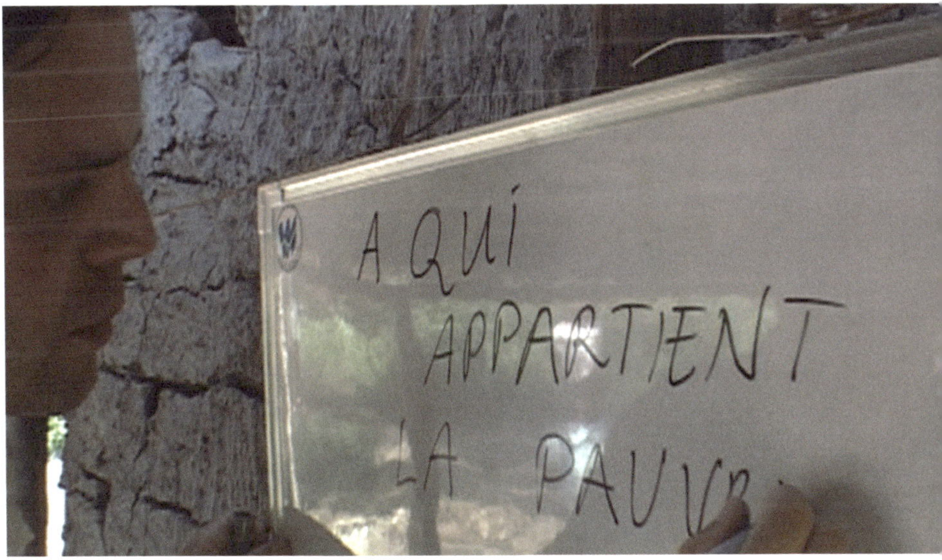

Renzo Martens, still from *Episode III (Enjoy Poverty)*, 2009

tizes: "You're not merely people in need of aid. You're also people that aid the rest of the world. So now we launch the publicity for the viewers back home or at gallery exhibits. Surely, they will be open to the idea that Africans are taking charge of their own re-sources." After starting up a generator, he turns on a large bluish neon sign attached to a makeshift wooden armature, which reads "Enjoy Poverty," with the word "please" blinking in red between the phrase, its on–off switch manually operated by a Congolese man who flips the button back and forth. As the light shines forth, a crowd of children become rapturous; drum music, singing, and dancing break out; and, in a perverse moment of pop-cultural *arte povera* performance, a young man plays air guitar with a rough piece of wood. A group of concerned men approach Martens, who explains, to their surprise, that no relief aid will follow the party;

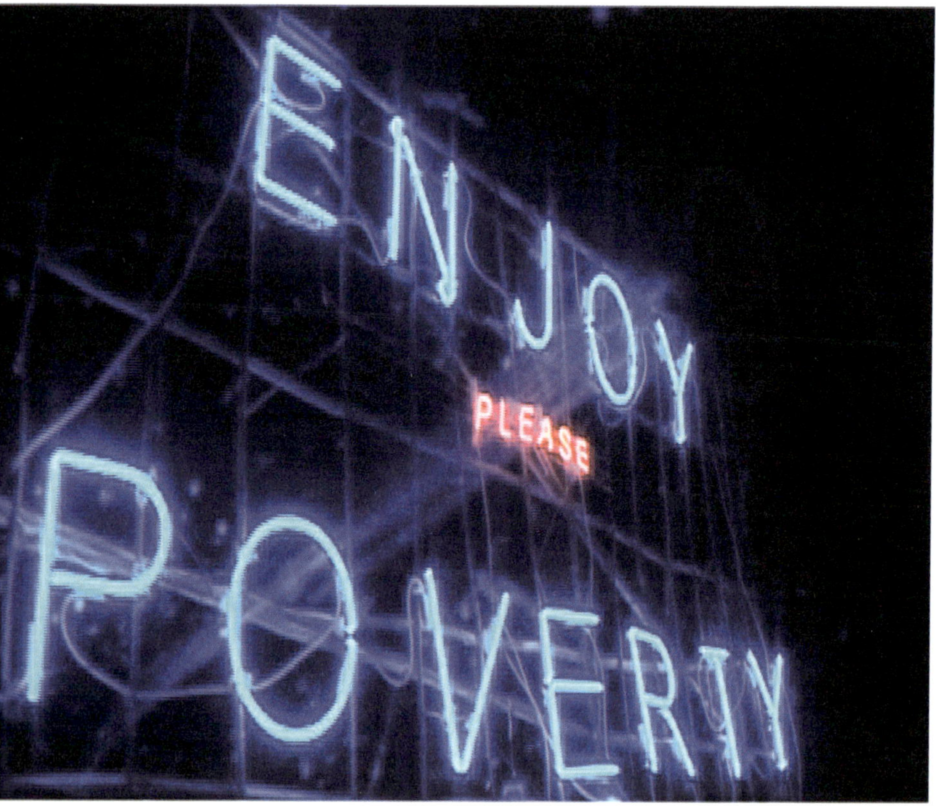

Renzo Martens, still from *Episode III (Enjoy Poverty)*, 2009

instead they are told, "You'd better enjoy poverty rather than fight it and be unhappy." They resignedly accept this idea: "We don't want to fight. We want to be happy despite poverty." In response, Martens ventriloquizes the ideal humanitarian self-aggrandizing sentiment, drawing applause: "Experiencing your suffering makes me a better person. You really help me. Thank you."

—

Martens's project seems like it was designed for failure all along, and in fact confronting that failure leads to the film's very lesson. When it comes to addressing the horrific living conditions, economic flounderings, appalling hunger, and senseless violence in the DRC, art, according to Martens, cannot offer an answer—not even its critical, documentary, or socially engaged forms. Rather, the artistic system, of which Martens's own project is exemplary, is shown to be consistent with the very same global arrangements that structure the inequalities of humanitarianism and the media. Such is exemplified in another of the film's parables in which the artist visits a photography exhibition in Kinshasa that displays black-and-white images of toiling plantation workers (one is marked "Workers for peace, Ndeke, the Congo"). Martens interviews one visitor, himself a white plantation owner, who explains that he bought several of the images of sweating laborers dressed in rags—most likely shot on his own plantation—for their "artistic" value.

More than a matter of a local ethical scandal, this scene dramatizes a widespread paradox of contemporary art, particularly that of video and photography. It occurs when "concerned" documentary images, intended to alleviate poverty or "work for peace," actually operate as commodity objects and are purchased by those who encourage or benefit from the very industries of inequality and exploitation against which concerned documentarians justify their practice. Or, to put it another way, the problem concerns mobilizing a "politics of aesthetics" (for example, imagery that reorganizes visibility so that those normally excluded from "what counts" now appear) in contexts such as commercial art galleries that perpetuate an exploitative "distribution of the sensible"—one of sheer consumerism and voyeuristic enjoyment. The situation expresses a false proximity to the victimized that grants spectators distance from their complicity in the wider situation of generalized economic inequality.[18] The problem is of course not new. In fact, it identifies art's difficult and longstanding location in a paradox endemic to liberalism, according to which art

18   I use the language of Jacques Rancière, whose work I believe helps us to critically analyze the situation, not fall into its trap, even though he neglects to deal with this paradox. See Rancière, *The Politics of Aesthetics*, trans. Gabriel Rockhill (London: Continuum, 2004).

offers, on the one hand, a sociocultural progressivism supportive of human rights, individual freedoms, equality in principle, and concerned expressions of political sympathy with the oppressed; and, on the other, the tacit acceptance (or at least the absence of a critique) of the wider economic system that perpetuates the very same social un-freedoms and global divisions against which said progressivism is posed—a paradox that has only grown more blatant in recent years. It is in this same context that we can locate the humanitarianism that has exploded since 1989, due partly to the end of ideological conflicts and the demolition of state welfare in the post-Cold War era. Humanitarianism has consequently supplanted the struggle for political agency and economic justice with depoliticized poverty relief and charitable giving. The current resurgence of political aesthetics in a globalizing art world funded by elite financial interests makes these critical considerations newly urgent.[19]

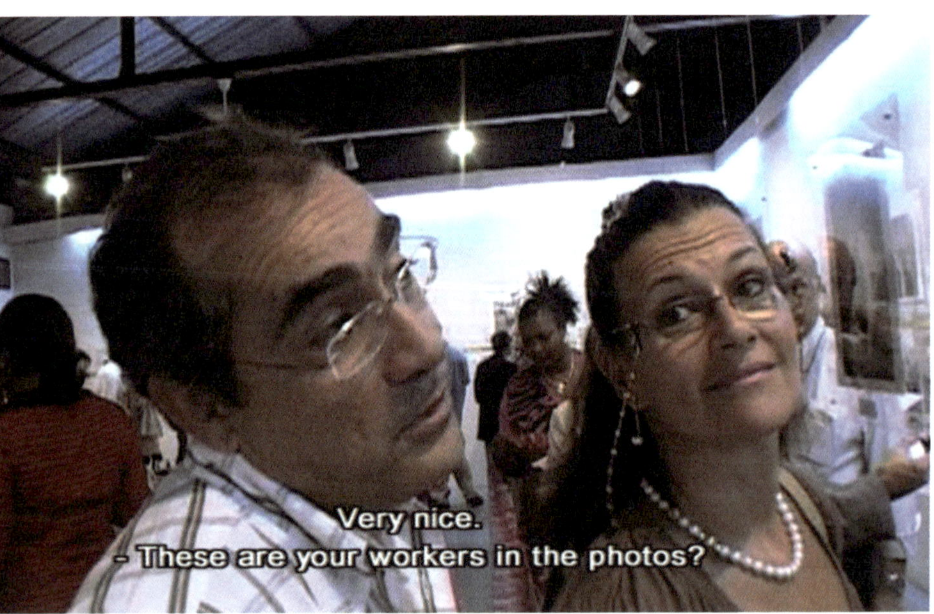

Renzo Martens, still from *Episode III (Enjoy Poverty)*, 2009

As artist and theorist Hito Steyerl has recently observed, the "blind spot" of contemporary political art dedicated to global crises is to overlook the often compromised local conditions of its own production and display—a situation reeking of the exploitation of armies of interns and financially driven by politically unsavory benefactors, such as multinational banks and arms dealers. In her view, "We could try to understand [art's] space as a political one instead of trying to represent a politics that is always happening elsewhere."[20] She is surely right to point out this negligence; but it is, in my view, a false choice. We can and must work on multiple fronts, not one *or* the other. This is the significance of Martens's work: to critically locate political images in networks of consumption and distribution that support forms of inequality, putting himself in the midst of those networks and its contradictions and failures—or rather his self-constructed avatar of the do-gooder artist—as he walks around for much of the time in the film with the camera trained on his own face in an insistent act of self-reflexive exposure and criticality. It is equally imperative for writers to reflect on these matters, too, in order to extend the debate via discourse and pedagogical contexts, to contribute to the growth of critical awareness. Instead of abandoning global politics for local art-world politics, we should try to connect them as overlapping spheres of complex entanglements.

At the same time, it is important to resist the potential reductiveness of such critiques—that politically conservative contexts, funding bodies, and commercial institutions somehow completely determine, as if by necessity, the meaning of art; or that politically engaging work cannot operate in unanticipated or strategic ways against the very contexts that frame it. Consider a recent comment by *Bidoun* editor Negar Azimi: "What is the good of engaged art—whether it take the form of governmental critique or institutional critique or otherwise—when it is subsumed back into the system?"[21] Or, as Andrea Fraser writes, speaking on behalf of artists: "If our only choice is to participate in this economy or abandon the art field entirely, at least we can stop rationalizing that participation in the name of critical or political art practice or—adding insult to injury—social justice. Any claim that we represent a progressive social force while our activities are directly subsidized by the engines of inequality can only contribute to the justification of that inequality."[22] But who is to say that such artwork, no matter where it is presented and no matter who funds it, cannot still encourage a politicization among unexpected viewers, contribute to unsuspected alliances with social movements outside the gallery, or even inspire protests and

19   On this subject, see the recent important essays by Andrea Fraser, including "L'1%, C'est Moi," *Texte zur Kunst*, no. 83 (September 2011); and "There's No Place Like Home," in *The Whitney Biennial 2012*, eds. Jay Sanders and Elisabeth Sussman (New York: Whitney Museum, 2012).

20   Hito Steyerl, "Politics of Art: Contemporary Art and the Transition to Post-Democracy," *e-flux*, no. 21 (December 2010).

21   Negar Azimi, "Good Intentions," *frieze*, no. 137 (March 2011).

22   Fraser, "L'1%, C'est Moi," 124.

manifestations? The problem with arguments that endow the "system" with a seemingly omnipotent power of co-optation is that they end up serving that very power, inadvertently licensing reactionary attacks on art's political ambition.

An exemplary retort is Judith Butler's inspiring consideration of the infamous digital images of Abu Ghraib prisoners made to perform degrading acts before the cameras of depraved US military contractors. Though initially an instrument of torture, those images escaped their own imprisoned context. "The photos have functioned in several ways," Butler explains: "as an incitement to brutality within the prison itself, as a threat of shame for the prisoners, as a chronicle of a war crime, as a testimony to the radical unacceptability of torture, and as archival and documentary work made available on the internet or displayed in museums in the US, including galleries and public spaces in a host of venues." The conclusion being that there is no final system that can contain images, only endless "frames" of possibility, each with its own interpretive potentiality that cannot always be predicted and never completely controlled. "We probably need to accept that the photograph neither tortures nor redeems, but can be instrumentalized in radically different directions, depending on how it is discursively framed and through what form of media presentation it is displayed."[23] Extrapolating this point for our consideration of *Enjoy Poverty*, it appears that even if Martens commits a transgression by reproducing the images of mediatized suffering, when reframed, those images can also lead toward critical understanding of the wider mechanisms of the economy of empathy. Would it not represent an act of intellectual laziness, even a defeated conservativism, to abandon the politics of aesthetics to institutions that are only too happy to instrumentalize them? Why not engage diverse approaches, assess them individually and critically, but without forcing simplistic choices and posing false alternatives?

—

In this vein, let's consider another model that critically investigates the nexus of the global image economy, humanitarian photojournalism, and critical seeing when it comes to a haunting spectacle of misery: *The Sound of Silence* (2006) by Alfredo Jaar. The Chilean-born artist has long focused on the documentary image's intersection with media and politics, including subjects such as labor and exploitation in the Global South—for example, gold mining in the Amazon (*Introduction to a Distant*

23   Judith Butler, "Torture and the Ethics of Photography: Thinking with Sontag," in *Frames of War: When Is Life Grievable?* (London: Verso, 2009), 92.

World, 1985, and *Rushes*, 1986), the oil industry's environmental despoliation in Nigeria (*Geography = War*, 1991), and corporate media's alternately spectacularizing and silencing approach to humanitarian emergencies in Africa, as with the 1994 genocide in Rwanda (*Untitled (Newsweek)*, 1994). The latter project includes seventeen reproductions of covers of the popular weekly magazine (between April 6 and August 1, 1994), along with text captions that elaborate the growing death tolls in Rwanda during that time. For example, with nearly a million deaths, and three months into the tragedy ("with still no sign of UN deployment," a caption reads), *Newsweek*, in a further sensationalist and vacuous choice for its covers, featured the O. J. Simpson trial story over the course of three issues. It was not until August that the magazine dedicated its first cover to Rwanda.

The Sound of Silence follows suit by taking up Kevin Carter's infamous 1993 photograph of starvation in Sudan—portraying a malnourished Sudanese girl resting on the ground, who appears near death while stalked by a hungry vulture—used initially to illustrate a *New York Times* article about the country's civil-war crisis. Jaar's complex installation presents an eight-minute silent film inside a large black-box container about the circumstances of Carter's making of the image. The spatial arrangement choreographs a carefully controlled experience, beginning with a wall of fluorescent lights placed on the structure's exterior, which blind viewers before they enter the dark architectural space (guided by a cue of green light). Inside, the film projects a running text, presented in a typewriter-like font, which recounts Carter's life as an antiapartheid South African photojournalist, and relays the circumstances of his taking the famous photograph. The photographer waited twenty minutes for a dramatic shot, hoping in vain that the creature would spread its wings, before he finally shot the image and chased the bird away. According to Jaar's account, he then "sat under a tree and lit a cigarette, talked to God, and cried." The film projects the ghastly image for an instant on the screen, curtailing the viewers' time to act as voyeurs, but only after four strobe lights surprise them with a flash, as if to give them a taste of photographic objectification. We learn that in the end "no one knows what happened to the child."

How does one relate to such an image in a gallery context, and to Carter's own ethical dilemma—whether to give immediate assistance to a girl in need or withhold that assistance in order to make the most powerful image he could in the hope of generating international aid? Was Carter not himself "another vulture on the scene," as one critic mentioned in Jaar's film asks,

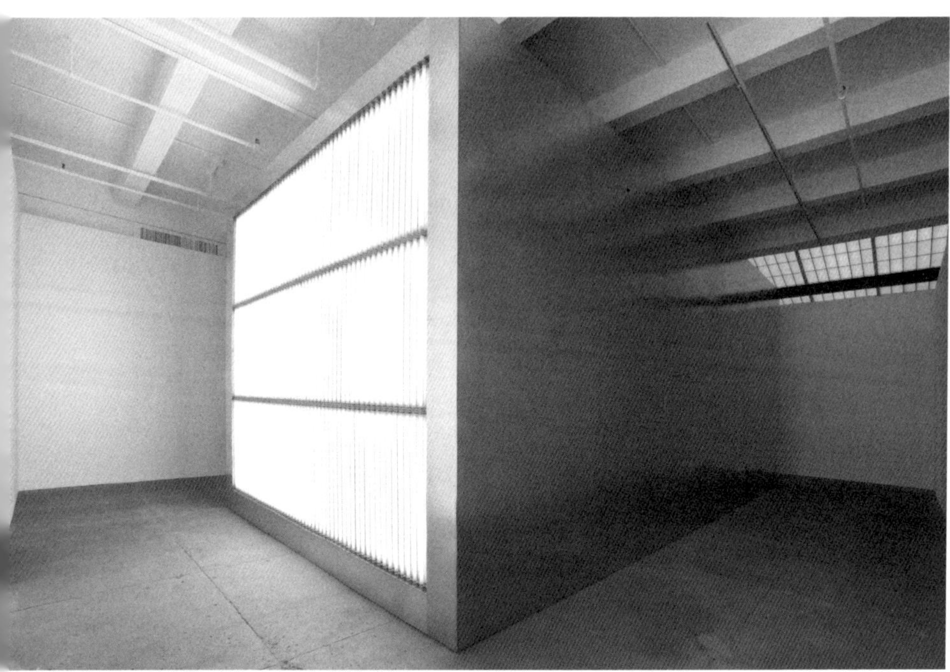

Installation view; Alfredo Jaar, *The Sound of Silence*, 2006

and do gallery visitors not become vampires in turn, faced with the dilemma of whether or not to look, and thereby either to become complicit in this spectacle of starvation or to remain ignorant of its visual cultural phenomenon? Clearly Jaar's work deals with exactly these thorny questions. For Jacques Rancière, Jaar's piece brings about a "different way of looking." By creating a "disruption of the normal relationships between textual messages and visible forms," the artist constructs a space "where a completely new interweaving of words and forms can give mass death or mass exile its resonance."[24] The solution to the problem of media's spectacle of misery, then, is not to look away (as *Newsweek* did), but rather to look again in a different way. Preempting the potential criticism of his position, Rancière writes, "The accusation of 'aestheticizing horror' is too convenient, shows too much ignorance of the complex entanglement between the aesthetic intensity of the exceptional situation taken in

24   Jacques Rancière, "Theater of Images," in *Alfredo Jaar: The Politics of Images*, ed. Nicole Schweizer (Zurich: JRP|Ringier, 2007), 78–79.

25   Ibid. Griselda Pollock argues similarly: "Jaar feels called upon, by his refusal to look away from what is happening in the world to and around Africa, to examine not only what our current regimes of representation do in this double bind of representation and the disposition of the viewer of the representation, but also the very conditions under which the artist can draw attention to the new complexities and ineffectuality of representation in a mediatic age that is ostensibly always watching but not always seeing." "Not-Forgetting Africa," in Schweizer, *Alfredo Jaar: The Politics of Images*, 117.

by a gaze, and the ethical or political concern to bear witness to the horror of a reality nobody is bothering to see."[25]

Yet in confronting that "complex entanglement," Rancière, I would argue, does not go far enough: it is crucial to identify the wider framework in which such images circulate, and to move

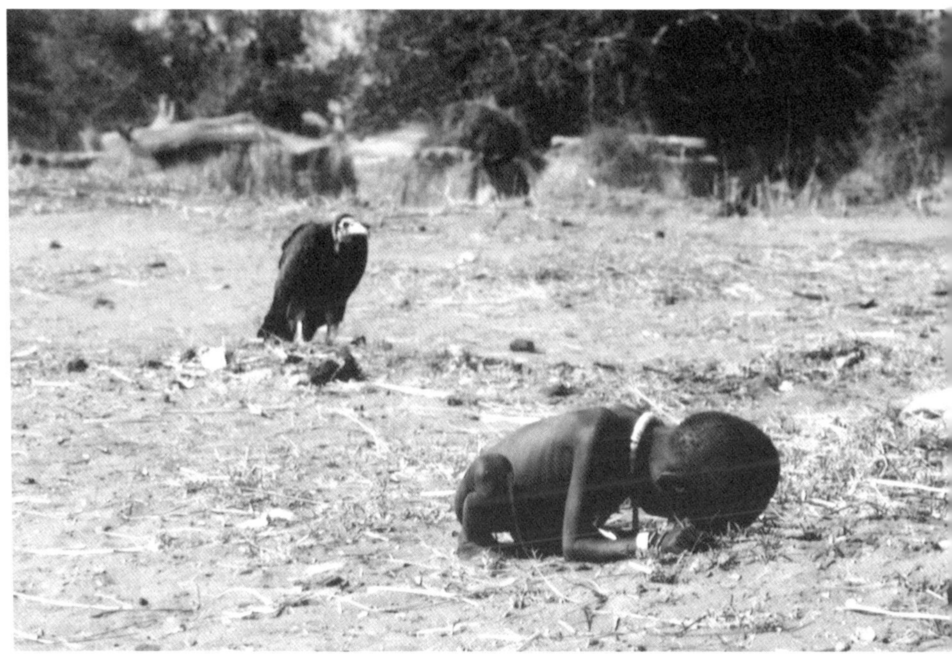

Kevin Carter, 1993

toward a systemic critique of humanitarianism and the media industry's economy of imagery. If we do "bother to see," then we need to look beyond the single image and, progressing from image to economy, take account of how "bearing witness" may play into a problematic logic of humanitarianism and documentarism in the service of empathy and hope. Photographs like Carter's can produce images that motor crises—most notably when perpetrators stage spectacles of violence readymade for cameras precisely to attract aid, as has happened repeatedly in Sudan, Sierra Leone, and Somalia.[26] Once we position ourselves as spectators and accept the ethical terms of the demands made on us—to be appalled at the horror, to sympathize, to bear witness—we have already

26 See Gourevitch, "Alms Dealers"; and Polman, *Crisis Caravan.*

been sucked into the logic of humanitarianism and risk becoming complicit in its larger situation. In this regard, it is significant that *The Sound of Silence* points out how, following Carter's suicide months after winning the Pulitzer Prize for his Sudan photograph, his surviving daughter came to inherit the image, and commissioned the Corbis Images photo agency, owned by Microsoft CEO Bill Gates, to manage its reproduction rights. As in Martens's film, this situation confronts us again with the fact that the world's poor cannot even own the images of their poverty, which become commodities traded in the Global North. It is this larger analysis of photojournalism's location within the disaster aid industry and the relation of humanitarianism to neoliberal globalization that need visibility.

Still, a tension persists between Martens's *Enjoy Poverty* and Jaar's *Sound of Silence*. The differences are in fact quite stark: whereas Jaar positions art as an exception to the media regime, one that can offer a critical perspective on the aesthetics and politics of (in)visibility by carefully reframing perceptual access to sensationalist imagery, Martens embraces and mimics that media regime in all its spectacular perversity. While Jaar relieves the viewer of complicity by promoting spectatorial criticality, Martens insists on showing how art objects—even those containing critical content—are immanent to an economy of exploitation. The issue is usefully elucidated by Fraser when she points to a contradictory duality endemic to much critical art, explaining how "formal, procedural, and iconographic investigation and performative experimentation are elaborated as figures of radical social and even economic critique, while the social and economic conditions of the works themselves and of their production and reception are completely ignored or recognized only in the most euphemized ways."[27] When art "speaks of that world [of economics] *so as not to speak of it*," it performs what Fraser terms a "negation" that serves to hold contradictions in suspension.[28] Certainly Jaar speaks of the world of economics—detailing how photojournalism is controlled and commodified not only by newspapers like the *New York Times*, but also by Gates's photo agency—but what of the implication of his own gallery-bound work in the market economy? Where is the confrontation with the fact that Jaar's critical exception may itself be marketed and instrumentalized in the art world in a way similar to Carter's image? When such matters are repressed, or negated, is that silencing not another source of a future haunting?

27 Fraser, "There's No Place Like Home," 30.

28 As Fraser explains: "Freud describes negation as a procedure through which 'the content of a repressed image or idea can make its way into consciousness,' even resulting in 'full intellectual acceptance'; and yet, repression remains in place because this 'intellectual function is separated from the affective process.' As such, negation functions as a mechanism of defense that produces a contradiction on the level of discourse that manifests but also aims to contain a conflict—between opposing impulses or affects; between a wish and a counterveiling imperative; or between a wish and a prohibition that negation itself may represent." Ibid., 31.

It is this structure of negation that *Enjoy Poverty* breaks down, doing so by placing documentary imagery and critiques of poverty in relation to systems of production and reception that produce inequality. Martens, first of all, shows how empathy is connected to the market, leading to perhaps the most difficult aspect of the film: the representation of the black body, and particularly the child's body, which is most vulnerable. In one galling scene, the film shows sick and starving children in an ill-equipped medical clinic (to which Martens has lead his troupe of photographers in a demonstration of the photojournalist's "money shot"); and in another, a Congolese man reveals to Martens's camera the suffering body and sore-infested anus of his young insomniac and malnourished daughter. It is at this point that we confront some of the most difficult questions regarding Martens's strategy. How can such depictions be justified, no matter what Martens's deconstructive intentions? Is this a case where even the last remaining dignity of an impoverished and dying human being is taken away by a debasing artistic portrayal? How does one validate or explain the exposure of a horror whose reality is a catastrophic failure on ethical, political, and humanitarian grounds? Is this *exposure* of bare life—stripped of political rights and humanitarian protections and reduced to mere biological existence—also an unacceptable *reproduction* of bare life, no matter what one's critical motivations?

When I posed these questions to Martens, he responded: "The conditions of these children are actually justified all the time. It's called the market, or African corruption, or pre-modern belief systems. Whatever the reasons, we thrive on it. I think it's unfair for the audiences to want to have it both ways: cheap labor on the one hand, and yet on the other being exempted from any confrontation with the results—malnourished and dying children, their parents feeling entirely helpless—on the grounds that representation of such lives would be immoral. Morality then serves profitability."[29] Still, what of the ethics of documentation? How can one stand by and record a child suffering and dying? How can one watch these images and write about them in turn? Martens himself asks: "How can I problematize the fact that children are maltreated, that their starvation is used in discourses that benefit many, but not these children? How to do that if the fact that, yes, they die, and yes, they are black, yes, they are malnourished, yes, their parents are so desperate, and no, no one is showing up to offer help, is all off limits? In

29   Quoted in T. J. Demos, "Toward a New Institutional Critique: A Conversation with Renzo Martens," *Atlántica*, no. 52 (February 2012): 93–94.

order to make viewing less painful, should we forget these facts
first?"[30]

    Enjoy Poverty does show these facts, and these scenes
are among the most disturbing in the film. They haunt precisely
because we as viewers can do nothing about the tragedies; we

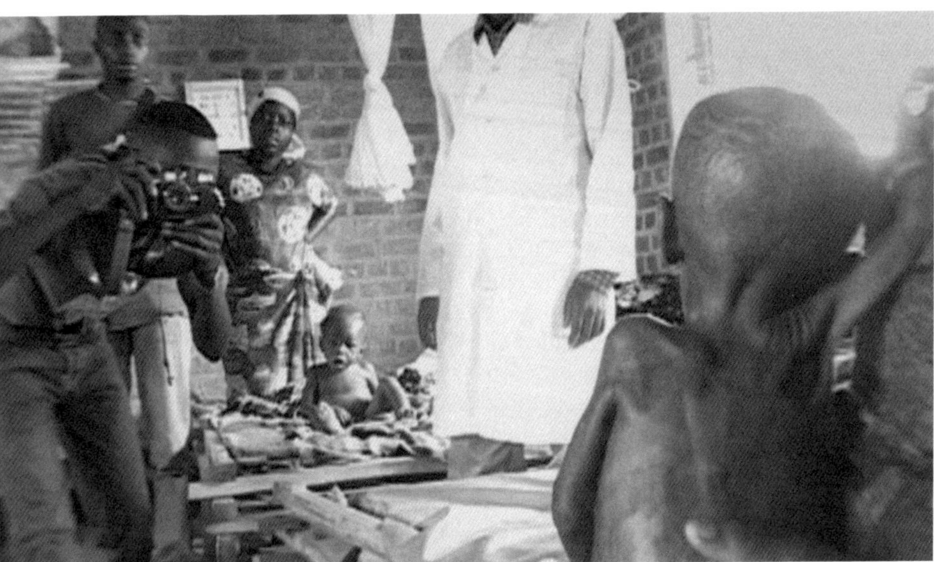

Renzo Martens, still from *Episode III (Enjoy Poverty)*, 2009

can only confront the impotency of the empathic response. They
haunt because of the insignificance of artistic critique when
compared to the monumentality of human suffering. But it's not
that these images should be stoically embraced by documentary
realists; rather, we need to critically address the larger economic
and political causes of such suffering, and thereby exorcize the
ineffective strategies and break the spell of the haunting. In this
regard, Martens's film shows—and importantly, problematizes—
social documentary's conventional production of "empathy" with
its represented victims, which nonetheless continues to gain
purchase among various practitioners and critics. For instance,
Susie Linfield has recently argued that without "empathy [...] the
politics of human rights [would] devolve into abstraction, romantic foolishness, and cruelty," and she finds the ability to foster
empathy to be one of photography's greatest
powers.[31] At the same time, her neo-humanist

argument offers no explanation for what the exact efficacy of empathy is, and fails to acknowledge the global image economy in which such imagery circulates and where "morality serves profitability." *Enjoy Poverty* clearly departs from this strategy, and, in this sense, rather takes seriously the warning of Susan Sontag:

> So far as we feel sympathy, we feel we are not accomplices to what caused the suffering. Our sympathy proclaims our innocence as well as our impotence. To that extent, it can be (for all our good intentions) an impertinent—if not an inappropriate—response. To set aside the sympathy we extend to others beset by war and murderous politics for a consideration of how our privileges are located on the same map as their suffering, and may—in ways that we prefer not to imagine—be linked to their suffering, as the wealth of some may imply the destitution of others, is a task for which the painful, stirring images supply only the initial spark.[32]

Martens's film hardly sets aside "painful, stirring images"; rather, it offers a massive dose of them, but does so in order to place our privileges "on the same map" as the suffering of others. The artist—playing up the cruelty of his character until the very end—tells the father of the girl whose sick body was presented to the camera earlier that he should expect no benefit from this film project. He goes on to explain to the man that if he has been working on a plantation for ten years and still doesn't have a TV or radio, bicycle, suit, leather shoes, etc., then he probably won't be able to afford such things anytime soon. For Martens, this exercise is intended to show "how making this film is in itself a process analogous to making chocolate, coffee, coltan, or gold. The power equation between those who consume and those who supply the raw material in those industries is the same, regardless of what specific product is produced."[33] In other words, art is no exception to these economies and offers no redemption to the world of inequality, exploitation, and cruelty, a point Martens frequently makes. In this regard, Martens embraces his film's own "inconsequentiality."[34] Acknowledging this failure of art's critical ambitions—documenting poverty for the sake of empathy—leads, however, to an uncertain politicization. Yet that may also be

31   Susie Linfield, preface to *The Cruel Radiance: Photography and Political Violence* (Chicago: Chicago University Press, 2010), xv. On page 129, she cites Hannah Arendt, who called compassion a "co-suffering" that produces a "community of interest with the oppressed and exploited." See Hannah Arendt, *On Revolution* (New York: Penguin, 1990), 88.

32   This passage was cited by Martens in Demos, "Toward a New Institutional Critique," 97. Sontag continues: "It seems too simple to elect sympathy (as a feeling generated by photographs). The imaginary proximity to the suffering inflicted on others that is granted by images suggests a link between the faraway sufferers—seen close-up on the television screen—and the privileged viewer that is simply untrue, that is yet once more a mystification of our real relations to power." *Regarding the Pain of Others* (New York: Picador, 2003), 102.

33   Martens, quoted in Demos, "Toward a New Institutional Critique," 91.

34   "I hope my piece shows this *cost* of art's inconsequentiality, and, in the same line, the cost of *beauty*," says Martens. Ibid., 98. On this point, also see Martens's comments in "Roundtable on *Episode III (Enjoy Poverty)*."

the point: though Martens's film doesn't identify what strategy one should follow in the wake of its deconstruction of a certain brand of political art, it leaves a vacuum in which we as viewers must determine the next step. As Thomas Keenan suggests: "The film seems to place a great deal of faith in our educability, in our ability to correct those mistakes, and in the capacity of its images to guide us to 'make choices,' 'to learn how to deal with life,' life as it is and not how we might hope it could be. [...] In the end, it hands over the responsibility for action and decision to us, and awaits our response."[35]

—

In a recent panel discussion on the "poverty pornography" that characterizes so many journalistic and artistic approaches to sub-Saharan Africa, Achille Mbembe questioned why such stereotyping and demeaning images continue to circulate and command critical attention.[36] Considering Martens's and Jaar's work, it is clear that what drives the industry is the conjunction of humanitarian concern and neoliberal incentive, and in this regard these projects are worthy of critical debate. But even while they importantly expose the financial causes that drive the political economy of poverty pornography, one can hardly disagree with Mbembe's important point: a danger remains of exhausting critical energies on such work while overlooking the many local practices that show positive representations of collective solidarity and political agency posed against the media spectacle of African misery (even though the either/or imperative is, once again, a false alternative).

Consider one last model, which approaches African poverty and neoliberal globalization from an African perspective: *Bamako*, by Malian director Abderrahmane Sissako. The feature-length 2006 film stages a political-legal theater in order to place the central financial institutions of globalization on trial for the disastrous effect they've had on African economies and standards of living, subjecting its peoples to malnutrition, chronic illiteracy, unemployment, and a lack of decent living conditions. The witnesses come successively before the court to tell their stories of how they have suffered under the austerity budgets forced onto struggling African nations by the World Bank, IMF, and "Paris Club" through immeasurable blackmail and coercion. One highlight is the testimony of Mali's former minister of culture, Aminata Traoré, who explains that

35   See Keenan's comments in "Roundtable on *Episode III (Enjoy Poverty)*," 12.

36   See the panel "Poverty Pornography? A Critical Analysis of Contemporary Photographic Practice in Africa," with Thembinkosi Guniwe, Khwezi Gule, Gabi Ngcobo, and Achille Mbembe, moderated by Ayana Jackson (Gallery MOMO, Johannesburg, August 5, 2010). Mbembe's statement is available online at: http://witspress.book.co.za/blog/2010/08/20/video-achille-mbembe-on-poverty-pornography/.

"Africa is rich in natural resources, yet has been exploited, brutalised and impoverished. [...] I am against the fact that Africa's main characteristic in the eyes of the world is its poverty. Africa is rather the victim of its wealth." Traoré continues: "I would rather talk about pauperization than poverty. In talking of pauperization, you pinpoint the mechanisms."[37] Her point is further clarified by witnesses who identify the outlandish disproportion of debt repayments foisted on African nations, repayments that typically take up nearly half of national budgets compared to the less than 10 percent they can then spend on social programs such as education, health care, and infrastructure. We thereby confront once again the global paradigm in which poverty doesn't simply exist as such—as if it were an uncontrollable natural disaster—but is the result of the neocolonial financial pillaging of Africa by G8 nations.[38]

Sissako studied in Moscow during the 1980s and thus represents one of the last in a line of filmmakers to produce revolutionary anticolonial African cinema, which stretches back to the 1960s and '70s, when figures such as Ousmane Sembène and Sarah Maldoror took part in skills exchange in the Soviet Union, generating a radical pedagogy and cinematic practice of resistance and politicization.[39] Although it appears as a vanishing history in today's post-Cold War context—without socialist nations to support militant cinema against neoliberal regimes, an NGOcracy of humanitarian depoliticization is the dominant response—Sissako importantly makes a crucial stand against the current forms of imperialism. He joins the ranks of other African artists and collectives who continue to struggle for political resistance, for decolonization from corporate globalization, and for practices that strengthen local communities, self-governance, and sovereign independence.[40] It is here that we find the solution that *Enjoy Poverty* fails to provide.

Rather than perpetuate the image economy of African poverty, *Bamako* generates a cinematic stage and communal space of politicization directed against global financial arrangements, which animate local protest culture and social movements. Building a makeshift set in the midst of a domestic courtyard, uniting international and community

37   Abderrahmane Sissako, dir., *Bamako* (New York: Louverture Films, 2006).

38   For further evidence, see James Ferguson, *Global Shadows: Africa in the Neoliberal World Order* (Durham, NC: Duke University Press, 2006); and Harrison, *Neoliberal Africa*. For proposed solutions that contest the approaches of the IMF and World Bank, see Cavanagh et al., *Alternatives to Economic Globalization*.

39   On this history, see "The Militant Image: A Ciné Geography," eds. Kodwo Eshun and Ros Gray, special issue, *Third Text* 25, no. 1 (January 2011).

40   Consider, for instance, Le Groupe Amos, founded in 1989 in Kinshasa: composed of social and political activists, they use pedagogical tools such as essays, pamphlets, cartoons, theatrical productions, and radio broadcasts to educate and raise awareness of violence against women, democratic election processes, and local histories and culture, and work with illiterate communities via vernacular languages such as Lingala, Kikongo, Swahili, and Tshiluba. See Okwui Enwezor, "The Production of Social Space as Artwork," in *Collectivism after Modernism: The Art of Social Imagination after 1945*, eds. Blake Stimson and Gregory Sholette (Minneapolis: University of Minnesota Press, 2007).

justice, the film interweaves legal testimony about the devastating effects of global financial instruments with scenes featuring the diversity, vibrancy, and also the banality of everyday life in Mali. In other words, the film goes beyond the negative fatalism of media and artistic stereotypes that haunt Western audiences. In this regard it is significant that *Bamako* has been screened not only in European film festivals, but also for local audiences in the same courtyard where the film was shot. In doing so, the film transcends divisions between North and South, and attempts to build political solidarity across those borders.

These still-emerging trade routes and communication networks—including the South–South axis that Mosquera calls to be further developed—do pose fresh possibilities for the circulation of imagery and information, joining transnational political alliances with artistic practices across the growing divisions of political, economic, and social inequality. Especially in the context of the ongoing right-wing movement of European and American political discourse and the widening gaps between North and South, it is crucial to develop these connections toward a transformative political project—one of social and economic justice—rather than allowing the forces of homogenization, economic inequality, and anti-democracy to continue unchallenged. If Martens and Jaar identify the barriers, Sissako points a way forward. At the end of *Bamako*'s trial, the court aptly sentences the World Bank and the IMF to serve humanity for perpetuity—in fidelity to their original mandate, to foster long-term development and poverty reduction. That is, even as one witness laments, "Why waste your time? No one will listen."

Still, Martens's work makes a substantial contribution to a new kind of institutional critique: it breaks out of the Western parochialism of such practice, obsessed as it often is with the ideological functions of museums and galleries; investigates the image economy of humanitarianism set in the expanded field of neoliberal globalization; and critically analyzes the production of Congolese poverty in relation to macroeconomic institutions like the World Bank and media enterprises like AFP.[41] Most importantly, *Enjoy Poverty* situates itself in these very conditions.

After viewing Martens's work, it becomes impossible to look at other documentary accounts in the same way—that is, without considering their embeddedness in the market and in the economy of images. As Butler argues: "If there is a critical role for visual culture during times of war it is precisely to thematize the forcible frame, the one that conducts the dehumanizing

41   On recent approaches to institutional critique, see Alexander Alberro and Blake Stimson, eds., *Institutional Critique: An Anthology of Artists' Writings* (Cambridge, MA: MIT Press, 2009); and Gerald Raunig and Gene Ray, eds., *Art and Contemporary Critical Practice: Reinventing Institutional Critique* (London: Mayfly, 2009).

norm, that restricts what is perceivable and, indeed, what can be."[42] Such is exactly what Martens has done, breaking through the typical layers of negation and structures of invisibility to lay bare the "forcible frame" of the image in which poverty is produced and consumed. He does so particularly where empathy figures as a dubious engine of political transformation, and, more often than not, an excuse for inaction. If *Enjoy Poverty* invites—without predetermining—a response, then it is one that, in my view, would reject the conditions witnessed in the film, abandon the pornography of poverty, and assess the unjust structures of globalization that are poverty's conditions of possibility. It would also entail the promotion of artistic and activist practices that facilitate positive social transformation in zones of conflict, rather than remaining enthralled and immobilized by poverty's spectacularized and commodified representations.[43]

[42] Butler, "Torture and the Ethics of Photography," 100.

[43] During the summer of 2012, Martens initiated a new five-year project in the DRC with his establishment of the Institute for Human Activities, which intends to bring economic development to the impoverished area of Boteka, near Mbandaka in the northwest of the country. The institute aims to realize its proposed model of "reverse gentrification"—whereby the site of artistic intervention will be unified with the site of artistic consumption—and thereby to escape the quandary Martens sees in so many other artistic projects, which base their interventions in Peru or Morocco but end up selling their videos and photographs in Chelsea and Berlin. See http://www.humanactivities.org.

5. A Postcolonial *Monstrum*: The Photographs of **Pieter Hugo**

We are presently "living in the aftermath of the many metanarratives that have shaped twentieth-century Africa—colonialism, independence, third-worldism, apartheid, post-apartheid, in the 'wreckages' of a set of utopias and dystopias." So explains South African cultural theorist Sarah Nuttall in a recent discussion on photography from South Africa. But the situation, as she continues to point out, is not all negative: "The idea is that living in the wreckage, in the ruins, of these grand schemes, can constitute a productive place [...] to think from, enabling us as it does to work with bits and pieces in order to make something else, something less coherent but more complex."[1] Nuttall's provocative insight is also an apt characterization of the historical context and geopolitical field in which South African photographer Pieter Hugo operates, his work pointing critically and creatively in many historical directions, mapping out the uncertain and complex present of the African postcolony.

Hugo is known for his quasi-documentary images of contemporary sub-Saharan Africa—the very status of the "documentary" being what his portrayals put into question. Like the work of Guy Tillim and Zwelethu Mthethwa—other notable South African photographers to whom Hugo could be productively compared—Hugo's work is frequently organized around the typological study of members of particular social groups, defined variously by their shared type of work, geographical context, or physical condition. These include a range of portraits from honey collectors, to those who have died from AIDS-related illnesses, people with albinism, inhabitants of the northern South African town of Musina, and victims of the Rwandan genocide. Organized in series, his photography engages with the complex dialectic between identity and difference that typically emerges in the formation of typologies, which is a well-established category of photographic practice in both contemporary and historical periods (think of the diverse models of David Goldblatt, Thomas Ruff, and Santu Mofokeng, and historically, the work of Eugène Atget, August Sander, and Walker Evans). Even while Hugo's photography explores distinct social categories, its emphasis falls on the singularity of his given subjects, indicated by the artist's practice of titling his images after the names of his sitters. As a result, his portraits stress a resistance to the potential homogeneity of the photographic series and the structure of representation, presenting viewers with the more complex disjunction between the standardization of a particular category and the differentiation that confers a specificity on *this* or *that* particular image. His work thereby

1   Sarah Nuttall, from her conversation with Tamar Garb, Achille Mbembe, Riason Naidoo, and Colin Richards, "Thinking from the South: Reflections on Image and Place," in *Figures & Fictions: Contemporary South African Photography*, ed. Tamar Garb (Göttingen: Steidl, 2011), 302.

offers a lesson about how photography can both engage with the readymade spectacle and uncover the singularity of lived experience in postcolonial Africa.

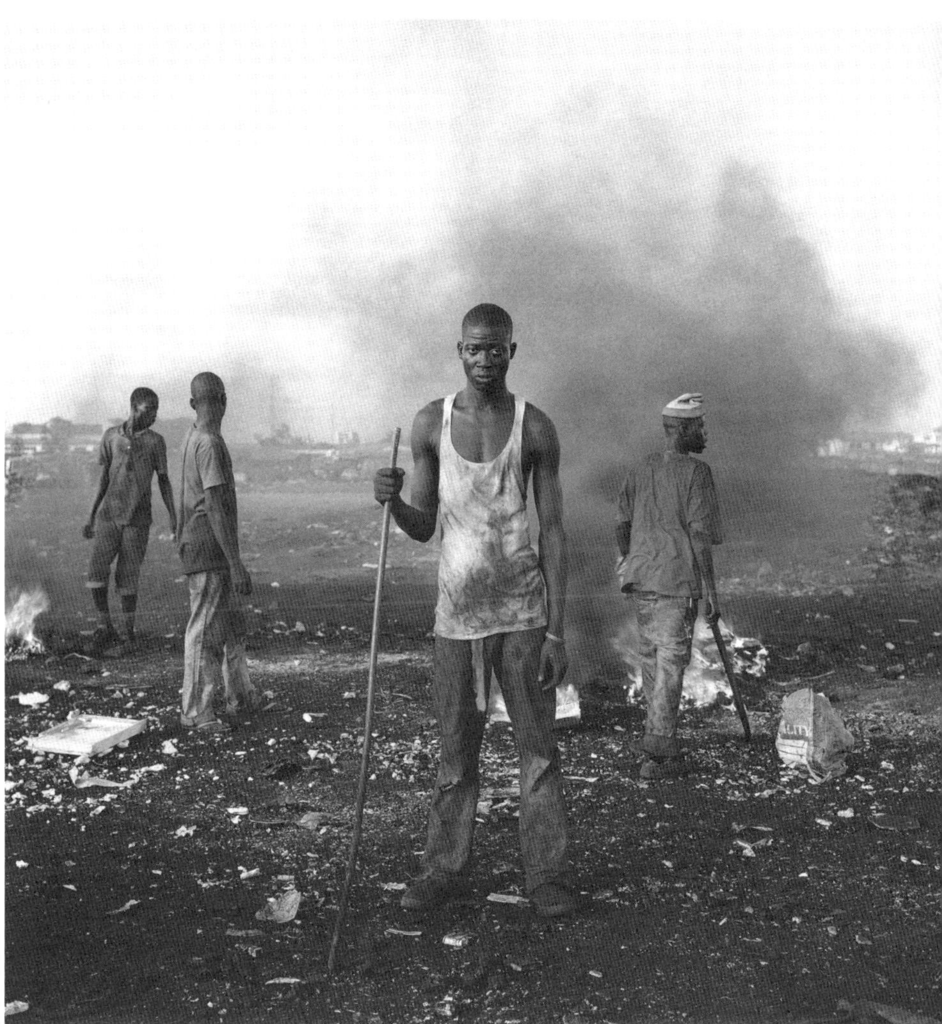

Pieter Hugo, *David Akore, Agbogbloshie Market, Accra, Ghana*, 2010

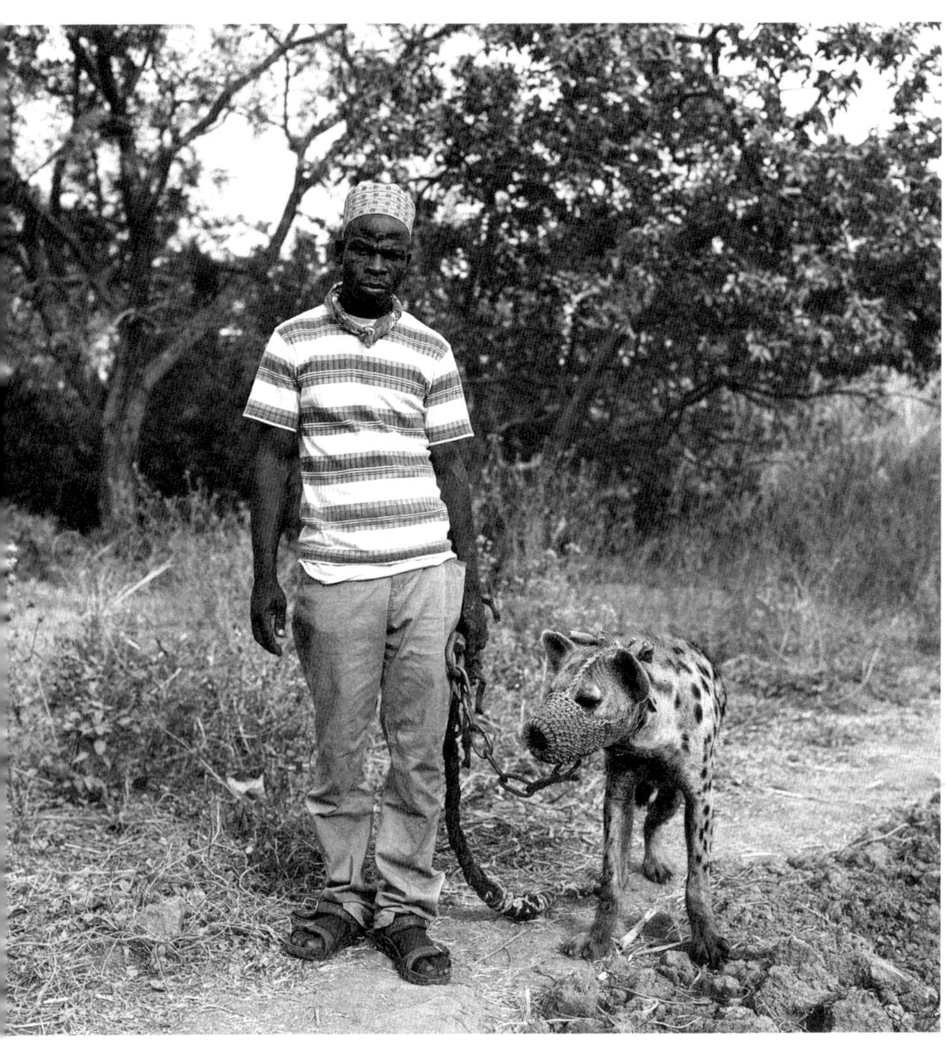

Pieter Hugo, *Abdullahi Ahmadu with Mainasara, Nigeria*, 2005

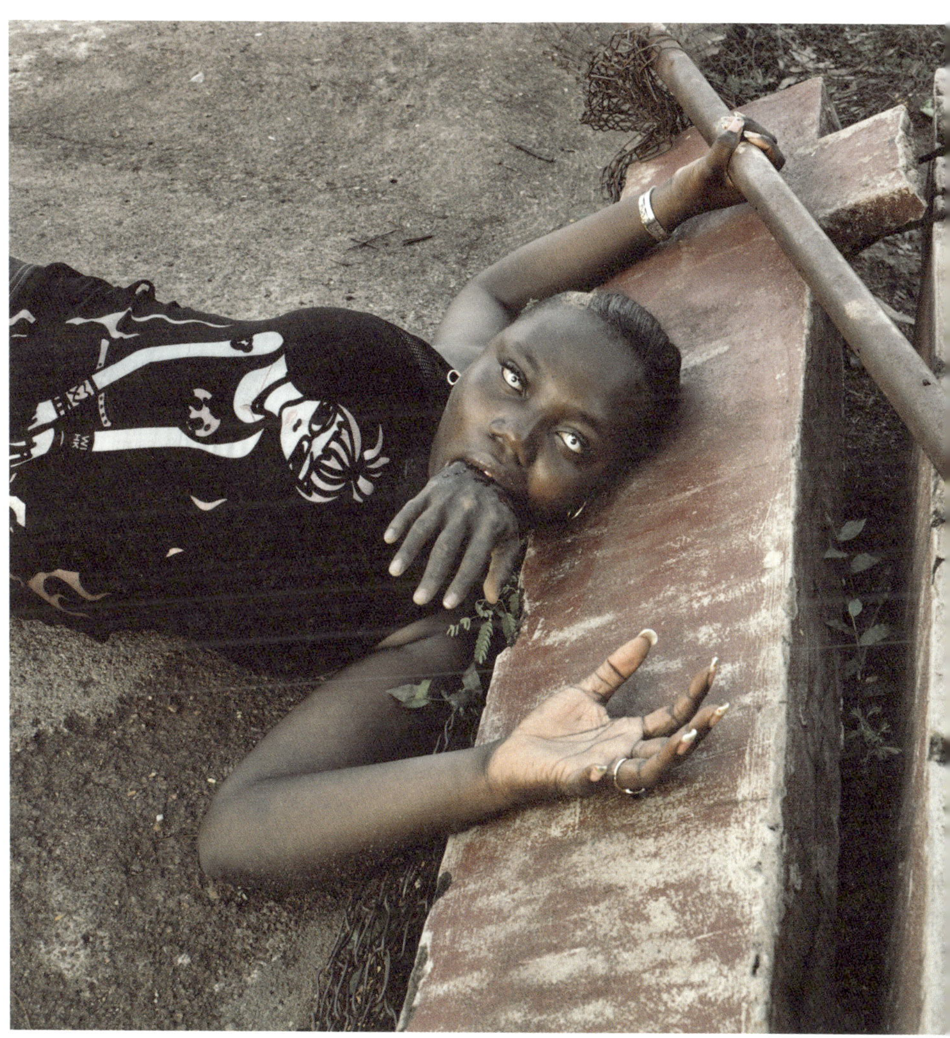

Pieter Hugo, *Princess Adaobi. Enugu, Nigeria*, 2008

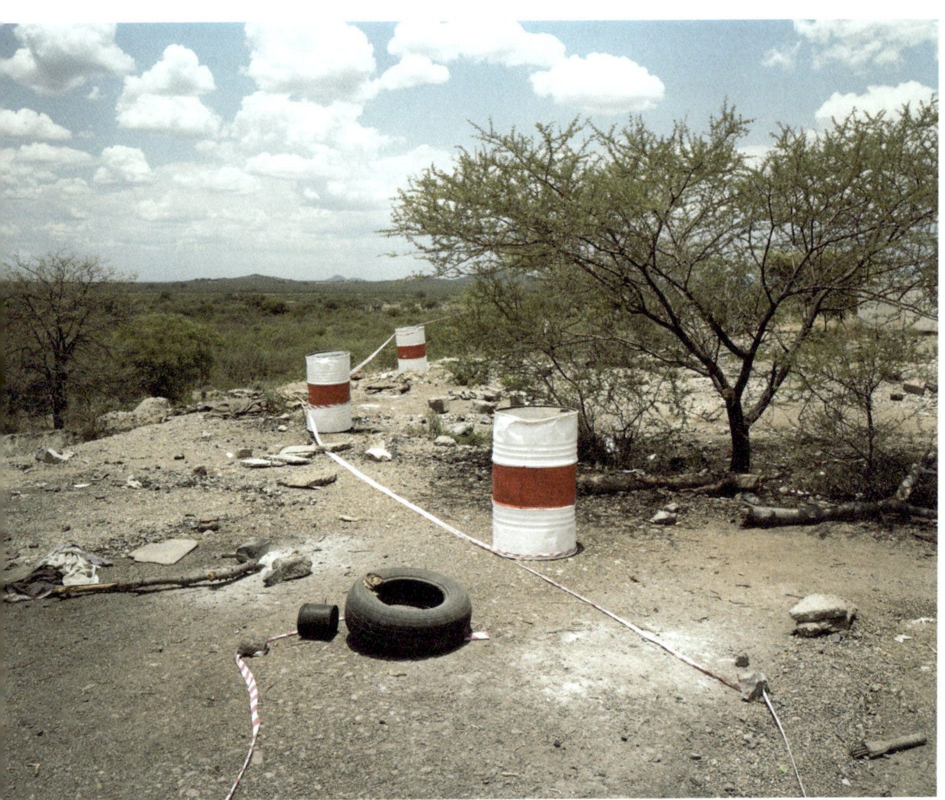

Pieter Hugo, *At the abandoned Campbell copper mine*, 2006

What does the postcolony look like in Hugo's portrayals? One particularly disturbing description is provided by Permanent Error (2009–10), a series that depicts the hellish zone of ecological disaster that is Agbogbloshie Market, the main center for e-waste "recycling" in Accra, Ghana. Rather than representing a model of the green reuse of electronic material, Hugo's images reveal an infernal operation that is a disastrous and toxic site of plastic-burning heaps of rubbish, picked through by forsaken scavengers hoping to extract a few bits of valuable metal. A very different image of the postcolony is offered in the carnivalesque iconography of The Hyena & Other Men (2005–07), for which Hugo focuses on a group of Nigerian men who have tamed wild hyenas, baboons, and snakes for display in sideshows, creatively profiting from local resources. Self-exoticizing figures, they define a mode of informal survival in the deteriorating economic

   A Postcolonial *Monstrum*: The Photographs of Pieter Hugo

circumstances of Nigeria's urban periphery and suggest forms of self-possession and independent organization in a world of lawlessness disarray. Still another vision emerges with Nollywood (2008–09), Hugo's study of the dramatic actors from the Nigerian film industry who are pictured in fantasy-based costumes posing for the camera off set. The cycle suggests a zone of fictionalization in everyday life where masquerading offers the possibility for experimental subjective construction and imaginative play. Yet another facet emerges in Messina/Musina (2006), which portrays a postapartheid space of ruins in the northernmost town in South Africa. There, on the border with Zimbabwe, Hugo investigated the social conditions in the era of desegregation and national rebuilding, finding the results far from even: impoverished economic existence pressures the appearance of social normality, while the signs of lingering racism and an artificial commonality are equally apparent.

In other words, Hugo's disparate imagery visualizes the postcolony as diverse zones of non-unifiable heterogeneity. His various portraits open onto seemingly infinite and localized cultures of social mixture, with geopolitical, economic, and social diversity within and between them, never offering a single moral, pat conclusion, or continuous geography. His imagery thereby reaffirms the complexity of existing views of sub-Saharan postcolonial African urbanism, which is frequently seen to exist between two interpretive poles. On the one hand, we have an image of cities in crisis undergoing spatial entropy, declining infrastructure, the unraveling of traditional institutions—with growing economic and political inequality, increasing violence and disorder, and corrupt governments dependent on foreign aid. On the other hand, there is the presence of dynamic energy despite the crumbling sociopolitical and economic environment, with great potential for creative urbanism, new formations of postcolonial identity and sociality, hopeful modes of informal survival, and the resurgence of political struggles for economic independence, social justice, and environmental sustainability.[2] Hugo's work indeed touches on the utopian possibilities and dystopian "wreckages" of African contemporaneity. Accordingly, his photographs approach Nuttall's hopeful point that the broken- down aftermath of twentieth-century African modernity can nevertheless constitute a "productive place to think from" and "to make something else."

2   For complex views of sub-Saharan African urbanism, postcolonial conditions, social experience, and economic reality, see Enwezor et al., *Under Siege*; AbdouMaliq Simone, *City Life from Jakarta to Dakar* (London: Routledge, 2010); Ferguson, *Global Shadows*; Harrison, *Neoliberal Africa*; and Wangari Maathai, *The Challenge for Africa* (New York: Arrow, 2010).

Set in numerous geopolitical situations, Hugo's work characterizes a new internationalism in postapartheid Africa open to white South Africans—that is, following the lifting of the prohibition on white South Africans traveling to other African countries during apartheid. Countries like Ghana and Nigeria once banned their entrance as an act of protest against the system of legal and institutional racial segregation enforced by the National Party governments of South Africa between 1948 and 1994, which, as is widely known, had severely restricted the rights of the country's majority "nonwhite" inhabitants and maintained white supremacy and minority rule by Afrikaners. Following the collapse of that system, there has been a newfound freedom for those with resources to travel the African continent, and Hugo has done so extensively, visiting Botswana for his series on judges; Durban, South Africa for his cycle on taxi washers; Abuja, Nigeria, for The Hyena & Other Men and Nollywood; Ghana for The Wild Honey Collectors and Barristers and Solicitors; Rwanda to photograph the vestiges of the genocide; and Ghana again for Permanent Error. In many ways, Hugo exemplifies the nomadic contemporary artist in the period of postcolonial globalization, and, more specifically, represents a new category of the "Afropolitan" as one who travels extensively on the continent in an era of postapartheid African reintegration.[3]

Travel may stimulate the potential for greater global insight and trans-African awareness, but also brings with it certain dangers. As Tamar Garb observes, with such itinerant projects, we must ask if we encounter the formation of a "new colonial gaze of the continent," one promoted by "the hunger and the markets that demand and consume these images in North America and Europe."[4] The point raises the specter of the presumed inequality between the African *subjects* of documentary portrayals and the privileged *viewers* and *collectors* in the North, a problematic relation continuous with the increasing global disparity within and between the North and South. In regard to this important question, one could also respond that patronage alone cannot determine the scope of photography's meanings and significance. Moreover, Hugo's photography operates critically in precisely this space of unequal relationality within and between former colonizer and colonized nations, between the exposure of economic and social devastation on the continent and the ethics of viewership outside of postcolonial Africa, as we shall see. Okwui Enwezor voiced a related concern in 1997, only a few years after the end of apartheid, in his

3   On nomadism in contemporary art, see T. J. Demos, "The Ends of Exile: Toward a Coming Universality," in *Altermodern: Tate Triennial 2009*, ed. Nicolas Bourriaud (London: Tate Britain, 2009). On the "Afropolitan," see Nuttall's comments in Garb et al., "Thinking from the South," 302.

4   Quoted in ibid., 307.

study of artistic representations of the black subject in contemporary art. He wrote:

> As we all know, for the greater part of European presence in South Africa, the spectres, the haunted and historical memory, the glow, the consciousness, the metaphorical speech of European identity has stood solidly, for half a millennium, on a nationalism of white supremacist ideology. [In the wake of apartheid, South Africa must confront] the huge task of decolonization [and] the inability of a once dominant white culture to deal with its diminished role and sense of superior entitlement in the cultural and political life of the nation.[5]

Enwezor raises an important point, even if it is questionable to relegate white South Africans who have lived on the continent for generations to a foreign "European presence." Still, a pertinent question remains whether or not this situation of apartheid nostalgia is still the case today. Much progress has been made in recent years in terms of the decolonization of racial categories, laws, and institutions in South Africa. However, the country continues to confront the prolongation of financial colonization by international donors and neoliberal arrangements, which keeps African nations—including South Africa—locked in a position of debt servitude and growing internal inequality. This brings with it the increase in crime and social breakdown that comes with the rise of poverty. The ghosts of colonial modernity live on in such economic disparity, governmental tyranny, corruption, and poverty.

Not that Hugo pictures this economic situation per se, but he does focus on the social and subjective aspects of life in the neocolonial conditions of Africa. Hugo's images show the present postcolony struggling with precarity and creative survival, while implicitly acknowledging the failures of past large-scale projects of state development in sub-Saharan Africa as they fell victim to the subsequent catastrophe of structural adjustment programs and economic shock therapy of the 1980s and '90s.[6] And if he grants insight to this complex history, he does so without any nostalgia for the unfulfilled project of apartheid. In the place of such nostalgia for that system of racialist political and social separation, Hugo offers, in my reading, a complex iconography, a *monstrum*—in the sense of both a revelation and a portentous manifestation—of both the current geography of social, subjective, economic,

5   Okwui Enwezor, "Reframing the Black Subject: Ideology and Fantasy in Contemporary South African Representation," *Third Text* 11, no. 40 (Autumn 1997): 25, 27.

6   Naomi Klein points out that "not only did the ANC [African National Congress under Thabo Mbeki] renege on Mandela's original pledge of 'the nationalization of the mines, banks and monopoly industry' but because of the debt, it was doing the opposite—selling off national assets to make good on the debts of its oppressors," which was mediated by the IMF and the World Bank. *Shock Doctrine*, 212.

and ecological wreckage, and the field of potentiality for local socioeconomic creativity and subjective imagination. This complex picture is clearly situated beyond and in contradiction to the stereotypical and exoticizing colonial gaze that Garb and Enwezor identify.

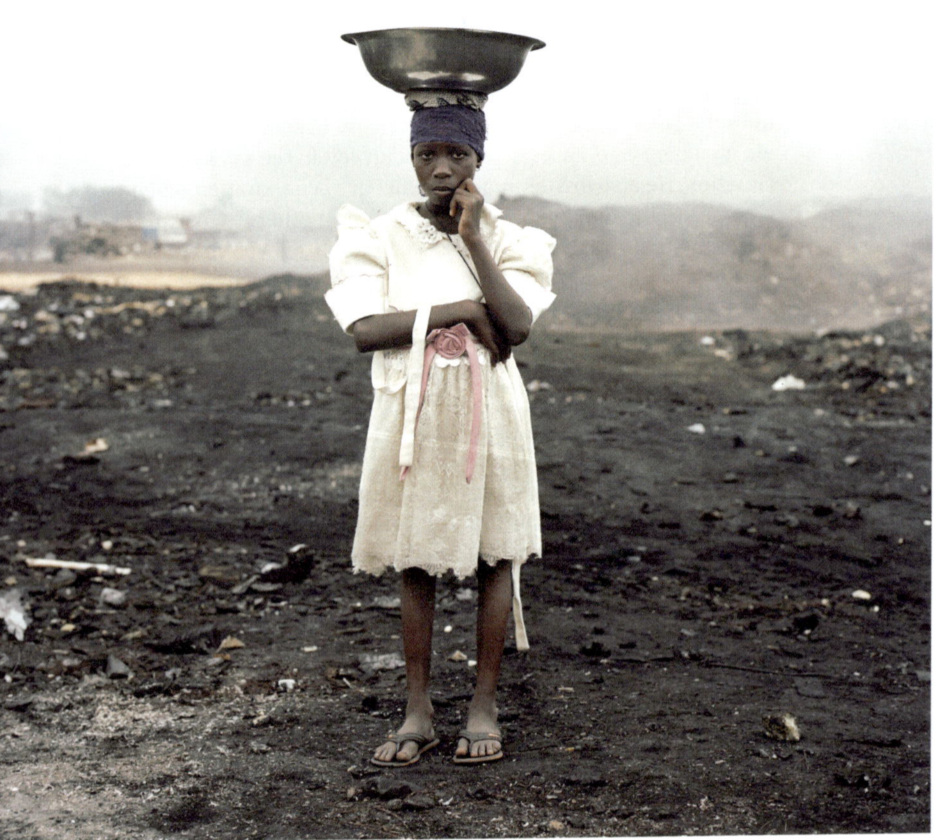

Pieter Hugo, *Naasra Yeti, Agbogbloshie Market, Accra, Ghana*, 2009

The tension between the two—in particular, between ecological disaster and creative survival—is palpable in Hugo's recent photographic series Permanent Error, which portrays the laborers and hellish landscape of the e-waste disaster site of Agbogbloshie Market. In one image, a teenage girl, Naasra Yeti, appears incongruously wearing a cream-colored dress and standing disjunctively amid an apocalyptic environment of blackened earth, burning fires of plastic devices, and noxious fumes. She looks directly into the camera, her collection bowl resting on her head. Her regard—an inquisitive address common in Hugo's numerous series—is arresting, suggesting that of the condemned, but one who is nevertheless self-possessed. The images present an astonishing dialectic between figure and environment. Bringing the two together—the overwhelming alien landscape that appears so deathly and the girl who, despite being situated in that context, remains as if supernaturally among the living—Hugo pressures the believability of his realism. The evident self-consciousness of the subject is an outcome of the artist's use of a large-format camera, making Hugo's presence undeniably felt in the photographic situation. He also invites an intersubjective collaboration when it comes to the making of images.[7] Sitters, in other words, are never presented as passive objects or objectified victims in his imagery, but rather appear as knowing agents who, like Yeti, are participating in the determination of their pose and appearance.

In other untitled photographs from the series, we see more of the blackened earth set alight with multiple fires, and in their dark plumes of gray smoke scavengers go about their business. Looking at the images, their untitled status intimating a place beyond words, one can almost smell the acrid fumes and taste the sooty air. In these other images of the series, Hugo reveals the human cost of technological progress by showing its dark ecological underside. Thanks to environmental activist organizations like Greenpeace, we know that around fifty million tons of e-waste are produced globally every year, which includes computer equipment, entertainment electronics, mobile phones, and other items such as television sets and refrigerators.[8] Yet only some 25 percent of the European Union's share is collected and treated effectively. The rest goes to dump sites in Africa, such as the Agbogbloshie Market, where informal and unregulated systems of recycling have sprung up to recover metals such as aluminum, copper, gold, silver, and platinum from the waste. To retrieve them, foragers commonly toss the equipment into open fires to melt away the worthless plastics, a process that releases

7   Hugo discusses his ethics of making images of others in his conversation with Joanna Lehan, in *Messina/Musina* (Rome: Punctum, 2007), n.p.

8   "Poisoning the Poor: Electronic Waste in Ghana," *Greenpeace*, August 5, 2008.

harmful carcinogens and neurotoxins into the air, which is clearly visible in the miasmic environments captured in Hugo's images.[9] Once incinerated, the bonfire refuse then finds its way into drainage ditches and waterways, as the toxic cocktail spikes the Densu River and leads into the Atlantic Ocean.

Making matters worse, much of this "recycling" work is carried out by children, and, indeed, Hugo's photographs show mostly young people engaged in this dangerous labor. Using their bare hands with no protective equipment, they interact with hazardous substances known to interfere with sexual reproduction and cause cancer. Sending used electronic equipment to "developing" countries is often hailed as bridging the digital divide, but in reality it means creating a toxic landfill that poisons the environment of the poor (and eventually the world), gradually destroying the natural resources of nations ill-equipped to deal with such hazardous waste. In fact, according to international treaties, the export of toxic waste—including e-waste—from wealthy developed countries is forbidden. However, in European legislation the term "reuse" offers a loophole, allowing opportunistic agents to ship old electronics to countries like Ghana and Nigeria, even though the majority of equipment is beyond repair.[10]

Hugo's images do not present the specifics of these legalistic details (although his catalog on the series does refer to the environmental reports); rather, the images focus with a bracing directness on the workers at the dump site, offering poignant portraits of people whose only apparent livelihood is to pick through the trash of the North, slowly killing themselves as they do so. The photographs thus capture the normally invisible "death-worlds" of the South, where the "necropolitics" of the postcolony are enacted, and the division between the living and the dead loses its clear definition.[11] Addressing the contemporary "wretched of the earth," Hugo's photographs nonetheless depict individual self-conscious subjects—as they do in The Hyena & Other Men, Nollywood, and Messina/Musina—extending dignity to these agents of their own appearance as much as the forlorn objects of the viewer's attention. Gazing into the camera, these figures connect visually with

9   In 2008, Greenpeace took samples of the burned soil in Agbogbloshie and found high concentrations of lead, mercury, thallium, hydrogen cyanide, and PVC. Hugo also includes a thorough list, based on the United Nations Environment Programme's account in 2009, in his catalog *Permanent Error* (Munich: Prestel, 2011), 11–13.

10   See Adrian Lewis, "Europe Breaking Electronic Waste Export Ban," *BBC News*, August 4, 2010.

11   Mbembe, "Necropolitics," 40.

12   Madhav Gadgil and Ramachandra Guha, "Ideologies of Environmentalism," in *Ecology and Equity: The Use and Abuse of Nature in Contemporary India* (London: Routledge, 1995), 98.

13   The series could also be positioned as a critical retort to the infamous comment of Lawrence Summers, at the time the World Bank's chief economist, who explained that developing countries are under-polluted: "A given amount of health-impairing pollution should be done in the country with the lowest cost, which will be the country with the lowest wages," he explained in a memo publicized by a critic of the World Bank's environmental record. "I think the economic logic behind dumping a load of toxic waste in the lowest-wage country is impeccable and we should face up to that." Quoted in "Furor on Memo at World Bank," *New York Times*, February 7, 1992.

the spectators of the photographs, as if asking us if we are aware of our complicity in this situation. Yet these photographs don't so much elicit an empathic regard for victims, as in conventional understandings of socially concerned documentary photography, but instead reveal the hidden truth of recycling—what Madhav Gadgil and Ramachandra Guha criticize as an "environmentalism born out of affluence"—which in effect means revealing how a hollow green rhetoric can mask the way in which the North's environmentalism ends up contributing to the misery of the less fortunate.[12] The photographic series thus reveals a conflict within environmentalism, making evident the imbalance and injustice in global systems divided between wealth and poverty, developed and underdeveloped.[13]

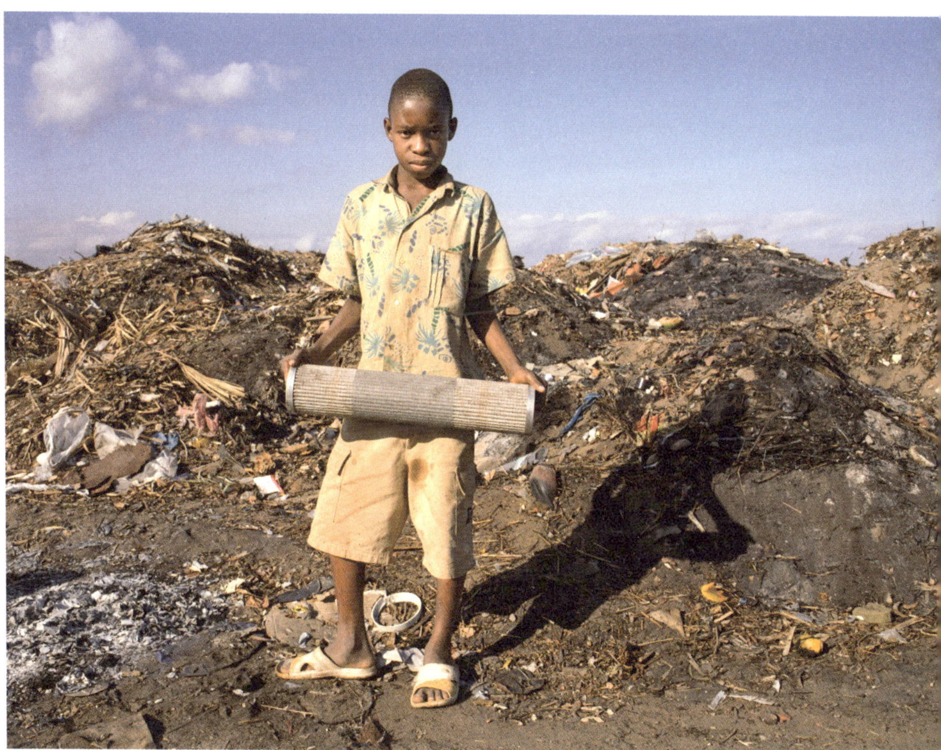

Zwelethu Mthethwa, *Untitled (Gladiator 5)*, 2008

    Return to the Postcolony

In this regard, Hugo's images resonate with the work of other South African photographers who also depict the economic inequality between developed and underdeveloped nations—including Goldblatt's images of squatters of trash dumps outside Johannesburg, and Mthethwa's photographs of child scavengers in Mozambique. They also connect with the work of other photographers who have focused on the "recycling" sites in Ghana, including that of Nyaba Leon Ouedraogo, a photographer from Burkina Faso whose series entitled The Hell of Copper (2008) offers an overview of the geographical sites, along with portraits of scavengers standing amid the burned and polluted environment. Such work insists that the worlds of affluence and abandonment be interconnected rather than dismissed in Europe's self-congratulatory greenwashing campaigns. Here, art proposes a redistributed form of appearance that suggests a different politics: by focusing on systems of inequality, it inspires demands for justice. Hugo's images do so by establishing a tension between the idealism of pictorial unity (presenting well-composed photographs, complete in and of themselves, within clearly organized typologies of compositional and formal consistency) and the relations of inequality between the image's subject and its privileged viewers, a relationality that forms part of the very critical traction that Hugo's work constructs. In addition, the photographs catalyze tensions between the luxury of Afropolitan mobility and the slavish immobility of the scavengers, a relation redoubled at the level of the disparity between the privileged viewer/consumer and the impoverished object of the gaze; these relations of inequality are exactly the expanded photographic terms in which viewers are implicated. In this way, his photographs not only *represent*, but also *act* politically, implicating viewers in the world the images depict. Here, we are also left with an aesthetics of haunting, where the afterlife of our technology that carries glimmers of immateriality and virtuality returns in infernal visions of its environmental destruction and deathly material social effects. By showing the waste cycles and environmental destruction of capitalism's systems of overproduction, Hugo's work politicizes this ecology and contests the normally hidden arrangements that allow innocent life to continue to be sacrificed in this way.

—

In his series Messina/Musina, which investigates the social environment of the northernmost town in South Africa, Hugo mixes environmental ecology with social anthropology. Formerly known as Messina, the town changed

14   Quoted in his conversation with Lehan, in *Messina/Musina*, n.p.

its name in 2002 to correct the colonial misspelling. Positioned on a major northern highway and located in the center of the Bushveld, the area is a destination for miners and farmworkers, and equally a hub for prostitution. Police monitor and control the porous border, where the smuggling of contraband and illegal migration is common. Hugo's photographs focus on individuals and families, interiors and landscapes, and—building on the tradition of Goldblatt's piercing model of social documentary—they reflect on "the wounds and scars of race, class and nationality that persist [in] a country in the process of self-destructing," as Hugo explains.[14]

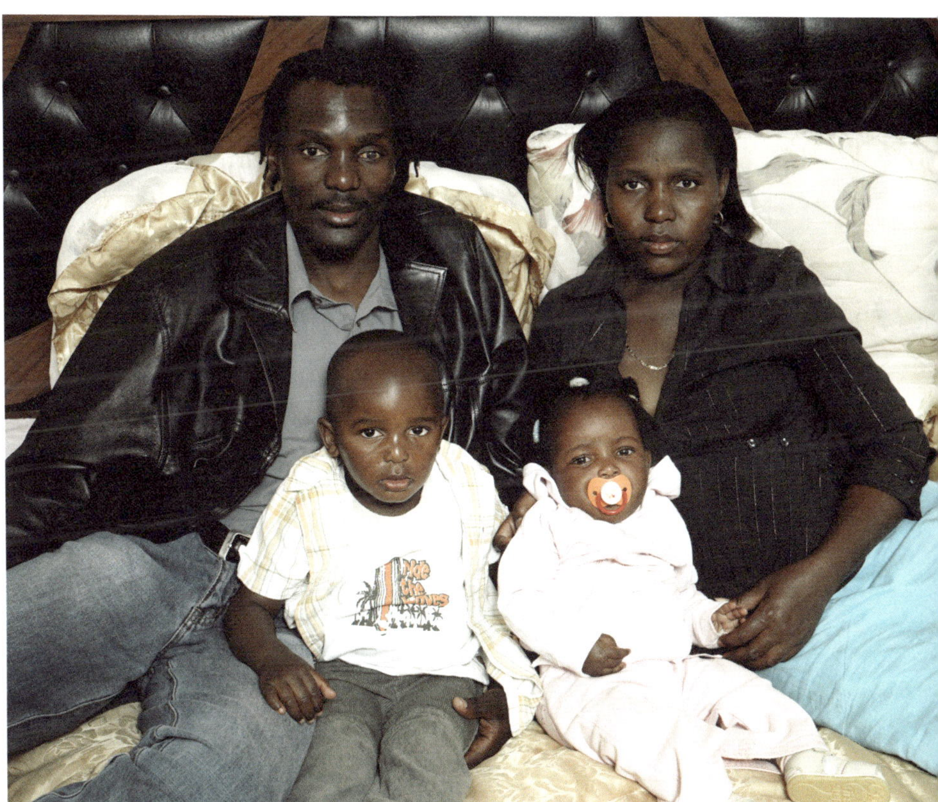

Pieter Hugo, *Kelly and Zanele Nggaba with their children Bongani and Mbali*, 2006

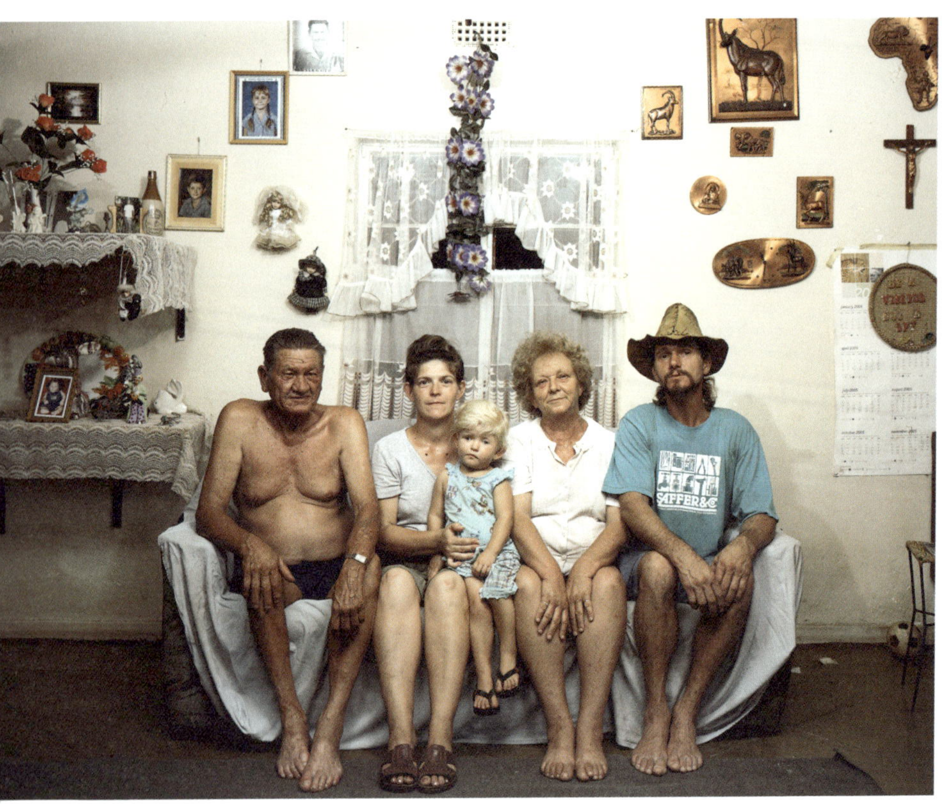

Pieter Hugo, *Jan, Martie, Kayala, Florence and Basil Meyer in their home*, 2006

There are various subcategories at work in Messina/ Musina, which together propose an archival study of the social systems and built environment of the area. Family portraits constitute the main subject—for instance, *Kelly and Zanele Nggaba with their children Bongani and Mbali* presents the black family close-up sitting on a couch and addressing the camera; *Martie and Morkel Smith, their son Stephen and his fiancée Illze Venter with their dog Snooze* offers a corresponding image of a white family, the father and son wearing matching baseball caps and jean vests filled with patches and buttons. These group portraits are intermixed with images that portray the littered and abandoned natural environment of apparent desolation, such as *Discarded tomatoes and chillies in the veld*, showing a brown field covered with the red fruits and vegetables that initially appear like flowers; and *The veld outside town*, a wasteland of trash amid a backdrop of wilderness, in a way similar to *Baobob and boxes*

140   A Postcolonial *Monstrum*: The Photographs of Pieter Hugo *in the veld*. Others show close-ups of roadkill, such as *On the high-way outside Musina*, which portrays an eviscerated fox, its organs spilled on the asphalt road, the shot taken from directly above so that it almost looks as though the grotesque carcass is standing. Still others depict cemeteries and the interiors of funeral homes, including *Graveyard and the town's sewerage pipe* and *Makhado Funeral Undertakers and Tombstones*, which, in a gesture of macabre humor, shows an infant-sized coffin leaning up against a brick wall near a portable hot plate. In the domestic scenes, families appear situated in awkward and artificial groupings—*Jan, Martie, Kayala, Florence and Basil Meyer in their home* is exemplary, showing the cramped figures sitting on a small couch surrounded by kitschy decoration like artificial flowers, copper plaques of animals, and lace curtains. That the chilling scenes of death and burial are decorated with the same type of kitschy ornaments proposes a provocative continuity between Musina's homely domesticity and the aesthetics of the grave. Like the armless and cheaply dressed mannequins presented in *General Dealer, Tshipise*, living people are intermixed with nonliving objects in this series. Hugo's images thus allow the worlds of life and death to blur, as social artifice is related to the negation of living individual differences.

It is therefore not surprising to learn from the photographer that for him the family portrait is "based on an unrealistic ideal," whereas "in truth, families are complex and [...] dysfunctional. So by taking on this aesthetic, I am subverting that [...] idealised notion."[15] The resulting tension is palpable between the photograph's pictorial unity and the stability of its typological conventions, and the complexity of social reality that inevitably expresses discomfort with those unities and conventions. This disjunction points to a fundamental structural tension that operates throughout Hugo's work: the discord between the semblance of unity and the truth of dissonance. The tension is not only pictorial, but also carries socioeconomic implications, metaphysical blurrings between life- and death-worlds, even geopolitical resonances. As Hugo explains in relation to his images of Musina: on one level, we encounter families from "different [...] socio-economic and racial" backgrounds, but on another, "what you find in these family and group portraits is that an economic homogeneity sets in, there's a forming of new identity, whether you see it in the furniture that's bought from the same stores, or the same art reproductions hung on the walls."[16] One gains insight into the artificiality and precariousness of South Africa's postapartheid social formation, which, according to Hugo's portrayal, seems to be in the grips of a downward spiral of econom-

15 Hugo, in conversation with Lehan, in *Messina/Musina*, n.p.

16 Ibid.

ic depression and standardization—metaphorically expressed by the images of death, funeral homes, and cemeteries—even while the potentiality of post-racial communities appears fragilely on the horizon.

In this sense, Hugo visualizes the condition in which nostalgic mourning for the uncompleted Afrikaners' project *might* indeed take place. Yet, in contrast to past documentary cycles that critically show the social and racial segregation of the apartheid years—for instance, Goldblatt's Some Afrikaners Photographed (1975) and In Boksburg (1979)—Hugo's are nonetheless also hopeful glimmerings of a newly emerging desegregated social reality, particularly in the interracial grouping of *Pieter and Maryna Vermeulen with Timana Phosiwa*. The white middle-aged couple are shown sitting on a maroon sofa with a black child resting on the woman's lap, suggesting the social cohesion of a family portrait. In fact, the poor and disabled couple (the man has a prosthetic leg) are looking after the child of their landlord, who was recently shot in the spine during a robbery. The image portrays the uncompleted project of postapartheid social democracy, where racist separation is overcome by the loving care of children, yet where pervasive poverty and self-destruction has equalized the playing field.[17] Still, how different are these images from Goldblatt's apartheid-era portrayals of East Rand's well-groomed suburbs, with children playing carefree outdoors, and the well-appointed domestic interiors with black subjects shown securely as outsiders or safely as servants, clearly expressing apartheid's social geography? Regarding these images, Goldblatt explains that "most of [the] townspeople pursue the family, social and civic concerns of respectable burghers anywhere, while locked into a deep and portentous fixity of self-elected, legislated whiteness. [...] Blacks are not of this town. They serve it, trade with it, receive charity from it and are ruled, rewarded and punished by its precepts. Some, on occasion, are its privileged guests. But all who go there do so by permit or invitation, never by right."[18] For Hugo, the postapartheid context presents the contemporary legacy of that history of institutionalized racism. His images represent a further example of the uneasy social reality between "the wreckages" of past utopias and dystopias, and a further place "to make something else," without offering any easy resolution. As he explains—with evident critical distance from the often clichéd documentary approach to such reality—"There's no such thing as a happy ending."[19]

17   For further discussion of this image, see Tamar Garb, "Figures and Fictions: South African Photography in the Perfect Tense," in Garb, *Figures & Fictions*; and Hugo's comments in his conversation with Lehan, *Messina/Musina*, n.p.

18   David Goldblatt, "Boksburg," in *David Goldblatt: Fifty-One Years* (Barcelona: Museu d'Art Contemporani de Barcelona, 2001), 251.

19   Hugo, in conversation with Lehan, *Messina/Musina*, n.p.

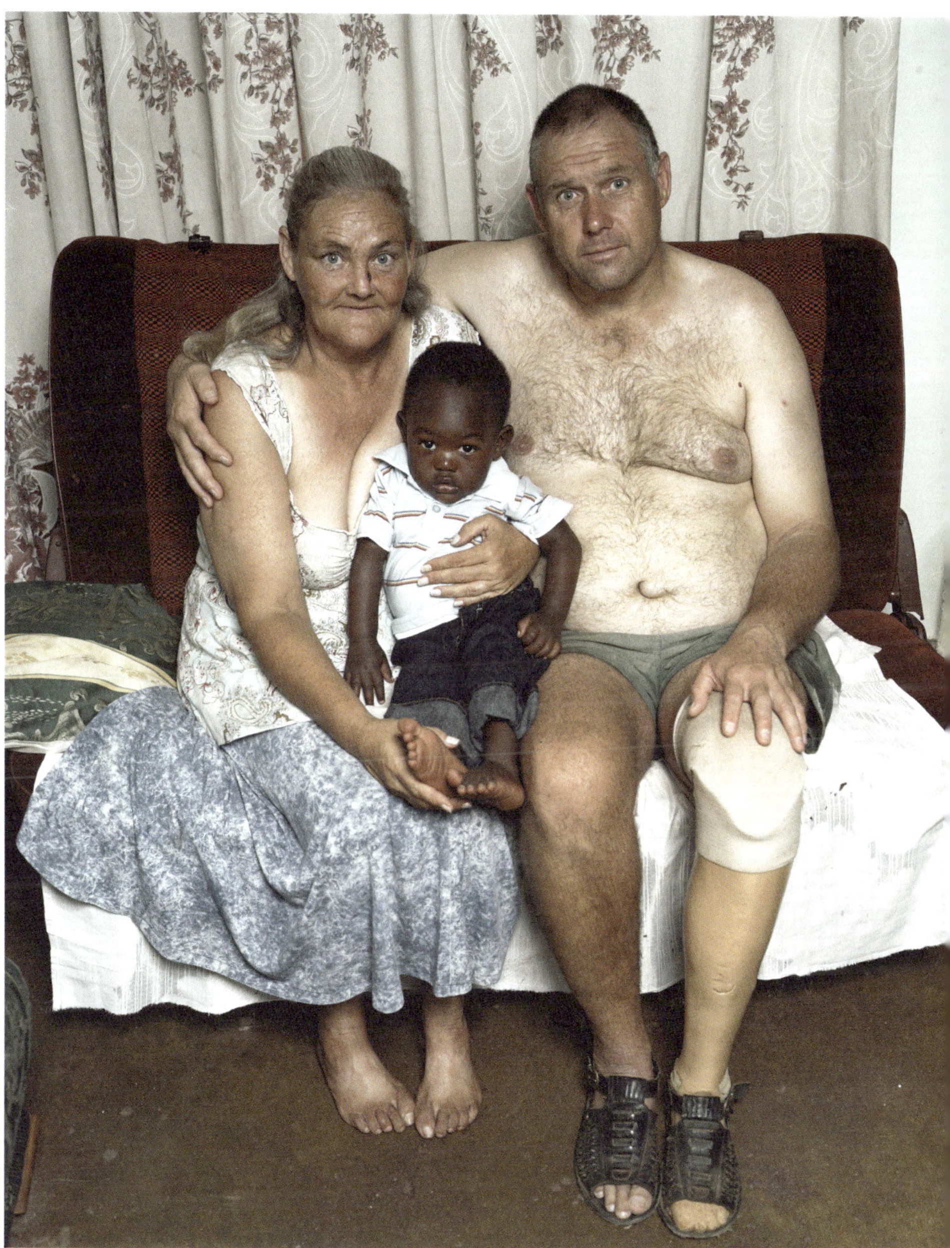

Pieter Hugo, *Pieter and Maryna Vermeulen with Timana Phosiwa, 2006*

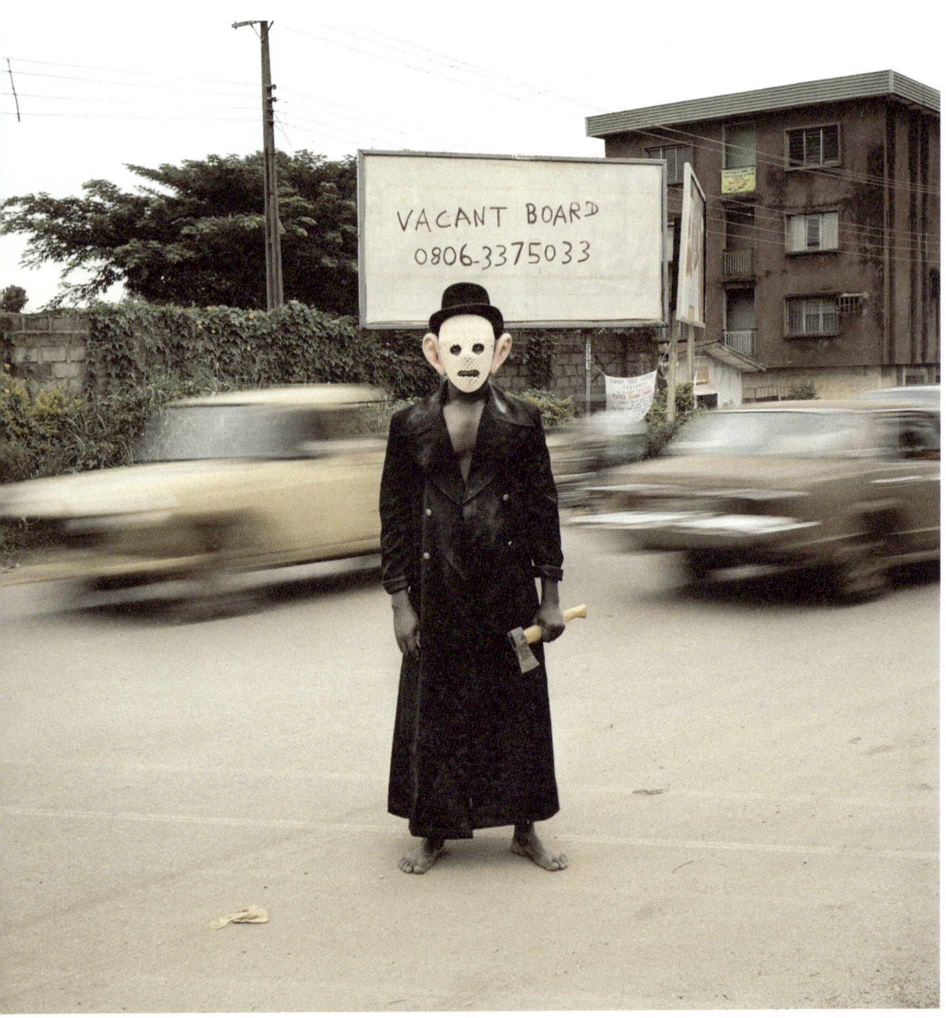

Pieter Hugo, *Escort Kama, Enugu, Nigeria*, 2008

—

Given the postcolony's chaotic pluralism, regimes of violence, broken infrastructures, mythologies of power, mass poverty, and economy of death,[20] it's not surprising that its visual culture might easily translate into a kind of horror film. And, in fact, the Nigerian film industry represents a burgeoning field for the production of precisely such allegories of social and political collapse, subjective

20 These are categories developed by Achille Mbembe to define the post-colony in his book *On the Postcolony*.

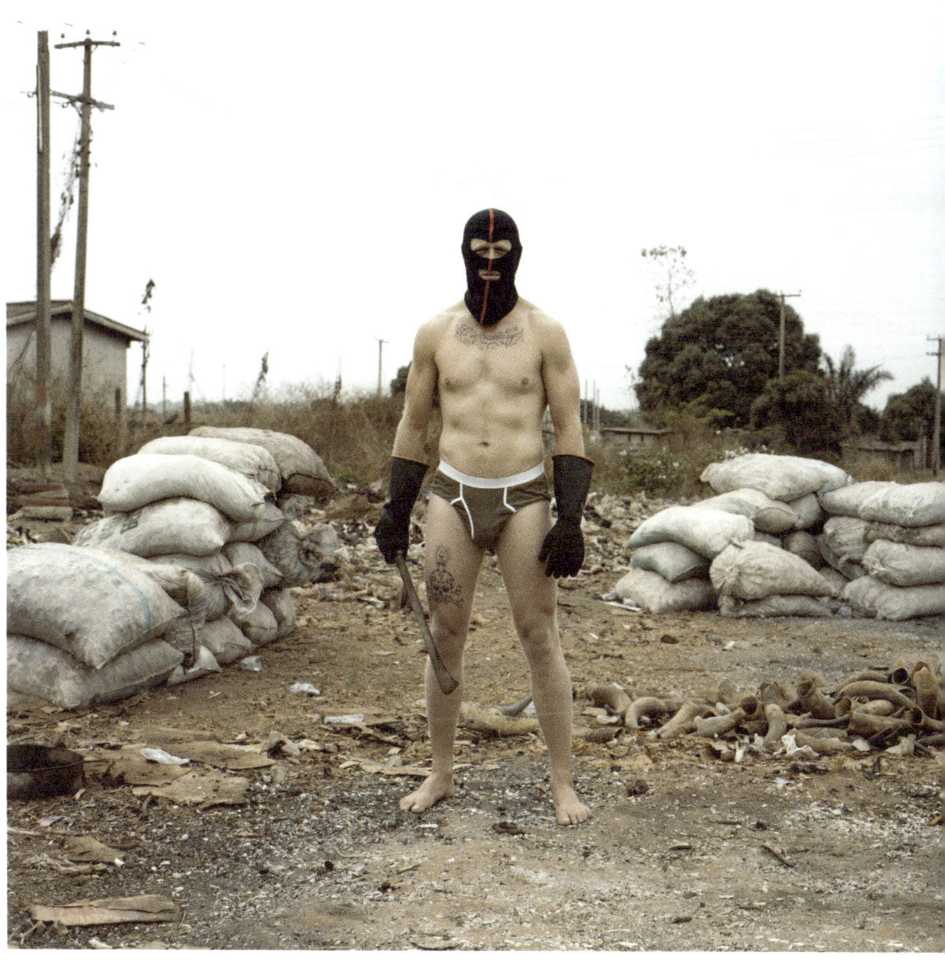

Pieter Hugo, *Pieter Hugo, Enugu, Nigeria*, 2009

devastation, and creative survival—the subject of Hugo's Nollywood series. The series presents portraits of film actors, generally those from Nollywood's most popular genre, "juju" or voodoo
horror, "supernatural thrillers involving spirits, vampires and
ghosts" meant "to provide emotionally-satisfying explanations
for wealth inequalities of injustices that abound in Nigeria."[21]
The characters wear monster-like costumes
and are oddly captured in everyday contexts.
For example, there are undead soldiers back

21   Zina Saro-Wiwa, "No Going Back,"
in Pieter Hugo, *Nollywood* (Munich:
Prestel, 2009), 22.

145   Return to the Postcolony

from the grave, female gangsters sporting machine guns, money-grubbing white-eyed zombies, and bloody-mouthed vampires, each posing for the camera off set in urban spaces such as the street, cafés, parking lots, next to garbage heaps, and ruined buildings. One particularly frightening figure is pictured standing barefoot wearing a black trench coat and a hockey mask with large pink ears, holding an axe in the middle of the road amid blurred cars speeding past, as a billboard with the handwritten words "VACANT BOARD" rises above him, adding to the disturbing quality of the scene (*Escort Kama, Enugu, Nigeria*, 2008). In another image, three "slaves" chained together wearing burlap rags seem to pause for a moment to comport themselves into a portrait in a dirty car park (*Emilia Ibeh, Doris Orji and Sharon Opiah, Enugu, Nigeria*, 2008). And in one of the stranger of the presentations, a naked man wearing a Darth Vader mask is shown standing defiantly before the camera in a dried-out riverbed (*Azuka Abindu, Enugu, Nigeria*, 2008). All the sitters address the camera directly in scenes that are obviously contrived, making for a paradoxical conjunction of theatricality, illusionistic characterization, and self-conscious exhibitionism. (And, acknowledging his own creative role in this production, as if ready for any difficult collaboration, the artist appears in one image dressed as a masked professional wrestler in balaclava and underpants holding a machete in the backyard of a slaughterhouse [*Pieter Hugo, Enugu, Nigeria*, 2009].)

In some ways, these images might be seen as offering a familiar "spectacle of Africa"—of primitivizing representations and exoticizing fantasies, clearly tantalizing for Western art markets—in a way similar to how orientalist portrayals of Middle Eastern harems and princely courts offered seductive fantasies for the nineteenth-century European gaze. Yet, such a spectacle is already contained within Nollywood productions, which are very much made for local, regional, and international audiences. As Hope Eghagha explains, "Nollywood gives to the world what Nigerians want to see."[22] In fact, Nollywood represents a strikingly successful model of postcolonial industriousness and local creative production in Africa. With an estimated 320 million dollar annual turnover, and one thousand to fifteen hundred films churned out each year, the Nigerian film industry has become the third largest in the world since its birth in the early 1990s, following Hollywood and Bollywood.[23] Films are typically made in haste, with entire features shot, cut, and packaged within a week at a cost of ten to fifty thousand dollars. While

[22]   Hope Eghagha, "Magical Realism and the 'Power' of Nollywood Home Video Films," *Film International* 5, no. 4 (July–August 2007): 74.

[23]   See Saro-Wiwa, "No Going Back," 17–20; and Jonathan Haynes, "Nollywood: What's in a Name?," *Film International* 5, no. 4 (July–August 2007): 106–8.

quality may suffer from the accelerated production rate, the consequent spontaneity and liveliness that is characteristic of Nollywood films offer a vitality often lost in overproduced and hyperprocessed Hollywood blockbusters. Films are distributed directly to DVD markets, as few multiplexes remain in Nigeria—many cinemas were converted to churches or warehouses in the '80s when videocassettes and VCRs became increasingly common. And unlike "embassy films"—those made for cinephilic audiences by francophone West African directors trained in Europe with European funding—Nollywood productions serve local markets and are shipped to destinations all over Africa.

Not only productive within emerging neoliberal capitalism, Nollywood is also symptomatic of neoliberalism's system and experiential conditions. Nollywood emerged in the wake of the structural adjustment policies implemented in Nigeria during the 1980s, which privatized the economics of filmmaking. The 1990s witnessed a migration of professionals from state-funded television studios to independent and privately funded digital video production studios, which were more accessible and affordable to use.[24] During these years, Nigeria, like many other African countries, entered into a difficult economic period marked by the collapse of state functions, infrastructure deterioration, increased social instability, and economic inequality. The escalation of government corruption and the growing arbitrariness of government power (defined by a succession of military coups) brought about the privatization of violence and exacerbated endemic social crises, with problems generally concentrated in the rapidly expanding and increasingly dysfunctional megacity of Lagos.[25]

In some ways, this dystopian description of Lagos is characteristic of the clichéd doomsday Western view of Africa,[26] though the alternate approach that celebrates the creativity of the country's informal economy and its "innovative" urbanism (as in Rem Koolhaas's sanguine approach to the city)[27] can be just as problematic for its ignoring of the negative costs, historical context, and structural macroeconomic causes of social, political, and economic breakdown. As the cultural geographer Matthew Gandy points out: "Under IMF tutelage, [General] Babangida [who came to power by military coup in 1986] immediately embarked on a full-spectrum Structural Adjustment Programme 'with Nigerian characteristics'—

24 Akin Adesokan, "Issues in the New Nigerian Cinema," *Black Camera* 21, no. 1 (2006): 7.

25 See Matthew Gandy, "Learning from Lagos," *New Left Review*, no. 33 (May–June 2005).

26 As presented in texts such as Robert Kaplan, *The Coming Anarchy* (New York: Random House, 2000), 5–15; and Pep Subirós, "Lagos: Surviving Hell," in *Africas: The Artist and the City; A Journey and an Exhibition* (Barcelona: Centre de Cultura Contemporania de Barcelona, 2001), 34–45.

27 See Rem Koolhaas's video *Lagos Wide and Close: An Interactive Journey into an Exploding City*, dir. Bregtje van der Haak, 2005; and Rem Koolhaas and Project on the City with students from Harvard Graduate School of Design, "Fragments of a Lecture on Lagos," in Enwezor et al., *Under Siege*, 129–51.

slashing tariffs and agricultural subsidies, devaluing the naira, stripping out what remained of public education provision, deregulating finance, selling off state-owned industries and indulging in narco-profiteering on a massive scale."[28] By the end of the 1990s, Nigeria—a country notably rich in natural resources including oil and gas—was reduced to a situation common in sub-Saharan African postcolonial states, spending the majority of its GDP servicing its debt, while education, health care, and infrastructure funding dwindled.

Nollywood was born in this conflicted context. Speaking of Lagos (although Hugo's images were taken in Enugu, an alternate site of Nollywood production about 250 miles west of the capital), film critic Jonathan Haynes points out, "The films are a means for Nigerians to come to terms—visually, dramatically, emotionally, morally, socially, politically, and spiritually—with the city and everything it embodies."[29] More specifically, one could argue that Nollywood offers an iconography of "capitalist monsterology," drawing on the "tales of body-snatching, vampirism, organ-theft, and zombie-economics" that "comprise multiple imaginings of the risks to bodily integrity that inhere in a society in which individual survival requires selling our life-energies to people on the market," as David McNally suggests.[30] Such an analysis, which acknowledges the multiple and complex determinations of Nollywood cinema, nevertheless argues for the significance of its relation to the phenomenology of the capitalist economy, drawing on Michael Taussig's investigations of commodity fetishism in South America, especially where he describes how "the feeling of atomization and bondage identifies the phenomenology of the market-based system."[31] The recognition of the monstrous conditions of capitalism, however, of course goes back even further, to the mid-nineteenth-century analysis of Marx, who famously remarked on how "capital is dead labour which, vampire-like, lives only by sucking living labour, and lives the more, the more labour it sucks."[32] It is not surprising then to learn that historians have dated the emergence of monstrous figures like vampires in the African cultural imaginary to the period *after* the imposition of colonialism,

28　Gandy, "Learning from Lagos," 46. On page 45 he expands: "In 1979, the US Federal Reserve's interest-rate hikes brought the decade of cheap loans and high oil rents shudderingly to a halt. Nigeria, with other Third World borrowers, was plunged into a spiral of rising debt repayments. The onset of global recession in 1981 and the collapse in oil prices threw the imbalances of the Nigerian economy into stark relief. Through the build-up of arrears and penalties for missed payments, the country's external debt rose from $13bn to $30bn between 1981 and 1989. Many of the infrastructure programmes of the 1970s—ports, airports, roads, bridges, oil refineries, steel mills—were abandoned incomplete, or left to deteriorate beyond repair."

29　Jonathan Haynes, "Nollywood in Lagos, Lagos in Nollywood Films," *Africa Today* 54, no. 2 (Fall 2007): 133.

30　David McNally, *Monsters of the Market: Zombies, Vampires and Global Capitalism* (London: Brill, 2011), 2, 3; esp. chap. 3, "African Vampires in the Age of Globalisation."

31　Michael Taussig, *The Devil and Commodity Fetishism in South America* (Chapel Hill: University of North Carolina Press, 1980), 27.

32　Elsewhere he describes capital's "werewolf-like hunger for surplus labour" and its "vampire thirst for the living blood of labour." Karl Marx, *Capital*, vol. I, trans. Ben Fowkes (Harmondsworth: Penguin Books, 1976), 342, 353, 367.

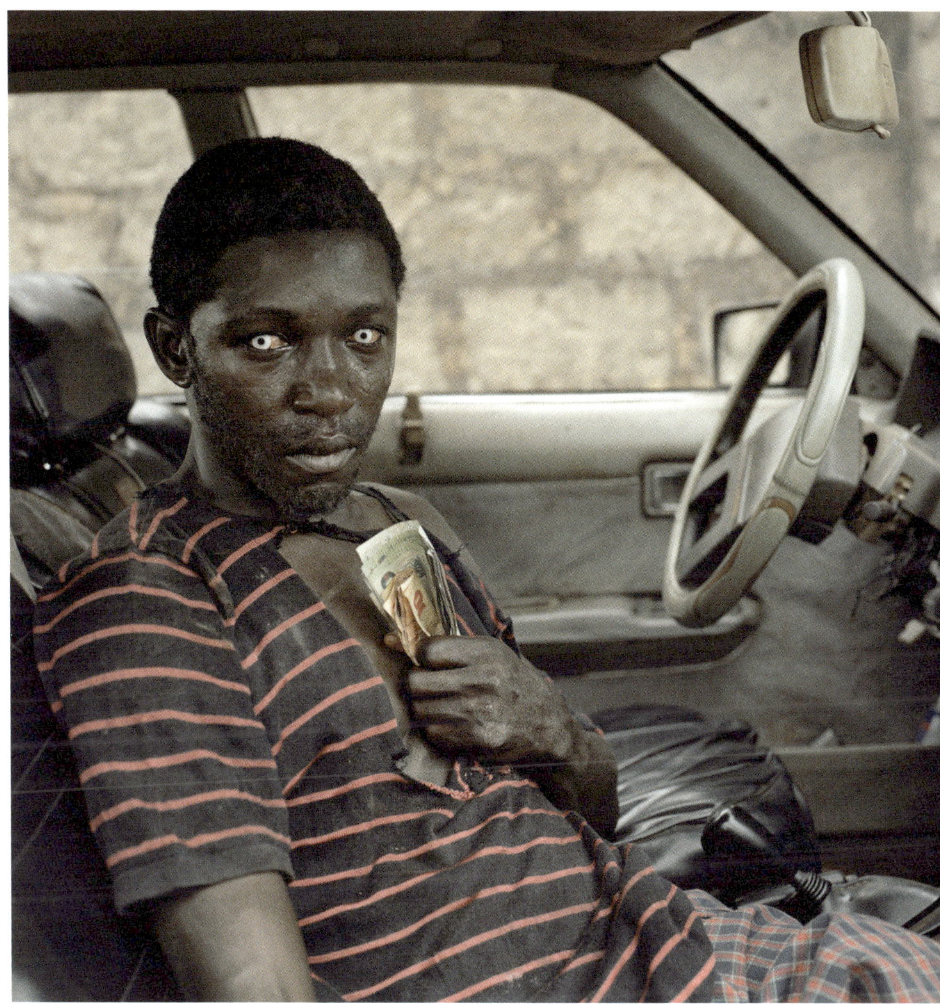

Pieter Hugo, *Thompson, Asaba, Nigeria*, 2008

in the twentieth century, following its introduction of capitalist value systems, labor regimes, and alienating and exploitative conditions.[33]

Nollywood represents "a mode of narration that naturalizes the supernatural; that is to say, a mode in which real and fantastic, natural and supernatural, are coherently represented in a state of rigorous equivalence—neither has a greater claim to truth or referentiality."[34] On the one

[33] See Louise White, *Speaking with Vampires: Rumor and History in Colonial Africa* (Berkeley: University of California Press, 2000).

[34] Eghagha, "Magical Realism," 73.

hand, the turn to the supernatural responds to and compensates for the widespread failures of the judicial system and the country's corrupt political institutions, which have inspired an alternate quest for justice and righteous life that is in part satisfied in the revenge plots common in the movies. On the other, Nigeria's cinema represents a positive and creative negotiation between the exploitation of modern technology's special effects and the unleashing of precolonial vestiges of ritualistic and tribal religious beliefs in the spirit world, which have survived alongside Christianity and Islam. Indeed, McNally argues that Nollywood's imagery delivers a "de-fetishizing charge" insofar as its monster tales contest the naturalness and universality of capitalist relations, drawing out its "zombie economics," worship of speculative finance, and mystifying immaterial value systems.[35]

This ambivalence and overdetermined complexity is also evident in Hugo's photographs, insofar as the series presents both "untitled film stills," in which actors are in character, and portraits, where cinematic narrative is not present and each subject is identified in the title by name. This fragmentary maneuver endows the images with a certain thematic ambiguity, which is matched by the appearance of the subjects caught between the fictional world of cinema and the documentary situation of Hugo's street photography. Similarly, the images of death and cannibalism are unnerving and sinister, as well as humorous and entertaining, suggesting a metaphorics expressive of postcolonial dystopia and a predatory capitalism gone berserk. Exemplary are the images of figures enthralled to money, such as the female visionary who, sitting in a chair wearing a blue dress, gazes out of her barred window with two coins placed over her eyes (*Ngozi Oltiri, Enugu, Nigeria*, 2009), or that of a white-eyed zombie who sits in a stationary automobile clutching a wad of British pounds in his hand (*Thompson, Asaba, Nigeria*, 2008). If "zombies present the 'human face' of capitalist monstrosity," then that is because capitalism gradually wears down the subject via the devalorization of living labor, to the point that all become so many scavengers and ragpickers sorting through garbage.[36] (One again recalls the infernal wasteland depicted in Permanent Error, and indeed, many of the shots from Hugo's Nollywood series take place in trash dumps or postindustrial architectural ruins.) These doomsday scenarios are played out in scenes that suggest an ongoing metaphysical battle between good and evil—a battle whose outcome is never reconciled.

35   See McNally, *Monsters of the Market*, 187, 203. For further discussions of the relations between postcolonial Africa, capitalism, and the monstrous, see Ben Fine, "Development as Zombieconomics in the Age of Neoliberalism," *Third World Quarterly* 30, no. 5 (2009); Chris Harman, *Zombie Capitalism: Global Crisis and the Relevance of Marx* (London: Bookmarks, 2009); and White, *Speaking with Vampires*.

36   Steven Shaviro, "Capitalist Monsters," *Historical Materialism* 10, no. 4 (2002): 283, 288.

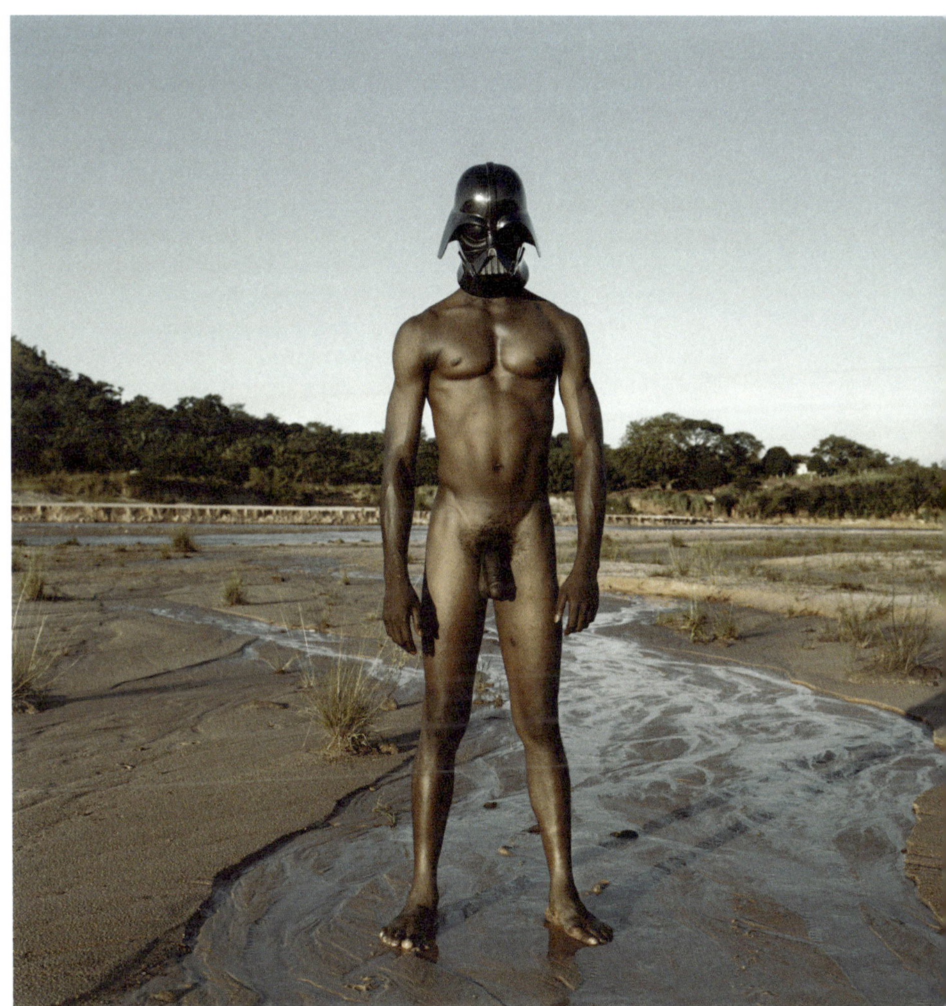

Pieter Hugo, *Azuka Adindu, Enugu, Nigeria*, 2008

Yet if Hugo's Nollywood proposes an indeterminate allegory that meditates social and economic crises, then it is realized via a collaborative performativity. Here too there is an important difference from Nollywood films, which naturalize the unnatural by depicting an everyday world filled with supernatural presence and significance, even while it simultaneously can be seen to denaturalize the capitalist market economy by its very dramatic estrangement. Conversely, and at its most provocative, Hugo's Nollywood series offers a gothic post-human inventiveness, a

151

constructive hybridity, where the monstrous takes on a complex value, expressing a morbid, crisis-ridden reality, and proposing the unconventional as a site of unrecognizability filled with potentiality and creative self-invention. The result is not so much a naturalization of the supernatural, but rather a repositioning of carnivalesque grotesquerie as a hallucinatory site of critical social allegory and imaginative survival. In this sense, Hugo's presentation is far from the familiar spectacle that pictures African social reality in the most negative of terms, and which continues to reign within conventional documentary practice.

In fact, indeterminacy and ambivalence appear as part of the very complex makeup of Hugo's monstrous characters—where the monstrous refers both to the vampires, devils, zombies, and undead, as well as to the bizarre hybrids mixing African bodies and global culture-industry props like the Darth Vader figure, or those that combine divergent temporalities with premodern and postcolonial references (such as the hairy wild man, a living fetish object, who appears seated with a bottle of Coca-Cola in a café). In this regard, the monstrous signifies a composite figure of heterogeneous origins, blurring the divisions between life and death, real and imaginary, past and present, North and South, the photographic and the cinematic. It also proposes a being that is not recognized or understood, that exists outside conventional categories. As Derrida explains: "A monster is a species for which we do not yet have a name, which does not mean that the species is abnormal, namely, the composition or hybridization of already known species. Simply, it *shows* itself [...] in something that is not yet shown and that therefore looks like a hallucination, it strikes the eye, it frightens precisely because no anticipation had prepared one to identify this figure."[37] Indeed, the word "monster" has roots in the Latin *monstrum*, which originates in *moneo* ("to warn," "to exhort") and is connected to *monstrare* ("to show," "to teach," "to prescribe a path that is to be followed").[38] As Stefan Nowotny and Gerald Raunig explain, "The monster consequently forms a kind of in-between figure or a figuration of the in-between emerging in a linguistic history process, which occupies a transition between an order of (initially given by the gods) exhortative instruction and an order of appearance."[39]

What exhortative instruction and what order of appearance do Hugo's figures offer? Importantly, they do not result from the devising of the artist alone; rather, with his

[37] Jacques Derrida, "Passages—From Traumatism to Promise," in *Points: Interviews, 1974–1994*, ed. Elisabeth Weber, trans. Peggy Kamuf (Stanford, CA: Stanford University Press, 1995), 386; italics and parentheses in original.

[38] See Émile Benveniste, *Le vocabulaire des institution indo-européenes*, vol. 2, *Pouvoir, droit, religion* (Paris: Les Éditions de Minuit, 1969), 257.

[39] Stefan Nowotny and Gerald Raunig, "On Police Ghosts and Multitudinous Monsters," trans. Aileen Derieg, *transversal* (May 2008).

Nollywood series, Hugo provides a context for Nigerian actors to obscure the divisions between film and everyday life, producing an uncertainty of meaning out of a collaborative scenario between photographer and subject, which is the constitutive basis of all his series. Hugo's images at their most complex thus create a double defamiliarization—estranging everyday life (including life's subjugation to capitalism's depredations) with the presence of unsettling performances, where the human becomes monstrous, or ceases to appear human; and conversely, comically showing the constructed nature of the make-believe figures in nontheatrical urban contexts, where their surprising entrance disturbs the banal proceedings of everyday life.These acts of defamiliarization thereby suggest hieroglyphs of an unrecognizable future located disjunctively and provocatively in the present.[40] Are the figures situated in a film set, or in real life? Are the images an ethnography of Nollywood, or do they participate in its cinematic spectacle, bringing it out of filmic space, where it might spark an imaginative intervention in the real? Do the photographs offer personifications of a dystopian and neoliberal postcoloniality, or allegories that attempt to work through its contradictions, traumas, and crises? Finally, as images that travel beyond the Nollywood context and into a parallel universe of artistic photography on the global market, do Hugo's images then come to express a hybridity of blurred networks that expand and transmute the very hybridity and global image economy of Nollywood? These questions are perhaps unanswerable; rather they form the very questions that Hugo's series opens up and leaves provocatively and pointedly unresolved.

If Hugo's photographs register the devastated social and subjective landscape of postapartheid South Africa, and, more broadly, that of a still-traumatized postcolonial sub-Saharan Africa, then they also catalyze the unfixing of categories and identities by theatricalizing everyday life. They thereby draw out the complexities and contradictions of photography's and portraiture's typological constructions. The portrayed subject is shown to be a site of potentiality and heterogeneity, self-possessed and participating collaboratively in the construction of his or her own image. In opening up this positive potential in the postcolonial zone of conflict, Hugo's photography defines a model that is both *representational* of a reality—itself shown to be unfixed and in the process of becoming—and *productive* of new subjective and social possibilities, where new realities might yet be created. It thereby challenges us to posi-

40   As Enwezor writes: "'My negritude is neither tower nor cathedral' [Aimé Césaire]. 'Black is … black ain't' [Ralph Ellison]: are there any more succinct ways to begin the delimitation of those fantasies which mark the black subject as abject, than to start with those two ideas of unfixed blackness, burgeoning into the expansive site of heterogeneity?" "Reframing the Black Subject," 39.

tion ourselves in relation to the postcolony, and to consider our own place in the production of its ruinous breakdown and upheavals, its unstable and shifting realities, and—with hope—its ongoing and future creative renewal.

Conclusion
Living with Ghosts, Justly

The European dream needs the Mediterranean dream, [...] the dream that once sent knights from all of Europe down the roads of the Orient; a dream that drew to the South so many emperors of Saint Empire, so many kings of France; a dream shared by Bonaparte in Egypt, Napoleon III in Algeria, Lyautey in Morocco. This dream was not so much a dream of conquest as a dream of civilization. [...] The wellspring has never run dry. We just need to unite our forces and it will all begin anew.

—Nicolas Sarkozy, 2007[1]

If further proof were needed that we live in the "colonial present," then the widely available and abundant evidence is concretely summarized by anthropologist James Ferguson, who writes, "It is equally clear that the latest round of worldwide capitalist restructuring, with its frenzied construction of 'the global economy,' has left little or no place for Africa outside of its old colonial role as provider of raw materials (especially mineral wealth)." Indeed, he goes on to specify the by-now familiar material effects of such a role:

> Mass poverty—that long-standing continental curse— is not only not improving but, in many areas, actually getting worse. The AIDS situation on the continent, meanwhile, has become so grim that it is difficult to overstate the magnitude of the tragedy. With only 10 percent of the world's population, Sub-Saharan Africa has fully two thirds of all the world's people living with HIV/AIDS (some 25 million), and in 2003, some 2.2 million Africans died of the disease (some three quarters of the world total), a rate of some 6,000 every day. Estimated life expectancies at birth in a number of African countries have dropped to the mid 30s and even lower, even as life spans almost everywhere else in the world continue to lengthen.[2]

Ferguson's condemnation of the catastrophe of the "Saint Empire" invoked in Sarkozy's dreamworld seems entirely justified. Yet while it is easy to criticize that fantasy, Sarkozy's is only the most visible attempt to render official the broader neo-revisionist politics that refuse to repent for the sins of past colonial injustices and misdeeds (and time will tell if the post-Sarkozy years will be significantly different). Where its adherents go so far as to redeem colonialism for its positive accomplishments,[3] such amnesiac refusals and nostalgic inventions have lead to the "provincialization" of

1 Nicolas Sarkozy, speeches in Toulon, February 2007, and Dakar, July 2007. Cited in Mbembe, "Provincializing France?," 107–8. Also see Alain Badiou, *The Meaning of Sarkozy*, trans. David Fernbach (London: Verso, 2010), in which Sarkozy figures as a symbol of "transcendent Pétainism," running on an agenda of pandering fear and xenophobia.

2 Ferguson, *Global Shadows*, 8.

3   Sarkozy continues: "The West has been long steeped in the sin of arrogance and ignorance. Many crimes and injustices were committed. But most of those who headed south were neither monsters nor exploiters. Many put their energies toward building roads, bridges, schools, and hospitals. Many wore themselves out cultivating a bit of thankless land that none had farmed before. Many went only to heal or teach. We must stop blackening the past. [...] We can disapprove of colonization from the point of view of our modern values. But we must respect the men and women of goodwill who honestly believed their work was useful for an ideal civilization in which they believed." Cited in Mbembe, "Provincializing France?," 107–8.

4   Ibid., 87. Also see Dipesh Chakrabarty, *Provincializing Europe: Postcolonial Thought and Historical Difference* (Princeton, NJ: Princeton University Press, 2000).

5   On the rightward trend of European politics, see Perry Anderson, *The New Old World* (London: Verso, 2009). Gregory explains that "while they may be displaced, distorted, and (most often) denied, the capacities that inhere within the colonial past are routinely reaffirmed and reactivated in the colonial present." *The Colonial Present*, 7. He cites Andreas Huyssen, "Present Pasts: Media, Politics, Amnesia," in *Globalization*, ed. Arjun Appadurai (Durham, NC: Duke University Press, 2001).

6   Mbembe, "Provincializing France?," 102.

7   See, for instance, C. L. R. James, *The Black Jacobins: Toussaint L'Ouverture and the San Domingo Revolution* (New York: Vintage Books, 1989). For the wider historical conflicts accompanying and determining enlightenment articulations of the universality of freedom, see Susan Buck-Morss, *Hegel, Haiti, and Universal History* (Pittsburgh, PA: University of Pittsburgh Press, 2009).

8   For instance, Chika Okeke-Agulu writes that "the strategies of European colonization, the failures of the postcolonial African states, and subsequent patterns of migration [...] can no longer be ignored in debates about national and continental identities in Europe." "Who Knows Tomorrow," *Art Journal* 69, no. 4 (Winter 2010): 50.

French politics and culture and "its regression on a planetary scale."[4] If herein we witness the disavowal of the negative effects and outcomes of the colonial past—which is in fact a European-wide tendency at the current time of the ascendency of its many right-wing governments—then can we not also expect the denial of the colonial present?[5] It is exactly such a connection that Mbembe maps in terms of France's "ailment of the spirit," which results from the persistence of two contradictory desires at the heart of the nation's constitutional basis: on the one hand, the yearning for the "phantasm of a polis without strangers," and, on the other, the wish for the "symbolic recognition and the expansion of citizenship, defended, in particular, by the minorities and their supporters."[6] This paradox—and, equally, still unresolved political conflict—can be traced back to the very origins of French revolutionary republicanism in the colonial late eighteenth century, when the competing claims between "freedom" and "property" pitted abolitionists against the slave-owning bourgeoisie, and when the universal ideals of the revolution were placed in question.[7]

Such a politics of disavowal belies hopeful claims that Europe has entered a new age of historical consciousness regarding its colonial past.[8] That may be true of minority and academic discourse. Yet when the particularly cruel elements of European colonization, the failures of postcolonial African states, and patterns of migration *are* ignored—as the history of murders and atrocities, the structural racism, the continued forms of inequality and repression are quite blatantly and commonly dismissed by leading government officials and their minions such as Jacques Brassinne de la Buissière—then that is where the haunting begins. Such refusals, denials, and disavowals unleash the spirits that materialize in what Avery Gordon calls so many "inarticulate experiences, [...] symptoms and screen memories, [and] spiraling affects of [...] modernity's violence and wounds," which come to figure as "the haunting reminder of the complex social relations in which we live."[9]

That "haunting reminder," as we've seen, is registered in a diverse range of micro-political artistic positions—yet with considerably more sensitivity and articulateness than when such symptoms are unconsciously acted out. There is Sven Augustijnen's film that stages a cinematic court for the witnessing of the perpetrator's defense; Vincent Meessen's hauntology in which the ghosts of Roland Barthes are conjured via a performative documentary and spectral historiography; Zarina Bhimji's cultural politics of affect, offering an acute aesthetic attention to the environmental and architectural traces of the colonial past; Renzo Martens's deconstruction of the media regime of poverty pornography, asking for the acknowledgment of our own participation in the production of inequality, and thereby opening up a yet to be invented relation to the impoverished; and Pieter Hugo's participatory documentary approach to postcolonial realities and monstrous fictions that visualizes the diversity and complexity of African cultural formations. I have tried to assess the aesthetic innovations and singularities of these practices, as well as their complex effects, political risks, and accomplishments. Yet my analysis makes no claim that these practices cohere into anything like a unified ethico-aesthetic paradigm—far from it. In effect, what we are left with is a number of speculative and experimental modelings of cinematic and photographic hauntologies, which, addressed in their singularity and in relation to specific historical and geopolitical contexts, presents us with the following conclusions.

First, in defiance of the neo-imperialist culture of disavowal, these practices reanimate an artistic advancement of postcolonial studies that offers a crucial antidote to a pervasive amnesia, insofar as they help to conjure the spirits that hover around the negations of historical consciousness. Indeed, it has been my operating assumption that the artistic practices considered here enter into alliance with this longstanding anti- and postcolonial critical discourse. As Ali Behdad insists, the field of postcolonial studies operates "on the side of memory"; it not only counters *amnesiac* histories of colonialism but also stages "a return of the repressed" to resist the seductions of *nostalgic* histories of colonialism.[10] In this way, the postcolony shows itself as a temporal entanglement comprised of continuities and discontinuities, overlapping histories and unacknowledged presences. One major accomplishment of the art considered here is that it proposes aesthetic mediations that pur-

9   Gordon, *Ghostly Matters*, 25.

10   Ali Behdad, *Belated Travelers: Orientalism in the Age of Colonial Dissolution* (Durham, NC: Duke University Press, 1996), 6, 8.

sue these historical linkages and interlinked geographies to critical ends—for instance, connecting one man's archive fever with the open wound of a Congolese political killing decades earlier; or exploring the temporal resonances that vibrate through architectural ruins in Gujarat, which links homesickness to traumatic exile.

Second, this entanglement is not only temporal, but also extends to the spatial realm; it identifies historical linkings and connects to cultural, financial, and environmental geographies—as when contemporary Congolese poverty is joined to global economic arrangements and historicized in relation to the colonial legacy. One way to specify the contemporaneity of Africa's colonial present is to stress what Mbembe terms the "spectralization" of the economy under neoliberalism. He writes: "Another configuration of terror and violence is embodied in a set of economic policies fostered by international financial institutions such as the World Bank and the IMF. The implementation of such policies in the absence of a significant reduction of African debt has led to the 'spectralization' of the economies of the continent."[11] That debt-infused spectralization—a term that usefully captures the speculative and possessive aspects of capitalism—has led to the increased corruption and greed of governing elites, the privatization of militia violence, modes of everyday impoverishment, and the crumbling of state provisions such as education, health care, and welfare services (exactly the brutal effects Martens finds in the Democratic Republic of the Congo, and which Hugo allegorizes in his images of Nollywood horror). In this regard, sub-Saharan Africa emerges not as an example of the anomaly or failure of neoliberalism—comprising the regime of deregulation, privatization, and the minimizing of state funding, which brings with it social insecurity and the growth of economic inequality—but rather as arguably the most advanced contemporary site of its development.[12] In this regard, it is not surprising that contemporary economic theorists have articulated its present form as one of "capitalist sorcery," offering a way to comprehend the capture and possession of contemporary neoliberalism in the West.[13] From here, economic spectralization appears as an element of capitalist sorcery. That connection also suggests an additional reason why images of African poverty, wanton violence, and governmental corruption haunt European viewers. The implication is that in viewing those disturbing scenes reflective of the advanced state of African neoliberalization, Westerners glimpse one potential dystopian future of their own politics of austerity, brought

11   Mbembe, quoted in Höller, "Africa in Motion," n.p.

12   See Harrison, "Neoliberal Africa," 19. For an overview of neoliberalism, see David Harvey, *A Brief History of Neoliberalism* (Oxford: Oxford University Press, 2005).

13   See Pignarre and Stengers, *Capitalist Sorcery.*

about by savage cutbacks to social spending, and privatizations of education, health care, and social security.[14]

Third, in this milieu of neoliberal globalization, the work of contemporary artists becomes especially urgent: their return to the postcolony insistently confronts the ghosts that European governments seem intent on keeping in the dark in order to carry on their destructive international arrangements. Is their "return"—insofar as they are retracing the steps of past generations of Europeans during colonialism—not then a speculative voyage to Africa's colonial present that also illuminates one potential future of the West? To create an aesthetics of the spectral, in this regard, suggests a complex ethico-political imperative: to recognize our debt to the oppressed of the past, and to support the practice of equality and international solidarity in the present and the future. That said, these artistic projects are not so much politically activist as aesthetically multivalent, channeling and negotiating discourses, affects, media imagery, and theoretical paradigms, and investigating the places where the specters of colonialism reside and cause havoc. Theirs is a critical reckoning with this transnational ghostly realm, which allows us—writers, students, cultural practitioners, activists, political agents, and artists—to address these matters with cultural, historical, and aesthetic precision and depth. Not that these experiments will reverse the neo-imperialist revisionism signaled in the directions of European politics. They do however contest its seductive nostalgia and insist on locating the failures of African politics and economics within a larger historical trajectory and expansive financial geography that connects to the legacy of Western imperialism. Opening up the disturbing visual and cultural effects of this repressed history by returning to the postcolony will not necessarily make the world a more comfortable place, yet it will let us live with a greater understanding of our situation, and, with hope, will open up possibilities for a different, better future.

Fourth, if within the entanglement of the postcolonial condition are the workings of a colonial present, then it's also important to acknowledge their *differences* from the colonial past. As Derek Gregory reminds us, the "commitment to a future free of colonial power and disposition is sustained in part by a critique of the continuities between the colonial past and the colonial present."[15] We must practice such a critique to invent a real *post*colonial condition today. Yet "because history is akin to witchcraft,

14   Which brings to fruition an observation made long ago by Michel Foucault: "It should never be forgotten that while colonization, with its techniques of political and juridical weapons, obviously transported European models to other continents, it also had a considerable boomerang effect on the mechanisms of power in the West, and on the apparatuses, institutions, and techniques of power. A whole series of colonial models was brought back to the West, and the result was that the West could practice something resembling colonization […] on itself." *"Society Must Be Defended": Lectures at the Collège de France 1975–1976*, trans. David Macey (New York: Picador, 2003), 103.

many feel the need to wear masks and to blame everything on the past," writes Mbembe. To live in the present, for him, requires the following:

> A renewal of the virtue of intellectual curiosity has to replace the current syndrome of victimization. Bridges have to be built between a new social science and the various domains of the humanities, including philosophy, the arts, music, architecture, film and design. Such would be some of the attributes of an Afro-cosmopolitanism firmly rooted in the continent, but mindful of the force and wealth Africa's multiple internal and external diasporas represent.[16]

In addition to considering African practices that work toward such a noble vision further, we must also ask: how can the *West* live in the postcolonial present? While artists can expect to have little effect on the dreams and practices of the political elites, they do possess the freedom to imagine other ways of living more justly in relation to the ghosts of the past and present —an important step in the right direction. Such a postcolonial imagination would build on past articulations that help illuminate the way forward. Let us remind ourselves, as Derrida once observed, that "no justice [...] seems possible or thinkable without the principle of some *responsibility*, beyond all living present, within that which disjoins the living present, before the ghosts of those who are not yet born or who are already dead, be they victims of wars, political or other kinds of violence, nationalist, racist, colonialist, sexist, or other kinds of exterminations, victims of the oppressions of capitalist imperialism or any of the forms of totalitarianism."[17] Without that sense of justice and responsibility—which comes from the commitment to connecting the dark moments of history to the failures of the present, as well as to building upon the inspiring precedents of past struggles today—how can we know who we are, where we're going, and where we're coming from?

To take responsibility means opening up the wounds of the colonial past, exploring the hidden archive of the violence of modernity and its relation to its erstwhile colonial possessions. It means acknowledging the history of inequality, domination, and oppression, which cling to the present in the current economic and political circumstances of corporate globalization.[18] Such a historical consciousness represents the achievement of the work of the artists presented here. If the historically past and the geographically distant

15 Gregory, *Colonial Present*, 7.

16 Mbembe, quoted in Höller, "Africa in Motion," n.p.

17 Derrida, exordium to *Specters of Marx*, xix.

18 For a compelling formation of a counter-politics to corporate globalization, see Cavanagh et al., *Alternatives to Economic Globalization*.

haunt the here and now, then this haunting animates an ethico-
political quest and an aesthetic set of imperatives: to learn to live
with ghosts, doing so by committing to justice in relation to the
past, and, in turn, to the struggle for the invention of a common
future on that basis.

Bibliography

Adesokan, Akin. "Issues in the New Nigerian Cinema." *Black Camera* 21, no. 1 (2006): 6–11.

Ahmed, Sara. *The Cultural Politics of Emotion.* Edinburgh: Edinburgh University Press, 2004.

Alberro, Alexander and Blake Stimson, eds. *Institutional Critique: An Anthology of Artists' Writings.* Cambridge, MA: MIT Press, 2009.

Alter, Nora M. "Translating the Essay into Film and Installation." *Journal of Visual Culture* 6, no. 1(2007): 44–57.

Anderson, Perry. *The New Old World.* London: Verso, 2009.

Arendt, Hannah. *On Revolution.* New York: Penguin, 1990.

Augustijnen, Sven. "An Interview with Colette Braeckman," *A Prior*, no. 14 (2007): n.p.
———. Preface to *Les Démoiselles de Bruxelles.* Amsterdam: De Appel, 2008.
———. "Qu'en pensez-vous Bwana Kitoko?" *A Prior*, no. 14 (2007): 6–145.

Azimi, Negar. "Good Intentions," *frieze*, no. 137 (March 2011): 110–15.

Azoulay, Ariella. *The Civil Contract of Photography.* Translated by Rela Melazi and Ruvik Danieli. New York: Zone Books, 2008.

Badiou, Alain. *The Meaning of Sarkozy.* Translated by David Fernbach. London: Verso, 2010.

Barthes, Roland. *Camera Lucida: Reflections on Photography.* Translated by Richard Howard. London: Vintage, 1993.
———. *Essais critiques.* Paris: Éditions du Seuil, 1981.
———. "Myth Today." In *Mythologies.* Translated by Annette Lavers, 109–59. New York: Noonday, 1972.
———. *The Preparation of the Novel: Lecture, Courses and Seminars at the Collège de France (1978–1979 and 1979–1980).* Translated by Kate Briggs. New York: Columbia University Press, 2010.

BBC. "War Haunts Eastern Congo Voters." August 1, 2006.

Behdad, Ali. *Belated Travelers: Orientalism in the Age of Colonial Dissolution.* Durham, NC: Duke University Press, 1996.

Benveniste, Émile. *Le vocabulaire des institution indo-européennes.* Vol. 2, *Pouvoir, droit, religion.* Paris: Les Éditions de Minuit, 1969.

Bhimji, Zarina. "Outline of a Film," *Art Journal* 69, no. 4 (Winter 2010): 74.
———. *Zarina Bhimji: I Will Always Be Here.* Birmingham: Ikon Gallery, 1991. Exhibition catalog.

Blanchot, Maurice. *The Step Not Beyond.* Translated by Lycette Nelson. Albany: State University of New York Press, 1992.
———. *The Writing of Disaster.* Translated by Ann Smock. Lincoln: University of Nebraska Press, 1986.

Braeckman, Colette. "Dix noms remis à la justice." *Le Soir*, June 24, 2011.

Brassinne, Jacques and Jean Kestergat. *Qui a tué Patrice Lumumba?* Paris: Duculot, 1991.

Breton, André, Roger Callois, René Char, René Crevel, Paul Eluard, J.-M. Monnerot, Benjamin Péret, Yves Tanguy, André Thirion, Pierre Unik, and Pierre Yoyotte. "Murderous Humanitarianism." Translated by Samuel Beckett. In *Negro: An Anthology.* Edited by Nancy Cunard, 352–53. London: Continuum, 2002.

Buchloh, Benjamin H. D. "The Anomic Archive." *October*, no. 88 (Spring 1999): 117–45.

Buck-Morss, Susan. *Hegel, Haiti, and Universal History.* Pittsburgh, PA: University of Pittsburgh Press, 2009.

Burch, Noël. *Life to Those Shadows.* Berkeley: University of California Press, 1990.

Buse, Peter and Andrew Scott, eds. *Ghosts: Deconstruction, Psychoanalysis, History.* London: Macmillan, 1999.

Butler, Judith. "Torture and the Ethics of Photography: Thinking with Sontag." In *Frames of War: When Is Life Grievable?*, 63–100. London: Verso, 2009.

Cadava, Eduardo. *Words of Light: Theses on the Photography of History.* Princeton, NJ: Princeton University Press, 1997.

Calhoun, Craig. "The Idea of Emergency: Humanitarian Action and Global (Dis)order." In *Contemporary States of Emergency: The Politics of Military and Humanitarian Interventions.* Edited by Didier Fassin and Mariella Pandolfi, 18–39. New York: Zone Books, 2010.

Cavanagh, John and Jerry Mander, eds. *Alternatives to Economic Globalization: A Better World Is Possible; A Report of the International Forum on Globalization*. San Francisco: Berrett-Koehler, 2002.

Césaire, Aimé. *Discourse on Colonialism*. Translated by Joan Pinkham. New York: Monthly Review Press, 2000.

Chakrabarty, Dipesh. *Provincializing Europe: Postcolonial Thought and Historical Difference*. Princeton, NJ: Princeton University Press, 2000.

Corrigan, Timothy. *The Essay Film: From Montaigne, After Marker*. Oxford: Oxford University Press, 2011.

Cramer, Phebe. *Protecting the Self: Defense Mechanisms in Action*. New York: Guilford Press, 2006.

Daily Mail. "'Making the Invisible, Visible': Haunting Pictures of America's Most Vulnerable People Shot by Photojournalists against Poverty." March 21, 2012.

Davis, Kristin. "Kenya's Dadaab Refugee Camp Is a Haunting Place." *Guardian*, July 14, 2011.

Deleuze, Gilles. *Cinema 2: The Time-Image*. Translated by Hugh Tomlinson and Robert Galeta. Minneapolis: University of Minnesota Press, 1989.

Demobour, Marie-Bénédicte. *Recalling the Belgian Congo: Conversations and Introspections*. Oxford: Berghahn Books, 2000.

Demos, T. J. "Auguste Orts: Sensing Politics." In *Auguste Orts: Correspondence*, 86–95. Antwerp: MuHKA, 2010. Exhibition catalog.
———. "The Ends of Exile: Toward a Coming Universality." In *Altermodern: Tate Triennial 2009*. Edited by Nicolas Bourriaud, 74–89. London: Tate Britain, 2009. Exhibition catalog.
———. "Is Another World Possible? The Politics of Utopia in Recent Exhibition Practice." In *On Horizons: A Critical Reader in Contemporary Art*. Edited by Maria Hlavajova, Simon Sheikh, and Jill Winder, 52–82. Utrecht: BAK, 2011.
———. *The Migrant Image: The Art and Politics of Documentary During Global Crisis*. Durham, NC: Duke University Press, 2013.
———. "Toward a New Institutional Critique: A Conversation with Renzo Martens." *Atlántica*, no. 52 (February 2012): 90–103.

Demos, T. J. and Hilde Van Gelder, eds. *In and Out of Brussels: Figuring Postcolonial Africa and Europe*. Leuven: Leuven University Press, 2012. See esp. Renzo Martens's introduction; "Roundtable on Renzo Martens' *Episode III (Enjoy Poverty)*, with Carles Guerra, Thomas Keenan, Toma Muteba Luntumbue, and Renzo Martens, moderated by T. J. Demos and Hilde Van Gelder," 5–34; and "Roundtable on Sven Augustijnen's *Spectres* (2011) with Sven Augustijnen, Filip De Boeck, Dirk Snauwaert, and Françoise Vergès, moderated by T. J. Demos and Hilde Van Gelder," 37–64.

Derrida, Jacques. "Passages—From Traumatism to Promise." In *Points: Interviews, 1974–1994*. Edited by Elisabeth Weber. Translated by Peggy Kamuf. Stanford, CA: Stanford University Press, 1995.
———. *Specters of Marx: The State of the Debt, the Work of Mourning, and the New International*. Translated by Peggy Kamuf. London: Routledge, 1994.

Dewan, Deepali. "Tender Metaphor: The Art of Zarina Bhimji." In Tawadros et al., *Fault Lines: Contemporary African Art and Shifting Landscapes*, 131–37.

Didi-Huberman, Georges. *Images in Spite of All: Four Photographs from Auschwitz*. Translated by Shane B. Lillis. Chicago: University of Chicago Press, 2008.

Dupont, Gilbert. "L'assassinat de Lumumba n'est pas prescript." *La Dernière Heure*, June 21, 2012.

Edwards, Steve. *Martha Rosler: The Bowery in two inadequate descriptive systems*. London: Afterall, 2012.

Eghagha, Hope. "Magical Realism and the 'Power' of Nollywood Home Video Films." *Film International* 5, no. 4 (July–August 2007): 71–76.

Enwezor, Okwui. "The Production of Social Space as Artwork." In *Collectivism after Modernism: The Art of Social Imagination after 1945*. Edited by Blake Stimson and Gregory Sholette, 223–52. Minneapolis: University of Minnesota Press, 2007.
———. "Reframing the Black Subject: Ideology and Fantasy in Contemporary South African Representation." *Third Text* 11, no. 40 (Autumn 1997): 376–99.
———. *Snap Judgments: New Positions in Contemporary African Photography*. New York: International Center of Photography, 2006.

Enwezor, Okwui, Carlos Basualdo, Ute Meta Bauer, Susanne Ghez, Sarat Maharaj, Mark Nash, and Octavio Zaya, eds. *Experiments with Truth: Transitional Justice and the Processes of Truth and Reconciliation.* Documenta11_Platform 2. Ostfildern: Hatje Cantz, 2002.
——— . *Under Siege: Four African Cities; Freetown, Johannesburg, Kinshasa, Lagos.* Documenta11_Platform 4. Ostfildern: Hatje Cantz, 2003.

Eshun, Kodwo and Ros Gray, eds. "The Militant Image: A Ciné Geography." Special issue, *Third Text* 25, no. 1 (January 2011).

Ewans, Martin. *European Atrocity, African Catastrophe: Leopold II, the Congo Free State and Its Aftermath.* London: Routledge, 2002.

Ferguson, James. *Global Shadows: Africa in the Neoliberal World Order.* Durham, NC: Duke University Press, 2006.

Fine, Ben. "Development as Zombie-conomics in the Age of Neoliberalism." *Third World Quarterly* 30, no. 5 (2009): 885–904.

Foster, Hal. "An Archival Impulse." *October,* no. 110 (Fall 2004): 3–22.
——— . "Death in America." *October,* no. 75 (Winter 1996): 35–59.

Foucault, Michel. *"Society Must Be Defended": Lectures at the Collège de France, 1975–1976.* Translated by David Macey. New York: Picador, 2003.
——— . "Subjectivity and Truth." In *The Politics of Truth.* Edited by Sylvère Lotringer. Translated by Lysa Hochroth and Catherine Porter, 147–68. Los Angeles: Semiotext(e), 2007.

Franke, Anselm, ed. *Animism: Modernity Through the Looking Glass.* Cologne: Verlag der Buchhandlung Walther König, 2011.

Franke, Anselm. "Introduction—'Animism.'" *e-flux journal,* no. 36 (July 2012). http://www.e-flux.com/journal/introduction—"animism"/.
——— . "Much Trouble in the Transportation of Souls, or: The Sudden Disorganization of Boundaries." In *Animism.* Edited by Anselm Franke, 11–51. Berlin: Sternberg Press, 2010.

Fraser, Andrea. "L'1%, C'est Moi." *Texte zur Kunst,* no. 83 (September 2011): 114–27.
——— . "There's No Place Like Home." In *The Whitney Biennial 2012.* Edited by Jay Sanders and Elisabeth Sussman, 28–33. New York: Whitney Museum, 2012. Exhibition catalog.

Freud, Anna. *Ego and Mechanisms of Defense.* Translated by Cecil Baines. London: Hogarth Press, 1968.

Freud, Sigmund. "Beyond the Pleasure Principle." In *The Standard Edition of the Complete Psychological Works of Sigmund Freud.* Edited and translated by James Strachey. Vol. 18, 1–64. London: Hogarth Press, 1953.

Gadgil, Madhav and Ramachandra Guha. "Ideologies of Environmentalism." In *Ecology and Equity: The Use and Abuse of Nature in Contemporary India,* 98–112. London: Routledge, 1995.

Gandy, Matthew. "Learning from Lagos." *New Left Review,* no. 33 (May–June 2005): 36–52.

Garb, Tamar, ed. *Figures & Fictions: Contemporary South African Photography.* Göttingen: Steidl, 2011.

Garb, Tamar. "Figures and Fictions: South African Photography in the Perfect Tense." In Garb, *Figures & Fictions: Contemporary South African Photography,* 10–85.

Garb, Tamar, Achille Mbembe, Riason Naidoo, Sarah Nuttall, and Colin Richards. "Thinking from the South: Reflections on Image and Place." In Garb, *Figures & Fictions: Contemporary South African Photography,* 302–30.

Ghosh, Amitav. *Sea of Poppies.* New York: Farrar, Straus and Giroux, 2008.

Gierstberg Frits, Maartje van den Heuvel, Hans Scholten, and Martijn Verhoeven, eds. *Documentary Now! Contemporary Strategies in Photography, Film and the Visual Arts.* Rotterdam: NAi Publishers, 2005.

Godfrey, Mark. "The Artist as Historian." *October,* no. 120 (Spring 2007): 140–72.

Goldblatt, David. "Boksburg." In *David Goldblatt: Fifty-One Years,* 248–77. Barcelona: Museu d'Art Contemporani de Barcelona, 2001. Exhibition catalog.

Gordon, Avery. *Ghostly Matters: Haunting and the Sociological Imagination*. Minneapolis: University of Minnesota Press, 2004.

Gourevitch, Philip. "Alms Dealers: Can You Provide Humanitarian Aid without Facilitating Conflicts?" *New Yorker*, October 11, 2010, 102–9.

Greenpeace. "Poisoning the Poor: Electronic Waste in Ghana." August 5, 2008. http://www.greenpeace.org/international /en/news/features/poisoning-the-poor-electroni/.

Gregory, Derek. *The Colonial Present*. Oxford: Blackwell, 2004.

Haak, Bregtje van der, dir. *Lagos Wide and Close: An Interactive Journey into an Exploding City*. Amsterdam: Submarine, 2005.

Hall, Stuart. "Maps of Emergency: Fault Lines and Tectonic Plates." In Tawadros et al., *Fault Lines: Contemporary African Art and Shifting Landscapes*, 31–42.

Hargreaves, Alec G. "A Neglected Precursor: Roland Barthes and the Origins of Postcolonialism." In *Postcolonial Theory and Francophone Literary Studies*. Edited by H. Adlai Murdoch and Anne Donadey, 55–64. Gainesville: University Press of Florida, 2005.

Harman, Chris. *Zombie Capitalism: Global Crisis and the Relevance of Marx*. London: Bookmarks, 2009.

Harman, Graham. *Towards Speculative Realism: Essays and Lectures*. Winchester: Zero Books, 2010.

Harrison, Graham. *Neoliberal Africa: The Impact of Global Social Engineering*. London: Zed Books, 2010. See esp. chap. 2, "Neoliberalism in Africa: A Failed Ideology."

Harvey, David. *A Brief History of Neoliberalism*. Oxford: Oxford University Press, 2005.
———. *The New Imperialism*. Oxford: Oxford University Press, 2003.

Haynes, Jonathan. "Nollywood in Lagos, Lagos in Nollywood Films." *Africa Today* 54, no. 2 (Fall 2007): 131–50.
———. "Nollywood: What's in a Name?" *Film International* 5, no. 4 (July–August 2007): 106–8.

Hill, M. F. *Permanent Way: The Story of the Kenya and Uganda Railway*. Nairobi: East African Railways and Harbours, 1949.

Hochschild, Adam. *King Leopold's Ghost: A Story of Greed, Terror, and Heroism in Colonial Africa*. London: Macmillan, 1999.

Höller, Christian. "Africa in Motion: An Interview with the Post-Colonialism Theoretician Achille Mbembe." *Springerin* 3, no. 2 (June 2002): n.p.

Hugo, Pierre. *Messina/Musina*. Rome: Punctum, 2007.
———. *Nollywood*. Munich: Prestel, 2009. See esp. Zina Saro-Wiwa, "No Going Back," 17–28.
———. *Permanent Error*. Munich: Prestel, 2011.

Huyssen, Andreas. "Present Pasts: Media, Politics, Amnesia." In *Globalization*. Edited by Arjun Appadurai, 57–77. Durham, NC: Duke University Press, 2001.

James, C. L. R. *The Black Jacobins: Toussaint L'Ouverture and the San Domingo Revolution*. New York: Vintage Books, 1989.

Jones, Pete. "The Material Stakes in the Democratic Republic of the Congo Elections." *Open Democracy*. December 5, 2011. http://www.opendemocracy.net/ pete-jones/material-stakes-in-democrat ic-republic-of-congo-elections.

Jørgensen, Jan Jelmert. *Uganda: A Modern History*. London: Taylor & Francis, 1981.

Kaplan, Robert. *The Coming Anarchy*. New York: Random House, 2000.

Keatley, Patrick. "Obituary: Idi Amin." *Guardian*, August 18, 2003. http://www. guardian.co.uk/news/2003/aug/18/ guardianobituaries.

Klein, Naomi. *The Shock Doctrine: The Rise of Disaster Capitalism*. London: Penguin, 2007.

Knight, Diana. *Barthes and Utopia: Space, Travel and Writing*. Oxford: Clarendon Press, 1997.

Knightley, Phillip. *The First Casualty: The War Correspondent as Hero, Propagandist, and Myth Maker from the Crimea to Kosovo*. London: Prion, 2000.

Koolhaas, Rem. "Fragments of a Lecture on Lagos." In Enwezor et al., *Under Siege: Four African Cities; Freetown, Johannesburg, Kinshasa, Lagos*, 129–51.

Lewis, Adrian. "Europe Breaking Electronic Waste Export Ban." *BBC News.* August 4, 2010. http://www.bbc.co.uk/news/world-europe-10846395.

Linfield, Susie. *The Cruel Radiance: Photography and Political Violence.* Chicago: Chicago University Press, 2010.

Lorés, Maite. Interview with Zarina Bhimji. *contemporary*, no. 49 (2003): 58–63.

Lumumba, Patrice. "Letter to Pauline Lumumba." In *Lumumba Speaks: The Speeches and Writings of Patrice Lumumba, 1958–1961.* Edited by Jean Van Lierde. Translated by Helen R. Lane, 412–23. Boston: Little, Brown and Company, 1972.

Lütticken, Sven. "Interzone: On Three Works by Wendelien van Oldenborgh." *Afterall* 29 (Spring 2012): 50–57.
———. "The Feathers of the Eagle." *New Left Review* 36 (November–December 2005): 109–25.

Maathai, Wangari. *The Challenge for Africa.* New York: Arrow, 2010.

Mackay, Robin, ed. "Speculative Realism." Special issue, *Collapse* 2 (March 2007).

Maharaj, Sarat. "Xeno-Epistemics: Makeshift Kit for Sounding Visual Art as Knowledge Production and the Retinal Regimes." In *Catalogue.* Documenta11_Platform 5, edited by Documenta und Museum Fridericianum Veranstaltungs-GmbHs, 71–84. Ostfildern: Hatje Cantz, 2002.

Mamdani, Mahmood. *Citizen and Subject: Contemporary Africa and the Legacy of Late Colonialism.* Princeton, NJ: Princeton University Press, 1996.
———. *From Citizen to Refugee: Uganda Asians Come to Britain.* London: Frances Pinter, 1973.

Martens, Renzo in conversation with Artur Žmijewski. "Artists Come to Create Beauty and Kindness." In *Forget Fear: 7th Berlin Biennale.* Edited by Artur Žmijewski and Joanna Warsza, 148–55. Cologne: Verlag der Buchhandlung Walther König, 2012.

Marx, Karl. *Capital.* Vol. I, translated by Ben Fowkes. Harmondsworth: Penguin Books, 1976.

Massumi, Brian. "The Autonomy of Affect." In *Parables for the Virtual: Movement, Affect, Sensation,* 23–45. Durham, NC: Duke University Press, 2002.

Mbembe, Achille. "Necropolitics." *Public Culture* 15, no. 1 (Winter 2003): 11–40.
———. *On the Postcolony.* Berkeley: University of California Press, 2001.
———. "Provincializing France?" *Public Culture* 23, no. 1 (2011): 85–119.
———. "Provisional Notes on the Postcolony." In Tawadros et al., *Fault Lines: Contemporary African Art and Shifting Landscapes*, 53–64.

McNally, David. *Monsters of the Market: Zombies, Vampires and Global Capitalism.* London: Brill, 2011. See esp. chap. 3, "African Vampires in the Age of Globalisation."

Mercer, Kobena. "Vincent Meessen." In *Ars 11.* Helsinki: Museum of Contemporary Art Kiasma, 2011. Exhibition catalog.

Mosquera, Gerardo. "Art and Cultural Interactions in a Globalised World." *Stedelijk Bureau Newsletter*, no. 120 (2011): n.p.

Mundt, Katrin. "A Conversation with Vincent Meessen." *A Prior*, no. 20 (2010): 20–30.

Mutibwa, Phares Mukasa. *Uganda Since Independence: A Story of Unfulfilled Hopes*, Trenton, NJ: Africa World Press, 1992. See esp. "Expulsion of the Asians," 92–97.

New York Times. "Furor on Memo at World Bank." February 7, 1992. http://www.nytimes.com/1992/02/07/business/furor-on-memo-at-world-bank.html.

Nichols, Bill. *Blurred Boundaries: Questions of Meaning in Contemporary Culture.* Bloomington: Indiana University Press, 1994.

Nkruma, Kwame. *Neo-Colonialism: The Last Stage of Imperialism.* London: Thomas Nelson & Sons, 1965.

Nowotny, Stefan and Gerald Raunig. "On Police Ghosts and Multitudinous Monsters." Translated by Aileen Derieg. *transversal* (June 2008). http://eipcp.net/transversal/0508/nowotnyraunig/en.

Okeke-Agulu, Chika. "Conversation with Zarina Bhimji." *Art Journal* 69, no. 4 (Winter 2010): 66–75.
———. "Who Knows Tomorrow." *Art Journal* 69, no. 4 (Winter 2010): 49–65.

Patel, Hasu H. "General Amin and the Indian Exodus from Uganda." *Issue: A Journal of Opinion* 2, no. 4 (1972): 12–22.

Peck, Raoul, dir. *Lumumba: Death of a Prophet*. Paris: Velvet Film, 1992.

Pethick, Emily. "Wendelien van Oldenborgh: 'The past is never dead. It's not even past.'" *Afterall* 29 (Spring 2012): 57–65.

Pignarre, Philippe and Isabelle Stengers. *Capitalist Sorcery: Breaking the Spell*. Translated by Andrew Goffey. New York: Palgrave Macmillan, 2011.

Pinney, Christopher. "What is to be done?" *Source*, no. 48 (Autumn 2006): 14–17.
———. *Photography and Anthropology*. London: Reaktion, 2011.

Pollock, Griselda. "Not-Forgetting Africa: The Dialectics of Attention/Inattention … in the Work of Alfredo Jaar." In Schweizer, *Alfredo Jaar: The Politics of Images*, 113–37.

Polman, Linda. *The Crisis Caravan: What's Wrong with Humanitarian Aid?* Translated by Liz Waters. New York: Metropolitan, 2010.
———. *War Games: The Story of Aid and War in Modern Times*. Translated by Liz Waters. London: Viking, 2011.

Prunier, Gérard. "The Eastern DR Congo: Dynamics of Conflict." *Open Democracy*. November 18, 2008. http://www.opendemocracy.net/article/war-in-the-dr-congo-group-nation-power-state.
———. *From Genocide to Continental War: The "Congolese" Conflict and the Crisis of Contemporary Africa*. London: Hurst, 2009.

Rabaté, Jean-Michel. "Roland Barthes, Ghostwriter of Modernity." In *The Ghosts of Modernity*, 67–83. Gainesville: University Press of Florida, 1996.

Rancière, Jacques. "Documentary Fiction: Marker and the Fiction of Memory." In *Film Fables*. Translated by Emiliano Battista, 157–70. London: Berg, 2006.
———. *The Politics of Aesthetics*. Translated by Gabriel Rockhill. London: Continuum, 2004
———. "Theater of Images." In Schweizer, *Alfredo Jaar: The Politics of Images*, 70–80.

Raunig, Gerald and Gene Ray, eds. *Art and Contemporary Critical Practice: Reinventing Institutional Critique*. London: Mayfly, 2009.

Renton, David, David Seddon, and Leo Zeilig. *The Congo: Plunder and Resistance*. London: Zed Books, 2007.

Rosler, Martha. "In, Around, and Afterthoughts (on Documentary Photography)." In *The Contest of Meaning: Critical Histories of Photography*. Edited by Richard Bolton, 303–42. Cambridge, MA: MIT Press, 1993.

Ross, Kristin. *May '68 and Its Afterlives*. Chicago: University of Chicago Press, 2002.

Salvadori, Cynthia, ed. *We Came in Dhows*. Nairobi: Paperchase Kenya, 1996.

Sandoval, Chela. *Methodology of the Oppressed*. Minneapolis: University of Minnesota Press, 2000.

Sartre, Jean-Paul. *Colonialism and Neocolonialism*. Translated by Steve Brewer, Azzedine Haddour, and Terry McWilliams. London: Routledge, 2001.

Schroeder, Barbet, dir. *General Idi Amin Dada: A Self-Portrait*. Paris: Le Figaro Films, 1974.

Schweizer, Nicole, ed. *Alfredo Jaar: The Politics of Images*. Zurich: JRP|Ringier, 2007.

Sekula, Allan. "Dismantling Modernism, Reinventing Documentary (Notes on the Politics of Representation)." *Massachusetts Review* 19, no. 4 (Winter 1978): 859–83.

Shaviro, Steven. "Capitalist Monsters." *Historical Materialism* 10, no. 4 (2002): 281–90.
———. "Specters of Marx." *The Pinocchio Theory* (blog), February 8, 2006. http://www.shaviro.com/Blog/?p=474.
———. *Post-Cinematic Affect*. Winchester: Zero Books, 2010.

Sillars, Laurence and Darren Pih. *Turner Prize 07*. Liverpool: Tate Liverpool, 2007. Exhibition catalog.

Silverman, Kaja. *The Threshold of the Visible World*. London: Routledge, 1996.

Simone, AbdouMaliq. *City Life from Jakarta to Dakar*. London: Routledge, 2010.

Sissako, Abderrahmane, dir. *Bamako*. New York: Louverture Films, 2006.

Sivan, Eyal. "Archive Images: Truth or Memory? The Case of Adolf Eichmann's Trial." In Enwezor et al., *Experiments with Truth: Transitional Justice and the Processes of Truth and Reconciliation*, 277–88.

Sompel, Ronald van de. "What a Day for a Daydream." *Mousse*, no. 27 (February–March 2011).

Sontag, Susan. *Regarding the Pain of Others*. New York: Picador, 2003.

Stengers, Isabelle. "Reclaiming Animism." *e-flux journal*, no. 36 (July 2012). http://www.e-flux.com/journal/reclaiming-animism/.

Steyerl, Hito. "Politics of Art: Contemporary Art and the Transition to Post-Democracy." *e-flux journal*, no. 21 (December 2010). http://www.e-flux.com/journal/politics-of-art-contemporary-art-and-the-transition-to-post-democracy/.

Subirós, Pep. "Lagos: Surviving Hell." In *Africas: The Artist and the City; A Journey and an Exhibition*, 34–45. Barcelona: Centre de Cultura Contemporania de Barcelona, 2001. Exhibition catalog.

Tallon, Steve and Emiliano Battista, eds. *Sven Augustijnen: Spectres*. Brussels: ASA Publishers, 2011.

Taussig, Michael. *The Devil and Commodity Fetishism in South America*. Chapel Hill: University of North Carolina Press, 1980.
———. *What Color Is the Sacred?* Chicago: University of Chicago Press, 2009.

Tawadros, Gilane. "The Revolution Stripped Bare." In Tawadros et al., *Fault Lines: Contemporary African Art and Shifting Landscapes*, 13–30.

Tawadros, Gilane and Sarah Campbell, eds. *Fault Lines: Contemporary African Art and Shifting Landscapes*. London: Iniva, 2003.

Todorov, Tzvetan. *Les Abus de la mémoire*. Paris: Alréa, 1995.

Verwoert, Jan. "The Practical Surrealism of Power." *A Prior*, no. 14 (2007): 147–55.

Waal, Alex De. *Famine Crimes: Politics & The Disaster Relief Industry in Africa*. London: African Rights & the International African Institute, 1997.

Weizman, Eyal. *The Least of All Possible Evils: Humanitarian Violence from Arendt to Gaza*. London: Verso, 2012.

White, Louise. *Speaking with Vampires: Rumor and History in Colonial Africa*. Berkeley: University of California Press, 2000.

Witte, Ludo De. *The Assassination of Lumumba*. Translated by Ann Wright and Renée Fenby. London: Verso, 2003.

Young, Robert J. C. *Postcolonialism: An Historical Introduction*. Oxford: Blackwell, 2001.

Image Credits

1. Sven Augustijnen's Spectropoetics

pp. 22, 31, 33, 40 Sven Augustijnen, *Spectres*, 2011. Video, color, 16:9, 104 min. Stills courtesy of the artist and Jan Mot, Brussels/Mexico City.

p. 24 Sven Augustijnen, "Spectres," WIELS Contemporary Art Centre, Brussels, 2011. Photo of exhibition by Marc Wathieu.

p. 27 Wendelien van Oldenborgh, *Maurits Script*, 2006. Video installation with two projections, 67 min. Still courtesy of Wilfried Lentz Rotterdam and the artist.

2. A Colonial Hauntology: Vincent Meessen's *Vita Nova*

pp. 47–51, 66 Vincent Meessen, *Vita Nova*, 2009. Video, color, 26 min. Stills courtesy of the artist.

p. 53 Vincent Meessen, *The Intruder*, 2005. Video, color, 7 min. 26 sec. Still courtesy of the artist.

p. 54 Vincent Meessen, *Dear Adviser*, 2009. Video, color, 8 min. Still courtesy of the artist.

pp. 61–63 Vincent Meessen, "My Last Life," Netwerk, Aalst, 2011/12. Exhibition views courtesy of the artist.

3. Ghostly Affect: Zarina Bhimji's *Yellow Patch*

pp. 72, 74, 91–94 Zarina Bhimji, *Yellow Patch*, 2011. 35 mm film, color, HD transfer, Dolby 5.1 sound, 29 min. 43 sec. Stills courtesy of the artist.

pp. 82–83 Zarina Bhimji, *Out of Blue*, 2002. 16 mm film, color, DVD transfer, 24 min. 25 sec. Stills courtesy of the artist.

p. 84 Black Audio Film Collective, *Handsworth Songs*, 1986. 16 mm film or video transfer, color, mono sound, 59 min. Still courtesy of David Lawson/Smoking Dogs Films.

p. 86 Steve McQueen, *Gravesend*, 2007. 35 mm transferred to HD, 17 min. 58 sec. Still courtesy of Marianne Goodman Gallery.

4. The Haunting: Renzo Martens's *Enjoy Poverty*

pp. 99, 102, 104, 107 (below), 108, 110, 118 Renzo Martens, *Episode III (Enjoy Poverty)*, 2009. PAL, 16:9, color, 90 min. Stills courtesy of the artist.

p. 100 Luis Ospina and Carlos Mayolo, *The Vampires of Poverty*, 1978. 16 mm, 28 min. Photo by Eduardo Carvajal.

p. 107 (above) Mark Boulos, *All That Is Solid Melts into Air*, 2008. Two-channel video, color, sound, 15 min. © Mark Boulos. Still courtesy of the artist and Galerie Diana Stigter, Amsterdam.

p. 114 Alfredo Jaar, *The Sound of Silence*, 2006. Wood, lights, flashes, video projection. 170 x 180 x 360 in. (431.8 x 457.2 x 914.4 cm). Installation view at Galerie Lelong, New York, 2009. © Alfredo Jaar. Courtesy of Galerie Lelong, New York.

p. 115 March 1993, Sudan. © Kevin Carter/Sygma/Corbis.

5. A Postcolonial *Monstrum*: The Photographs of Pieter Hugo

p. 127 Pieter Hugo, *David Akore, Agbogbloshie Market, Accra, Ghana*, 2010. From the series Permanent Error. C-Print, image: 82 x 82 cm, paper: 98 x 98 cm. © Pieter Hugo. Courtesy of Stevenson, Cape Town and Yossi Milo, New York.

p. 128 Pieter Hugo, *Abdullahi Ahmadu with Mainasara, Nigeria*, 2005. From the series The Hyena & Other Men. Archival pigment ink on cotton rag paper, image: 51 x 51 cm, paper: 63 x 61 cm. © Pieter Hugo. Courtesy of Stevenson, Cape Town and Yossi Milo, New York.

p. 129 Pieter Hugo, *Princess Adaobi. Enugu, Nigeria*, 2008. From the series Nollywood. C-Print, image: 102 x 102 cm, paper: 110 x 110 cm. © Pieter Hugo. Courtesy of Stevenson, Cape Town and Yossi Milo, New York.

p. 130 Pieter Hugo, *At the abandoned Campbell copper mine*, 2006. From the series Messina/Musina. C-Print, image: 76 x 95 cm, paper: 102.5 x 121.5 cm. © Pieter Hugo. Courtesy of Stevenson, Cape Town and Yossi Milo, New York.

p. 134 Pieter Hugo, *Naasra Yeti, Agbogbloshie Market, Accra, Ghana*, 2009. From the series Permanent Error. C-Print, image: 82 x 82 cm, paper: 98 x 98 cm. © Pieter Hugo. Courtesy of Stevenson, Cape Town and Yossi Milo, New York.

p. 137 Zwelethu Mthethwa, *Untitled (Gladiator 5)*, 2008. From the series Contemporary Gladiators. C-Print, 81.3 x 104.1 cm. Courtesy of the artist and Jack Shainman Gallery, New York.

p. 139 Pieter Hugo, *Kelly and Zanele Nggaba with their children Bongani and Mbali*, 2006. From the series Messina/Musina. C-Print, image: 76 x 95 cm, paper: 102.5 x 121.5 cm. © Pieter Hugo. Courtesy of Stevenson, Cape Town and Yossi Milo, New York.

p. 140 Pieter Hugo, *Jan, Martie, Kayala, Florence and Basil Meyer in their home*, 2006. From the series Messina/Musina. C-Print, image: 76 x 95 cm, paper: 102.5 x 121.5 cm. © Pieter Hugo. Courtesy of Stevenson, Cape Town and Yossi Milo, New York.

p. 143 Pieter Hugo, *Pieter and Maryna Vermeulen with Timana Phosiwa*, 2006. From the series Messina/Musina. C-Print, image: 95 x 76 cm, paper: 121.5 x 102.5 cm. © Pieter Hugo. Courtesy of Stevenson, Cape Town and Yossi Milo, New York.

p. 144 Pieter Hugo, *Escort Kama, Enugu, Nigeria*, 2008. From the series Nollywood. C-Print, image: 102 x 102 cm, paper: 110 x 110 cm. © Pieter Hugo. Courtesy of Stevenson, Cape Town and Yossi Milo, New York.

p. 145 Pieter Hugo, *Pieter Hugo, Enugu, Nigeria*, 2009. From the series Nollywood. C-Print, image: 102 x 102 cm, paper: 110 x 110 cm. © Pieter Hugo. Courtesy of Stevenson, Cape Town and Yossi Milo, New York.

p. 149 Pieter Hugo, *Thompson. Asaba, Nigeria*, 2008. From the series Nollywood. C-Print, image: 102 x 102 cm, paper: 110 x 110 cm. © Pieter Hugo. Courtesy of Stevenson, Cape Town and Yossi Milo, New York.

p. 151 Pieter Hugo, *Azuka Adindu, Enugu, Nigeria*, 2008. From the series Nollywood. C-Print, image: 102 x 102 cm, paper: 110 x 110 cm. © Pieter Hugo. Courtesy of Stevenson, Cape Town and Yossi Milo, New York.

Acknowledgments

Thanks are due to many colleagues, friends, artists, and family members for their gestures of support small and large, which have made this research possible, better than what it would have been otherwise, and worthwhile in multiple ways. I am greatly indebted to Sven Lütticken, Sarah James, Alex Alberro, Chris Pinney, Tamara Trodd, Tamar Garb, Stephanie Schwartz, Stuart Comer, Eric de Bruyn, Anjalika Sagar, and Kodwo Eshun for the many critical discussions of things ghostly and postcolonial, and for their incisive feedback, occasional skepticism, and generous readings of all or parts of this book at various stages. My sincere appreciation goes to my colleagues and students in the Department of Art History and the Centre for the Study of Contemporary Art at University College London for helping to advance my research and providing ever-productive feedback.

During the development of this book, I was able to present my work at various institutions and I gratefully acknowledge my generous hosts—including Tamara Trodd and Angela Dimitrakaki at the Art History Department at University of Edinburgh, Eu Jin Chua and Catherine Elwes at Chelsea College of Art and Design, Sara Knelman at the Photographer's Gallery, Stuart Comer at Tate Modern, and Saskia Ooms at Netwerk, among others—and my diverse audiences for their perceptive responses. Thanks also to Aliocha Imhoff and Kantuta Quiros of Le peuple qui manque and Morad Montazami, who organized the conference "The Artist as Ethnographer" at Musée du Quai Branly, Paris, where I was able to present material on Renzo Martens's film *Episode III (Enjoy Poverty)*; and to Alfredo Jaar for his critical appraisal of chapter 4.

This book has been greatly aided and informed by my collaboration with Hilde Van Gelder on the research project that led to the publication of *In and Out of Brussels: Figuring Postcolonial Africa and Europe in the Films of Herman Asselberghs, Sven Augustijnen, Renzo Martens, and Els Opsomer* (Leuven University Press, 2012). She has been a much appreciated and engaged colleague and a generous, encouraging friend along the way. I remain indebted to Dirk Snauwaert of WIELS, Jelle Bouwhuis of the Stedelijk Bureau, Curt Holtz of Prestel, Saskia Ooms of Netwerk, and Achim Borchardt-Hume (formerly) of Whitechapel Gallery, whose invitations provided

the opportunity for me to publish earlier versions of some
of the essays presented here.

For her enthusiasm and support for this project, I thank
Caroline Schneider, publisher of Sternberg Press, and for her
fantastic and rigorous editing, Leah Whitman-Salkin. I am
ever grateful to the artists Sven Augustijnen, Zarina Bhimji,
Pieter Hugo, Renzo Martens, and Vincent Meessen for their
continual encouragement, many insightful conversations,
and, most of all, their inspiring work. My deepest appreciation goes to Joy Schendledecker for her sustaining compan-
ionship, and to Zoe and Leila Demos for giving generously
without thinking twice; I dedicate this book to them.

T. J. Demos is critic and Reader in the Department of Art History, University College London. He is the author of *The Migrant Image: The Art and Politics of Documentary During Global Crisis* (Duke University Press, 2013), *Dara Birnbaum: Technology/Transformation: Wonder Woman* (Afterall Press, 2010), and *The Exiles of Marcel Duchamp* (MIT Press, 2007).

T. J. Demos
Return to the Postcolony:
Specters of Colonialism in
Contemporary Art

Published by Sternberg Press

Editor: Leah Whitman-Salkin
Proofreader: Max Bach
Design: Kummer & Herrman
Printing and binding: BUD
Potsdam

ISBN 978-3-943365-42-9

© 2013 T. J. Demos,
Sternberg Press

Sternberg Press
Caroline Schneider
Karl-Marx-Allee 78
D-10243 Berlin
www.sternberg-press.com